GOD AND GEORGE W. BUSH

Also by the Author

God and Ronald Reagan

GOD

a n d

GEORGE W. BUSH

a spiritual life

PAUL KENGOR, Ph.D.

ReganBooks

An Imprint of HarperCollins*Publishers*

A hardcover edition of this book was published in 2004 by ReganBooks, an imprint of Harper-Collins Publishers.

FIRST PAPERBACK EDITION PUBLISHED 2005

Designed by Kris Tobiassen

The Library of Congress has cataloged the hardcover edition as follows:

Kengor, Paul, 1966-
    God and George W. Bush : a spiritual life / Paul Kengor.—1st ed.
        p. cm.
    Includes bibliographical references and index.
    ISBN 0-06-076050-8 (alk. paper)
    1. Church and state—United States. 2. Bush, George W. (George Walker), 1946—
religion. 3. Religion and state—United States. 4. Religion and politics—United States.
5. United States—Religion. I. Title.

BR516 .K
973.931'092—dc22
[B]
                                                                    2004051083

ISBN 10: 0-06-077956-X (pbk.)
ISBN 13: 978-0-06-077956-6 (pbk.)

05 06 07 08 09 WBC/RRD 10 9 8 7 6 5 4 3 2 1

For Billy Graham, preacher to presidents

CONTENTS

PREFACE: TWO HYMNS AND A PURPOSE

"We are not this story's author, who fills time and eternity with His purpose. Yet His purpose is achieved in our duty."

—*George W. Bush, inaugural address, January 2001*

During his campaign for the White House, Governor George W. Bush was asked to name his favorite philosopher. Without hesitation, Bush cited Jesus Christ as the philosopher—and leader—he most admired. Christ is George W.'s philosopher-king.

Two hymns, "Amazing Grace" and "A Charge to Keep," embody the spiritual life and presidency of George W. Bush. "Amazing Grace" symbolizes Bush's conversion in the mid-1980s, before which Bush says that Jesus had not yet "changed my heart." Only today can a "found" Bush tell the world, "I believe in grace because I have seen it."[1]

"A Charge to Keep," the hymn by Charles Wesley, is also the title of Bush's prepresidential memoir. Associated with the New Testament's 1 Corinthians 4:2, the hymn underscores a Christian's need "to serve the present age" and "to do my master's will"; that is the "calling to fulfill." "'A Charge to Keep' calls us to our highest and best," Bush has said. "It speaks of purpose and direction."[2] A painting inspired by the hymn hangs next to his desk in the Oval Office; earlier it hung on the wall in Bush's office in Austin.

A special purpose came to define Bush's presidency on September 11, 2001. President Theodore Roosevelt is reported to have said that no one would remember some guy named Lincoln if not for the Civil War. TR saw it as his curse that no world-shaking battles transpired during his tenure. He saw it as doubly his curse that Woodrow Wilson, whom he despised, got a major war. Presidents usually do not get to pick and choose their turning points in world history, but they do get to choose how to respond. George W. Bush has responded by declaring a war on terror, and his administration will seek to undermine those that commit or support terrorism. This bold objective, declared immediately after September 11, has defined the Bush presidency and the reactions of both friends and foes.

Historical analogies, though sometimes laden with oversimplification, can often enhance our understanding. The Cold War holds some lessons for the War on Terror: neither war was formally declared, though Congress appropriated huge sums to fight each of them. September 11, terrorism, and Iraq are to the Bush presidency what the Cold War, communism, and the Soviet Union were to previous presidencies. Osama bin Laden's Al-Qaeda and Saddam Hussein's Iraq are Bush's Evil Empire. The president used the word *evil* so often in 2002 that the search engine for the *Presidential Documents* that year simply lists "200+" references.

It became Bush's personal purpose to rid the world of that evil. His supporters and those of a conservative religious stripe have expressed a sense that God has dropped Bush into this grand moment to undertake this purpose. For every evangelical who proffers such an assertion, a liberal Christian or agnostic begs to differ. Despite the perceptions of his detractors, the president himself has avoided such grandiose claims.

Nonetheless, George W. Bush believes that God charts his ultimate course, and that his duty is to accept God's calling and forge ahead. In so doing, he says that he relies on his faith for guidance and forbearance in a battle against what he views, unequivocally, as pure evil. This is his "charge to keep" on his spiritual journey.

1.

Robin and Growing Up

"Unconditional love is the greatest gift a parent can give a child."

—*George W. Bush*[1]

To this day, George W. Bush is sure he saw her. Swears by it. He caught her small head barely rising above the backseat of his parents' green Oldsmobile as it pulled in front of Sam Houston Elementary School in Midland, Texas, in the fall of 1953. Seven-year-old George happened to be strolling down an outdoor corridor with his friend Bill Sallee, carrying a Victrola record player to the principal's office. The moment he saw the car, he set down the phonograph and sprinted ahead to his teacher. "My mom, dad, and sister are home," he shouted. "Can I go see them?"[2]

His parents had been in New York, where they were tending to

George's little sister, Robin. He knew she was sick, but had no idea *how* sick. The three-year-old was dying from leukemia.

George's parents returned with an empty backseat and emptier news. "I run over to the car," said Bush almost half a century later, "and there's no Robin."[3] She was not coming home. "I was sad, and stunned," recalls Bush. "I knew Robin had been sick, but death was hard for me to imagine. Minutes before, I had had a little sister, and now, suddenly, I did not." Bush says that those minutes remain the "starkest memory" of his childhood—"a sharp pain in the midst of an otherwise happy blur."[4] When asked about the incident in an interview, his eyes welled with tears and he stammered his response.[5]

Pauline Robinson "Robin" Bush started to show symptoms in February 1953, just after the birth of her baby brother Jeb. She simply wanted to lie down all day. Mysterious bruises began appearing on her body. The Bushes took her to Dr. Dorothy Wyvell, renowned in West Texas pediatrics, who was shocked by the test results. She told the Bushes that the child's white blood cell count was the highest she had ever seen, and the cancer was already too advanced to treat. She recommended they simply take Robin home and allow nature to take its course, sparing all of them the agony of futile medications.[6]

The Bushes couldn't do that. George's father, George H. W. Bush, had an uncle in New York who was president of Memorial Sloan-Kettering Cancer Center. They agreed to do everything they could in the hope of some kind of breakthrough.[7]

Barbara Bush was constantly at Robin's side during the hospital stay. Her husband shuttled between New York and Midland. Each morning of Robin's New York stay, her father dropped by the family's Midland church at 6:30 A.M. to hold his own private prayer vigil. Only the custodian was there, and he let him in. One morning, Pastor Matthew Lynn joined him. They never talked; they just prayed.[8]

Robin never had a chance. Eventually, the medicine that labored to try to control the evil in her frail frame caused its own set of problems, and George H. W. was summoned from Texas immediately. He flew all night to get there, but by the time he arrived Robin had slipped into a coma and she died peacefully. "One minute she was there, and the next she was gone," remembered her mother. "I truly felt her soul go out of that beautiful little body. For one last time I combed her hair, and we held our precious little girl. I never felt the presence of God more strongly than at that moment."[9]

It all happened so fast; Robin died weeks before her fourth birthday.[10] The tragedy devastated the Bushes; it is likely the reason Barbara Bush turned prematurely gray.[11] She had been the strong one who held Robin's hand when she received blood transfusions at the cancer center; Robin's father had to leave the room.[12]

"We awakened night after night in great physical pain—it hurt that much," Barbara recalled.[13] Her husband said that he "learned the true meaning of grief when Robin died." Even though he believed that Robin was now "in God's loving arms," the distress never disappeared. The former president told CNN's Larry King in November 1999, "We hurt now." Five years after Robin's death, in the summer of 1958, George H. W. wrote a long letter to his mother. It was a sort of poem, with a dozen lines that began, "We need . . ." Each line stressed how much he and Barbara missed having a little girl around the house, amid the four boys. "We need a girl," Robin's father concluded.[14] (The Bushes were blessed with a daughter the next summer— their final child, Dorothy, who today raises four children of her own in Maryland.)

After Robin's death, the Bush family struggled to put their lives back together. One Friday night, they decided to attend a high-school football game with friends. Everyone avoided the hurtful subject on all minds. The silence was broken by young George, who stood on his tiptoes in the bleachers, craning his neck to see the field over the tall heads. Suddenly, he announced to everyone's dismay, "Dad, I wish I was Robin." A terrible silence ensued. His father visibly blanched. "Gee," his dad tenderly responded, "why would you say that, George?" Because Robin is in heaven, George explained: "She can probably see the game better from up there than we can from down here."[15] Robin had the best seat in the house.

George W. Bush is a rugged guy, a kind of cowboy—an image that works both for him and against him, usually depending upon the ideology of the source. He rightly says that his personality is "more complex than one or two events."[16] Yet his public image belies a more emotional side.

Robin's death hit Bush hard. A childhood friend named Randall Roden remembers spending the night at the Bush house; when George awoke screaming, his mother rushed in to comfort him. "I knew what it was about," said Roden. "He had nightmares for some period of time. It was one of the most realistic experiences I have ever had about death and . . . it had a profound effect on him."[17] Eight years later, at prep school in the Northeast, when young George was asked to write about a soul-stirring experience in his life, he wrote about Robin.[18]

Though he remembers being very sad, Bush says that his parents loved him enough that the death did not traumatize him. He learned never to take life for granted, to live it to the fullest. "Rather than making me fearful," he said, "the close reach of death made me determined to enjoy whatever life might bring, to live each day."[19]

It is telling that when George W. later wrote his life story, he began it with Robin.[20] She is the first subject in his memoir, and her picture is among the first. She stands next to her proud big brother, who rises a foot taller. She is wearing a buttoned shirt and white sweater. He is wearing a striped tie with a long clip and white pants and white shirt. His arm is around her; both are beaming. The resemblance is clear: she is undoubtedly a Bush.

Robin's death got her seven-year-old brother thinking about God and eternity. Before her passing, the beyond was a vague and distant concept for him. The experience also taught him about finding security in a heavenly father. He found comfort in the assurance that Robin was safe in heaven, from where she could watch them. One September day forty years after her death, the Bushes were attending Sunday service at St. Ann's by the Sea, their church in Kennebunkport, Maine; the theme was about being "prepared to go home." Pensively, George W. stared at a stained-glass window of Jesus Christ holding out His arms to a child, and told his mother, "That makes me think of Robin."[21]

GEORGE WALKER BUSH WAS BORN ON JULY 6, 1946, IN New Haven, Connecticut, where the family resided while his father, George Herbert Walker Bush, finished his undergraduate degree at Yale. They were there because his father had ignored the advice of Secretary of War Henry L. Stimson's commencement address to the 1942 prep-school class, in which Stimson had advised the senior Bush and his classmates to finish their education before considering military service. No, said Bush. Instead, he enlisted, postponing college to become the youngest navy pilot commissioned in the war.[22]

He and Barbara met and were married in Connecticut. George was born a year later. According to Barbara, her husband is the only man she ever kissed; no matter where George H. W. traveled, he called his wife and they prayed together before bed.[23]

When little George turned two, the family moved to the West

Texas town of Midland, where his father joined the oil industry. It is important to understand that while George H. W. was a northeasterner, George W. has always been pure Texan, of which he takes immense pride. Years later, in his first piece of political fund-raising mail, sent out as a gubernatorial candidate, he told his fellow Texans: "I view Texas as a way of life, a state of mind, a way to think."[24] He has said repeatedly that he loves Texas; it gave him his roots and shaped his character. To know Texas—and Midland in particular—is to know Bush.

Midland is where it all began for George W. in the late 1940s and 1950s. *Washington Post* reporters George Lardner Jr. and Lois Romano noted that while he was the only Bush child not born in Texas, George W. is "the one who would become the truest Texan, who had memories of the oil business, of sleeping in the back seat of the station wagon while his father waited for a well to come in."[25] Of all the Bushes, he has the most Texas in his blood.

In those days, the dry, dusty Midland had a frontier feeling— sandstorms whirled, tumbleweeds tossed. When he arrived at school in the morning, he dusted sand off his desk. One time, a pounding rain that followed a long dry spell left frogs everywhere, croaking in fields and on porches, like the biblical plague.[26]

It was a small town, where families watched out for one another and everyone went to church on Sunday. When they did, Midland's flock left their doors unlocked.

The Bush family attended the First Presbyterian Church in Midland. That was a switch for George's father, who had been reared in the Episcopal church. George H. W. was raised in a home where each morning at the breakfast table his Connecticut mother or father read a Bible lesson to the children. On Sundays, they attended services at Christ Church in Greenwich. George H. W.'s grandfather, whose full name was the familiar George Herbert Walker, had been born into a devout Catholic family in St. Louis, and was named after the seventeenth-century religious poet George Herbert.[27]

Now in Midland, the Episcopalian became a Presbyterian—the denomination of his wife—so that the entire family could attend one church.[28] There, at First Presbyterian, he taught Sunday school. The family spent eleven good years at that church before leaving Midland in 1959. More than twenty years later, when George W. returned to that same church, he too would teach Sunday school.

George's earliest memories of Midland involve baseball, which he played in the buffalo wallow behind the family's house on Sentinel Street. The game is his lifelong love. In those days, Texas had no major league baseball team: George W.'s big chance to watch professional baseball came when he visited his grandparents in the East. The New York Giants were his favorite team, and Willie Mays his idol. He wanted to be Willie.[29]

To this day, Bush says he can recite the entire lineup of the 1954 Giants.[30] Though he goes to bed early, he likes to try to watch *Sports-Center* on ESPN, where he catches the latest from the baseball diamond. He cites *Field of Dreams* as his favorite film—a movie about a father and son and their love for each other and for baseball. As president, he recently read the latest biography of Dodgers great Sandy Koufax.

His father had been a southpaw first baseman at Yale, where he rose to be captain of the team before withdrawing from college to fly in combat. George W.'s neighborhood buddies were in awe when his father caught the ball behind his back. They all tried to imitate the feat. George was a catcher; he still fondly remembers the moment his father told him, "Son, you've arrived. I can throw it to you as hard as I want to."[31]

He also played football, a natural outgrowth of the weekly community pilgrimage to high-school football games on Friday nights, a Texas tradition. In seventh grade, George was the quarterback for the football team.

For six years, Bush attended school at Sam Houston Elementary. He completed seventh grade at San Jacinto Junior High, where he was popular. There, for the first time, he ran for president, and won. To this day, he has yet to lose a presidential bid.[32]

His life changed in 1959 when the family moved to Houston, so that his father could be closer to his oil rigs. This was a major shift for George—and, while it broadened his borders, he was saddened to leave his friends. Though he adjusted, he never fully recovered; privately, he longed for West Texas.

Nonetheless, George H. W.'s financial prospects were finally looking up. One thing that has not been generally understood about the Bushes is that while George H. W.'s relations had money, at first he and Barbara did not. Before he had an oil well, the senior Bush was a clerk; his family's home was a tiny box in a low-income section of town, purchased with an FHA loan. Before that, George and his parents had settled for an apartment in a shotgun house, where they shared a bathroom with two prostitutes who lived next door.[33] This was not the Greenwich Country Club.

It was during these earliest years that George came by his lifelong ability to roll with the punches. By his teen years, the Bush brood had expanded substantially. Robin was gone, but George had three brothers: Jeb, a baby when Robin died, was followed by Neil and Marvin. They were soon joined by a sister, Dorothy, the last of the Bush kin. Huddled in the car, the family drove 744 miles eastward across the flat plains to Houston. The fourteen-hour drive toward the Gulf of Mexico brought a different climate: Houston was green, and it had rain.

In Houston, George made his first shift in religious denominations. The family went back to his father's roots, joining St. Martin's Episcopal Church at the corner of Sage and Woodway. George became an altar boy, and remained so until he left for prep school. In his early teen years, he served Communion at the 8:00 A.M. service and relished the Episcopal trappings. "I loved the formality, the ritual, the candles," he said, "and there, I felt the first stirrings of a faith that would be years in the shaping."[34]

MOM AND DAD

During those earliest Texas days, mothers were the rock in the family. Most of the fathers in the Bushes' social circle were in the oil business, which meant they were often away at drilling sites. This left the mothers with the task of driving children to and from ball games. This does not mean that George's father—whom he always refers to simply as "Dad"—was an absent father.

Today, Bush says that "unconditional love is the greatest gift a parent can give a child" and that the unconditional love his parents bestowed on him and his siblings "freed" them.[35] Growing up, they knew that "while they might not approve of everything we did . . . our mother and dad would always love us. Always. Forever. Unwaveringly. Without question. They said it and showed it." During his father's twelve years as vice president and president, he stresses, his father was never too busy to take a call from his children or to write them lengthy letters.[36]

There are parallels between how Bush views his earthly parents and his heavenly one. He has likewise expressed the conviction that faith in God frees individuals, and that God wishes His children to be free. Like his perception of his parents, he views God as loving all His children unconditionally, though he may not approve of their many missteps. Bush himself has frequently drawn this connection between the love of God and the love of a parent.

The bond between George and his mother tightened after Robin's death. Following the loss, George H. W. got back on the road with the oil business. At home alone with the two boys, though, Barbara suffered great despair after her daughter's death. And her oldest son, deeply aware of his mother's anguish, worked to make her feel better by becoming a jokester, a cutup.

Rather than go out with his friends, Bush stayed home to try to cheer her up. Barbara once said that this did not dawn on her until she overheard George telling friends that he could not play because he had to stay home and play with his mother. "I was thinking, 'Well, I'm being there for him,'" she remembered. "But the truth was he was being there for me."[37]

The fact that his father was on the road so much brought George and his mother ever closer. Once, in the mid-1960s, George drove his mother to the hospital while she was having a miscarriage. When she worried that she would not be able to walk out of the car, George told her he would carry her into the emergency room. She spent the night in the hospital and lost the baby. The next day, Barbara's son sternly asked, "Don't you think we ought to talk about this before you have more children?"[38]

While he looks like his father and shares many of his mannerisms, friends and relatives say that George's personality comes from his mother. The two of them speak to each other in a way father and son do not; they disagree candidly, sparring and even respectfully sassing each other. An illustration of these personalities was evident in George's first marathon. His parents stood and cheered at the nineteen-mile mark. As his father cheered him on—"There's my boy!"—his mother shouted and teased: "There are some elderly women ahead of you! Why are you running so slow?"[39]

Teddy Roosevelt has been quoted as saying that his father was the greatest man he ever knew. George W. has said the same about *his* father. At the dedication of his father's presidential library, he called him "the world's greatest dad." At the start of his Republican convention speech in Philadelphia in August 2000, in a subtle reference to President Bill Clinton allegedly calling him "daddy's boy" two days earlier, George W. looked toward his father's seat and proclaimed before a national audience, "I am *proud* to be your son."

To the Northeast

The teenage George had settled into a contented life in Houston when his parents started talking of sending him to Phillips Academy in Andover, Massachusetts, one of the nation's most exclusive college prep schools and his father's alma mater. "My parents wanted me to learn not only the academics," said Bush, "but also how to thrive on my own."[40] In 1961, he was accepted and enrolled at the age of fifteen. Andover, he soon found, was nothing like Texas. Unlike school at Sam Houston, he ditched his T-shirt and blue jeans for a coat and tie. There were no girls at all.

Bush attended chapel at Phillips every day except Wednesday and Saturday, and served as a deacon at the chapel, though the extent to which his attendance was a pious one is difficult to determine. One journalist reported that the deacon role at Phillips had long since lost any serious religious significance.[41] Chapel services were required, though they often served as school-wide meetings featuring general announcements and guest speakers. Sunday services were led by a Protestant minister named A. Graham Baldwin.[42]

Bush made friends fast in Andover, earning the nicknames "Tweeds" and "Lip." He played varsity baseball and basketball and JV football, was head cheerleader and a member of the Athletic Advisory Board, Student Congress, Spanish Club, and the Phillips Society, and was proctor at the America House. He was bestowed the mock honor of High Commissioner of Stickball,[43] and finished second in voting for Big Man on Campus. At the academy George W. also learned discipline, how to think, and to read and write with proficiency. A teacher named Tom Lyons imparted to George a lifelong love of history, which he majored in at Yale a few years later. To this day, his books of choice are more often than not works of history.

In his memoir, after describing his first taste of politics in Andover, he wrote about how the people there encouraged him "to rise to the occasion."[44] One of the most surprising aspects of Bush the politician is that he is able to call on this talent at key moments. Friendly and unfriendly observers alike have marveled at his unexpectedly strong performances in the public arena; he seems to have discovered that surprising ability at Phillips.

Much of that surprise has been expressed by modern pundits, born of their continual underestimation of Bush. Though the president has never pretended to be a genius, he is far cleverer than many give him credit for being. At Andover, Bush learned not to try to forge a phony pretense regarding intelligence. He still remembers the first paper he wrote, for which he pulled out a thesaurus and substituted fancy, flowery words to describe his emotions. Instead of simply saying that "tears" ran down a face, he wrote that "lacerates" fell. The paper was returned with a giant zero, carved so emphatically that it could be seen from the back side of the blue book.[45]

It has always been tough to stereotype Bush, particularly during his younger years. At every elite school he attended, classmates remember him as a swaggering kind of good ol' boy from Texas. Yet not even the snobs seem to have held that against him; by all accounts he fit right in and was perennially popular. He had a peculiar tendency to be a snob against snobbery, despising showy displays of wealth and valuing humility over ostentation.

Bush spent his next four years at Yale, where he earned a bachelor's degree in history in 1968. Rather than absorbing spiritual enrichment, Bush gained a reputation as a partygoer at college. Though a fairly serious student, Bush remained a prankster, the president of a fraternity, and someone with whom anyone could have a good time.

As he had been at Phillips, at Yale Bush was greatly bothered by "intellectual snobbery."[46] He was popular, seemed to enjoy himself, and did well academically. He had entered with a score of 1206 on his SATs, a high score by the stricter SAT scoring of that era. The *Washington Post* gained access to a copy of his grade transcript. Though it did not publish Bush's grades, the *Post* did note, by comparison, that Vice President Al Gore's grades in his sophomore year at Harvard were lower than any semester recorded on Bush's transcript from Yale.[47]

Yale also offered reinforcement of the comfort with issues of race he had learned at home. In a time when Martin Luther King Jr. was killed, Bush was buddies with Yale football star and future NFL all-pro Calvin Hill. To this day, he vividly recounts a talk about being a "Negro in America" by Dick Gregory, the black activist, at a Yale graduation event. Thirty years later, in his memoir, he would quote from Gregory's speech.[48]

This was not a time of punctilious churchgoing for Bush. One of his few encounters with a minister was a visit he paid to Yale chaplain William Sloane Coffin, who was well known as an antiwar, radical left theologian. When Bush had some questions about the Vietnam

War, about the protests and upheaval he saw around him, his father suggested he drop in and talk to Coffin for advice. According to Bush, not only was Coffin unhelpful, but he also insulted his father. At the time, Bush Sr. had just lost a close Texas race for the U.S. Senate to a liberal Democrat named Ralph Yarborough. "I knew your father," Bush remembers Coffin commenting, "and your father lost to a better man."[49] It was not the only time the younger Bush would encounter a rude reception from a liberal theologian.

For the record, Coffin later said that he had no recollection of a conversation with Bush—and that if he had said anything of the kind it would have been in jest. Yet Bush told his parents of the incident right away, and to this day they remember how clearly it affected him. His mother has said that Coffin's comment was "shattering" to her son. "And it was a very awful thing for a chaplain to say to a freshman at college," she continued, "particularly if he might have wanted to have seen him in church. I'm not sure that George ever put his foot again [in the school chapel]."[50] Yet Bush himself never forgot "how to pray," he has said, regardless of whether or not he did so inside a house of worship.[51]

THE REAL WORLD

Spiritually, the late 1960s and 1970s found George W. Bush spending less time searching his soul, and more trying to find a gainful place in the world.

In 1968, eager to follow in his father's footsteps, Bush joined the Texas Air National Guard and became an F-102 fighter pilot. Spending fifty-five weeks on active duty before graduating in December 1969, he logged thousands of miles and discovered a new lifelong love.

From there, Bush did some job-hopping, some volunteer campaign work, some travel. He did a stint as a management trainee with an agribusiness company in Houston, a job with stability but little satisfaction. This was a notably unclear time in his life.

Then Bush took a low-profile job that had a profound influence on his life and thinking. He accepted a full-time position with Project PULL (Professional United Leadership League), an inner-city poverty program located at 1711 McGowen Street in the heart of the slums of Houston's Third Ward. PULL recruited professional athletes during the off-season to offer their time as role models for young black boys under the age of seventeen. A recruiter for the program, Bush also became a mentor himself.

John L. White, a former tight end with the Houston Oilers, had asked Bush's father to help him with the program after the two met during George H. W.'s 1970 Senate campaign. Behind the scenes, his father asked White to find his son a place in the program. He wanted his son to see that side of life, and perhaps improve his focus in the process.

Bush was the only white person on all of McGowen Street. "Any white guy that showed up on McGowen was gonna get caught in some tough situations," said one of PULL's founders. "You better be able to handle yourself." George W. "stood out like a sore thumb," according to one of PULL's senior counselors. With his shabby casual clothes and beat-up car, Bush the sloppy bachelor looked nothing like an Ivy Leaguer.[52]

By his own account, PULL introduced Bush to a world he had never seen: a tableau of homelessness, drug and alcohol abuse, fatherless children, single mothers, teens who could not read, boys who hid guns under their shirts. "It was tragic, heartbreaking," said Bush, but also "uplifting." It was his introduction to what a well-meaning non-profit organization could do—his first lesson in what he would later call compassionate conservatism.

One employee remembered Bush's devotion: "[He] came early and stayed late." Bush wrestled with the boys, played basketball, and took them on field trips to juvenile jails as a deterrent to crime. He taught them not to run when police drove by. He was also creative in settling them down: One day he took a group of raucous boys for a plane ride. When one of the teens started getting rough, Bush stalled the engine, scaring the teen and his friends into obedient silence.[53]

"Big Cat" Ernie Ladd, an NFL star, spoke glowingly of Bush at PULL. "He was a super, super guy," said Ladd, who promised he would call Bush "a stinker" if he was one. "Everybody loved him so much. He had a way with people. . . . They didn't want him to leave."[54]

The biggest impact Bush made at PULL was on a six- or seven-year-old boy named Jimmy Dean; likewise, the boy seems to have made a strong impact on Bush. Bush has said that Jimmy became like a little brother to him. Edgar Arnold, a PULL director, called Jimmy an "adorable kid." "Everybody liked him, but he bypassed all these famous athletes, all these giants, and picked out George Bush, and vice versa."[55]

The two were inseparable: Bush called Jimmy his "adopted little brother." In the morning, the boy waited for him at the curb. During the day, he rode around on Bush's shoulders. One day, when Jimmy showed up without sneakers, the future president bought him a pair. One night George drove Jimmy home. The boy's house was a dump. His mother answered the door stoned on dope. "I was incredibly sad to leave him there," said Bush.[56]

Bush eventually left the job to go to Harvard. White advised that he could do a lot more for those kids one day if he got a Harvard degree.

When White died a few years later, Bush returned to deliver the eulogy. There he learned that little Jimmy had been shot and killed in the ghetto.[57] In later years, Bush said that Project PULL reinforced his biblical belief that "we are all equal in the eyes of a loving God."[58]

George W. opted for an MBA at Harvard Business School, which he called the West Point of capitalism. "I was there to learn," remembered the focused Bush, "and that's exactly what I did." He lived alone in an apartment, jogged, rode his bike, studied a lot, and graduated in June 1975.[59]

Once again, he detested the intellectual vanity around him. In a way, he literally spit at it. "One of my first recollections of him," said Marty Kahn, a Harvard classmate, "was sitting in class and hearing the unmistakable sound of someone spitting tobacco. I turned around and there was George sitting in the back of the room in his [Air Guard] bomber jacket spitting in a cup." "You have to remember," Kahn continued, "this was Harvard Business School. You just didn't see that kind of thing."[60] Whether in Cambridge, New Haven, or Andover, you couldn't remove the Texan from George W. Bush.

After getting his master's from Harvard, he tossed everything he had into his blue 1970 Cutlass and headed back to Texas. He could get along in New England, as he had in the previous decade, but it still left him with a fish-out-of-water feeling. He returned to his roots, his comfort zone, and went searching for meaning in Midland—cowboy country, oil country. "West Texas," he recognized, "was in my blood."[61]

Back in Midland, he started at rock bottom in the oil business, where he hoped to find success and perhaps a sense of calling. His company, Arbusto, missed black gold everywhere it poked. Rival drillers started calling Arbusto "Ar-busted." Bush started drinking.

Two years after returning to Midland, in 1977, he met Laura

Welch, a Midland girl who had gone to elementary school at James Bowie, not far from Sam Houston.

Laura had earned a bachelor's degree in education in 1968 from Southern Methodist University. After teaching for a while at schools in Dallas and Houston, she entered the University of Texas at Austin and earned a master's degree in library science in 1973. After that, she worked at the Houston Public Library before returning to Austin in 1974. Then she became a public school librarian at Dawson Elementary School, where she remained until her marriage.

In November 1977, only a few months after they met, George and Laura—both thirty-one—were married. Naturally, they made their first home in Midland.

They both desperately wanted children, but pregnancy proved elusive. Just as they were starting to think about adoption, however, they were blessed. On November 25, 1981, they became the parents of twin girls, whom they named after the twins' grandmothers, Barbara and Jenna.

Settling in Midland also meant it was time for George to get on track spiritually. For a time, he and Laura attended both her church, the First United Methodist Church in Midland, and his, the First Presbyterian Church in Midland. At the Presbyterian church, George W.'s increasing seriousness was evident: soon he was teaching Sunday school, just as his father had done years before at that same church.

After the twins' baptism in 1982, George officially joined Laura's church. Like his father, he deferred to his wife's denomination, deciding to join one church as a family. After years of flipping between Protestant denominations, mainly Episcopal and Presbyterian, this switch to the Methodist faith was permanent.

George immediately became active in the Methodist church, where he served on the finance committee. On Sundays it was his job to count the money collected from the congregation, then spend Sunday afternoons at meetings of the administrative committee. He also became involved with the United Way and chaired one of its campaigns. In this time of personal volunteer service with faith-related groups, George W. Bush was taking a step forward in his faith and his life. Now a husband and a father—and a man undergoing a serious stage of spiritual growth—Bush must have known that moving back to Midland had been the right thing to do.

Nonetheless, Bush still had a way to go. Blaise Pascal believed that in every heart there is a God-shaped vacuum that only God can fill[62]; in these years, the hole in George W.'s heart was at best partly full. It was an encounter at the family vacation home in Maine that would forever change and define him.

2.

"Mustard Seed" and Compassionate Conservatism

"Faith changes lives. I know, because faith has changed mine."

—*Governor George W. Bush*[1]

In the summer of 1985, the Bush family gathered in beautiful Kennebunkport, Maine. The idyllic New England town dates back to the early seventeenth century. At that time, this section of Maine was not known for religious fervor. According to an early history, the prevailing opinion was that the area was peopled by those "too immoral and irreligious" to be allowed to remain in the other colonies. One of the few places of piety was the home of, ironically, a man named Bush—a Mr. John Bush (no relation)—who, according to historian

Charles Bradbury, did what he could to satisfy the "want of regular religious and moral instruction" among the wanting.[2]

In Kennebunkport three and a half centuries later, there was another individual in want of religious and moral instruction—George W. Bush. And yet another Bush, George H. W., tried to supply the need through the help of a dear friend: the Reverend Billy Graham. The Bush family had for years owned a vacation home in Kennebunkport, and George W. had spent many lazy summers there. The summer of 1985, though, was different. George was about to be affected so profoundly that, arguably, without the events of this weekend he could never have become president.

Near the Bushes' home was a small summer church called St. Ann's by the Sea. It was not every Sunday at little St. Ann's that the world's most famous evangelist ascended the pulpit. Billy Graham was in town, at the invitation of the elder Bush. After the service, George's father asked Graham if he would field questions from the big group of Bushes gathered that weekend. Graham said he would be happy to comply.

Though George W. today swears he cannot remember specifically what Graham said, something he did "sparked a change" in Bush's heart. He has said that it was as much the crusader's "power of example"—his demeanor, how he comported himself—as his words that affected him. As Christians might put it, it was how he "modeled the faith."

The next day Bush and Graham went for a stroll at Walker's Point, and had a heart-to-heart conversation. "I knew I was in the presence of a great man," said Bush. "He was like a magnet; I felt drawn to seek something different. He didn't lecture or admonish; he shared warmth and concern. Billy Graham didn't make you feel guilty; he made you feel loved." It was the kind of Christianity that

Bush himself would later emulate. This moment became the forma-
tive faith experience in his life. Reverend Graham "planted a mustard
seed in my soul," Bush later wrote. "He led me to the path, and I began walking."[3]

Graham didn't criticize Bush. He didn't tell the Texan he was
headed for Hell. He embraced Bush. He was exactly the right messenger at the right time.

It is easy to overdramatize the Graham encounter. It was not a
lightning bolt that suddenly made Bush a Christian. He had thought
about God and the hereafter from the earliest days of his life, beginning with Robin's death and the churches of his youth. Before meeting with Graham, he had even taught Sunday school. As Bush recalls
today, "I had always been a religious person." Yet that weekend his
faith "took on new meaning." In retrospect, he saw it as "the beginning of a new walk where I would recommit my heart to Jesus Christ."[4]

Some believers fall away; their earnestness ebbs and flows. Bush
may or may not have fallen in that category during this hard time.
Nonetheless, something clicked with Graham. Bush took a larger step
that would make him the deeply devout Christian he remains today.
Bush describes what began under Graham, and the recommitment
that followed, not as a "born-again" experience—a word he is uncomfortable using—but, rather, as a "renewal of faith," or a "rededication"
to God, or flatly, "an acceptance of Christ."[5] Bush has referred to Graham as a "messenger," who simply "lit a spark inside me that kindled a
flame over time."[6] As governor, he explained: "By chance, or maybe it
wasn't chance . . . I got to spend a weekend with the great Billy Graham. And as a result of our conversations and his inspiration, I
searched my heart and recommitted my life to Jesus Christ."[7]

Understood this way, Bush's spiritual trek began with the baby
steps of his youth, with Robin and the Midland church, then the

teenage steps as an altar boy in Houston, and the adult steps teaching Sunday school. Then came the encounter with Graham, who pointed him toward the light—Bush's most meaningful step toward enlightenment. More would follow. Bush has said that his faith was "years in the shaping," and that he is still growing spiritually.[8] It is a life's journey.

When Bush returned to Midland after the Graham weekend, his friend Don Evans,[9] a committed Christian, asked him to join a Bible study group. Bush jumped at the opportunity, and never turned back.[10]

STILL, GEORGE W.'S LIFE CHANGE HARDLY CAME OVER-night, or over one Bible study. His was no Saul-like conversion; he continued to struggle for nearly a year.

That was painfully obvious one April 1986 evening, when Bush approached husband-and-wife journalists Al Hunt and Judy Wood-ruff at a Mexican restaurant and cursed out Hunt in front of the couple's four-year-old. Hunt had recently predicted that Jack Kemp would defeat Bush's father for the 1988 presidential nomination.[11] "You [expletive] son of a bitch," Hunt remembered Bush saying. "I saw what you wrote. We're not going to forget this." Hunt and Woodruff were embarrassed. Bush, rude and crude, was not; after all, he'd been drinking. By his own admission, a reporter's criticism of his father could set him on "the warpath." Referring to his father's cam-paign, he called himself "a warrior for George Bush."[12]

On that occasion, to Hunt and Woodruff and their innocent child, Bush acted like a wretch, blind to grace. This was the "once I was lost" George W. That precious grace had not yet appeared.

Three months later, Bush turned forty—and this birthday marked a true turning point for the wayward son. Several of his friends also turned forty that year, and they gathered in Colorado Springs on Don Evans's birthday for a collective celebration. That, of course, meant drinking. Though Bush and others maintain that he was never an alcoholic, once he began guzzling beer, he did not seem eager to stop. "Once he got started," said Don Evans, "he couldn't, didn't, shut it off. He didn't have the discipline."[13]

That birthday bash was no exception. By Bush's account they had a "big time" at a dinner at the Broadmoor Hotel. He woke the next day with a terrific hangover. As he had done every day for the past fourteen years, he hopped out of bed and went for a three-mile run—which, for Bush, is a literal run more than a jog. This dash, however, was not like the others. When he returned he felt awful. He went back to the hotel and informed Laura flatly, "I'm quitting drinking." He is not sure she believed him. Yet he was serious. He did stop, for good.[14]

This was a full year after his meeting with Graham. The encounter had grown on him, prompting a spiritual seriousness that later helped him overcome the bottle once he resolved to kick it. "I quit drinking in 1986 and haven't had a drop since then," Bush now declares. "It wasn't because of a government program. . . . I heard a higher calling."[15]

After becoming president, he told a group of clergy: "I had a drinking problem. Right now I should be in a bar in Texas, not the Oval Office. There is only one reason that I am in the Oval Office and not in a bar. I found faith. I found God."[16] On another occasion, he told pastoral social workers in Nashville: "I would not be president today if I hadn't stopped drinking seventeen years ago. And I could only do that with the grace of God."[17]

Bush himself has listed other reasons for quitting the bottle. Among them may have been the fact that his public drunkenness at times embarrassed his father. Still, Bush himself contends that faith was the one undeniable force that carried him through.

For many men, the forties are a time of doubt and midlife crisis. For Bush, they were the start of an upsurge, of personal rebuilding, of improvement.

COMMITMENT

The role of George's parents should not be excluded from this equation. His parents raised him to believe in God. His "introduction to faith" came from them; they "laid the framework for eventually what came to be."[18] Even the pivotal Graham incident came about because of his parents' invitation to the preacher. George H. W. had long been a fan: "I love Billy Graham," he wrote in a July 1982 letter.[19]

Back in Midland, Bush began his Bible study with Don Evans. A bellwether of his seriousness was the evening he and his buddies gave up *Monday Night Football* for Monday-night Bible. "For the first time," said a still-surprised and thrilled Laura, her husband and his pals "weren't just spending their time sitting around kicking back with hamburgers and beer."[20]

The group Bush joined was part of Community Bible Study, a national nondenominational program devised by a group of Christians in Washington, D.C. The rigorous study met weekly in groups of ten to twelve members at the home of local dentist Robert Henry, focusing each year on just one book of the New Testament. The class integrated outside sources and featured group discussion. Each gathering took several hours of preparation, reading assigned chapters and contemplating questions.[21] Bush looked forward to the discussions, and his interest in reading the Bible "grew stronger and stronger." The words became clearer to him and more meaningful.[22]

The group zeroed in on the writings of the historian and physician Luke, spending the first year on his Book of Acts and the second year on his Gospel. Luke's is the third and longest of the New Testament's four Gospels. Acts, which follows the last of the four Gospels, is the third-lengthiest book in the New Testament; it examines the initial days of the Christian church. In all, these writings constitute more than one quarter of the New Testament. Luke is hailed by both liberal and conservative scholars for his erudition, painstaking attention to facts, and historical reliability.[23]

Outside of Luke and the Gospel writers, the most important New Testament author was Paul, the onetime relentless persecutor of Christ. Of the New Testament's twenty-one Letters, thirteen were penned by Paul. Together, the learned Paul and Luke provided the majority of the New Testament's text. Martin Luther called Paul's Letter to the Romans "the principal part of the New Testament." Bush admired Paul's conversion from a wolf pursuing Christians to a lamb that defended his Messiah, from persecutor to persecuted. "A prisoner for the Lord," Paul called himself.

Bush went well beyond a shallow understanding of the faith. His grasp of Christianity was more than just "a kind of fraternity handshake," as the New York Times's Bill Keller put it.[24] Keller and others have characterized Bush's personal God as "his 12-step program" to meet a midlife crisis and drinking problem. "This kind of born-again epiphany is common in much of America—the red-state version of psychotherapy," Keller judged.[25] Where some middle-aged men get a sports car, by this logic, and others get a girlfriend or perhaps a psychiatrist, Bush got Jesus.

Yet it is a mistake to view Bush's faith as merely emotional, filling a psychological need. It developed over many years of reflection and experience, of listening to sermons and serving in a variety of functions within a diversity of Protestant denominations, of discussions with theologians and preachers, of teaching and attending Sunday school and Bible study, and from daily reading of the Bible and devotionals.

The Midland Bible study really never ended for Bush; it uncorked a yet deeper examination of Christianity. "That's when I began to read the Bible every day," he recalled.[26] He "began to have a better understanding" of the Christian faith.[27] Yet, it was more than that: the Bible study, said Bush at the time, "changed my life."[28]

At the Methodist church, he continued to read the Bible daily, using an intense "one-year" Bible given to him by Evans. It featured 365 daily readings, each excerpting a section from both the Old and New Testaments, and, in addition, the Book of Psalms and Proverbs—four separate sections for each day. Altogether, this was a significant amount of text—arguably too much, unless the reader is quick, disciplined, and sets aside the time, which Bush did.[29] In fact, Bush now reads through that same one-year Bible every other year. During the years in between, he picks up a regular Bible and studies different books at different times, guided by his interests and curiosity.[30] He has read the Bible from cover to cover a number of times.

All along, as Bush dug in, the Scriptures took on greater meaning and he grew more in his "confidence and understanding" of his faith. At the First Methodist Church in Midland, he and Laura participated in a number of family programs, including a series on raising children produced by James Dobson's *Focus on the Family*.[31]

STEPPING UP — THE GOVERNOR

After this period of renewal, Bush began achieving his greatest professional successes. In 1988 he worked on his father's victorious presidential campaign, in which one of his chief duties was to try to draw Christian conservatives. Biographer Bill Minutaglio called him "his father's constant arm to the hard Christian Right." He actively sought the support of men like Jerry Falwell and Jim Bakker. As one 1988 campaign staffer later told Minutaglio, "The first time I ever met Dr. Jim Dobson, it was in George W.'s office in the '88 campaign." Having recently committed himself so strongly to Christianity, George W. was a natural liaison to this political contingent, and these men were always more comfortable spiritually with him than with his father.[32]

After the presidential campaign, Bush assembled a group of partners who purchased the Texas Rangers baseball franchise in 1989. Bush himself served as managing general partner of the club; his dream of being involved with major league baseball had finally come true.

Anchored by a hardening bedrock of faith, Bush now learned to take both wins and losses in stride. He now had that saving grace that had so long eluded him; it was like a salve when in November 1992 a new Bush coped with his father's failed reelection bid. He, his father, and campaign director Mary Matalin sat on Air Force One and cried as they listened to the Oak Ridge Boys sing "Amazing Grace" while they absorbed his dad's impending defeat.[33] A few years earlier, Bush would have lashed out. Now a God-granted grace was helping him to respond to turmoil with dignity.

In 1993, shortly after his defeated father handed over the White House to former Arkansas governor Bill Clinton, Bush resolved to run for governor of Texas. Immediately, he was under unusually high pressure to articulate what he believed. Everyone, even sympathizers, wanted to be sure he was not just running on his father's name. The problem was that the campaign did not have its wheels down yet. Bush privately took the initiative. He sat down and penned what his staff called his "I believe" statement—a series of roughly a dozen remarks that instituted a working mission statement. "It was brilliant," said Brian Berry, who met Bush in 1993 and managed his first gubernatorial bid. "A big hit. We didn't expect it. It became a part of press releases, direct mail, fund-raising mail, his kickoff speech for the primary. It really worked. It was just what we needed."[34]

About the only item Bush steered clear of in the political document was his faith. That, however, quickly became clear to his staff. Campaign manager Brian Berry, who helped the new governor hire his team, said of Bush's faith: "I saw it in the way he conducted himself in office and with other people. He won't quote you the book and Scripture verse. He knows it but doesn't go around saying it. Having said that, he lives the so-called Word. You see his faith in the way he acts." Berry was struck by his candidate's compassion: "The guy really *loves* people. I mean that. He is not just very personable, kind, and gentle, but is also a handholding kind of guy. He literally will hold your hand while he chats with you." Berry believes that to the extent that this "love" comes from Bush's faith, it is based in the lessons of the New Testament. "I see him as a New Testament kind of Christian," says Berry. "A Sermon on the Mount type. He is not fire and brimstone." Berry, who manages political campaigns for Republicans, has met conservatives he dubs "Old Testament Christians." Bush, he says, is a different story.[35]

Bush's 1994 campaign against Governor Ann Richards was tough. Richards was the odds-on favorite; even Barbara Bush advised her son not to run against the popular incumbent.[36]

One thing that might have fired his drive to unseat Richards was the fusillade of personal comments she made about Bush's father during her keynote address at the 1988 Democratic convention in Atlanta. "Pooooooor George!" Richards belted in a bellyaching Texas drawl, "He caaan't help it! He was born with a silver foot in his

mouth!" The audience of Democratic faithful went wild over the dig
at the Bush family's wealth and class. Barbara Bush was so sickened by
the insult that she felt physically ill.[37] Her son was furious.

Now, six years later, the man from Midland took her on—and
prevailed. Bush was elected governor on November 8, 1994, grabbing
53.5 percent of the vote.

Two months later, Bush awakened in eager anticipation of the inaugural ceremony. His mother handed him a letter from his father.
"Your mother and I," wrote the forty-first president, "have total confidence in your ability." He said they had "an overflowing sense of
pride" in their son. "You have given us more than we ever could have
deserved. . . . Now it is our turn. We love you." He signed it "Devot-
edly, Dad." To this day, the letter brings a lump to George W.'s
throat.[38]

At noon, the younger Bush placed his hand on Governor Sam
Houston's worn Bible and took the oath. A proud Billy Graham, who
had sworn in George's father as president in 1989, was on hand to
provide the invocation. The preacher pointed to the "moral and spiritual example [Bush's] mother and father set for us all."[39]

In his inaugural address, Bush promised fellow Texans: "The duties that I assume can best be met with the guidance of One greater
than ourselves. I ask for God's help."[40] It was the first of Bush's many
acknowledgments that he could not do the job without God's guidance. He ended by saying that the history of the "special land" of
Texas tells its citizens "that what Texans can dream, Texans can
do. . . . To be your governor is an unimaginable honor. Thank you for
your confidence in me and God bless Texas."

He had begun the day with a church service, where the hymn "A
Charge to Keep" was sung. A few weeks later, two friends from the
Midland days, Joe and Jan O'Neill, telephoned. Struck by Bush's

choice of the Charles Wesley hymn, they told their old friend that they happened to own a painting inspired by the song. The work of artist W. H. D. Koerner, it had been given to them by Joe's father as a wedding present. They offered to loan it to the new governor for his wall in his state office.[41]

Bush jumped at the offer and soon found a perfect fit on the wall across from his desk. That April he sent a memo to his staff telling them about the painting and how it "epitomizes" his mission for Texas. He asked that when they came to his office, they pause and look at the work. In this "beautiful painting of a horseman determinedly charging up what appears to be a steep and rough trail," he advised, they should recognize that "This is us." In the memo, he stressed the core message of the painting/hymn: "that we serve One greater than ourselves."[42]

This same thinking was evident in a speech Bush gave two years later, on July 8, 1997, in a dedication ceremony for the Jesse H. Jones Power Center, a ministry created by the Windsor Village United Methodist Church, an African-American church in Houston. The pastor at Windsor Village is Bush friend Kirbyjon H. Caldwell; two months later, Bush would appoint him to the University of Houston System of Board of Regents. Bush's address at the Power Center was his most spiritually revealing statement to date.

In the speech, Bush averred, "I am convinced that faith is *exactly* [his emphasis] what we need to help solve the Number One problem facing America today—and that is a culture which has failed." He listed symptoms of cultural failure: child abuse, poverty, teen births, violent crime, and the general decay of family life. The governor noted that in searching for the right course of action for correcting these problems "a good place to start" could be found in the words of Dr. Tony Evans, a prominent African-American minister in Dallas.

Bush then, for possibly the first time, shared an anecdote from Evans that he would return to repeatedly in the years ahead: Evans maintained that fixing America's societal problems was like fixing a cracked wall. When Evans spotted a crack in one of his walls, he called a painter, who promptly plastered and painted over the line— only to watch it reemerge a few weeks later with yet more zigzags. Evans called in a better painter, but this painter told him, "Sir, the crack on your wall is not the problem. That's just an ugly symptom. Your problem is that you have a shifting foundation. Fix the foundation first, and you will solve the cracks on your wall." To Evans, and to Bush, this was a parable for American society: "We have serious cracks in our culture that no amount of plaster will fix," observed Bush, "*unless* we shore up our moral foundation."[43]

Bush said that government could help with these ills—but only so much, since "all the laws in the world cannot make people love one another." Government "cannot fill the spiritual well from which we draw strength every day. Only faith can do that." "Purely secular solutions to social problems" have not worked. This, he told his audience, would be the essence of his approach to government, which he called "compassionate conservatism." "One of my missions as governor is to call on people of faith and people of goodwill to unleash their compassion," Bush said. He would mobilize "armies of compassion"— fellow citizens helping their brothers and sisters. Bush said that he wanted neighbor to help neighbor, quoting Martin Luther King Jr.: "My neighbor . . . is any needy man on one of the numerous Jericho roads of life. . . . He is a part of me and I am a part of him. His agony diminishes me and his salvation enlarges me."

Bush shared another revealing anecdote with the faithful at the Power Center. He joked about a minister who Sunday after Sunday had his sermons interrupted by a parishioner who yelled out, "Use me

Lord! Use me!" Finally, one Sunday the minister pulled the man aside and told him that the Lord had answered his prayer: "God would like you to sand down all the pews before next Sunday." The pastor figured he had heard the last interruption from the congregant—until the next Sunday, when the man called out again: "Use me Lord! Use me—but only in an *advisory* capacity." America had plenty of advisers, said the governor: "What we need is more doers."[44]

Bush followed by commending the Texas legislature, which, at his urging, had passed new laws that allowed and encouraged faith-based charities "to bring their compassion and hope" to the delivery of the state's social services. This was a precursor to the faith-based initiatives he would champion at the national level once he reached the White House. Bush found these faith-based groups superior to the traditional solutions offered by what he called "soulless bureaucracy."

GOVERNOR BUSH WAS REELECTED ON NOVEMBER 3, 1998, in a landslide, taking 68.6 percent of the ballots cast, and becoming the first governor in Texas history to be elected to consecutive four-year terms. He would serve six years as the forty-sixth governor of Texas.

In his January 1999 inaugural speech, written partly by himself, Bush called upon Texas to become a "moral and spiritual center." Only then, he said, would true prosperity be attainable. "All of us have worth," he said. "We're all made in the image of God. We're all equal in God's eyes. And all of our citizens must know they have an equal chance to succeed." But that could never happen, the governor declared, if government insisted on dismissing people as the victims of outside forces beyond their control. Rather, people must realize that "they have a worth, a dignity, and a free will given by God, not by government."[45]

The Religious Governor

Though he is Methodist by membership, it is difficult to wed Bush to a particular denomination. It has been said that he mixes a Wesleyan theology of personal transformation and personal relationship with God with a Calvinist understanding of a God who has laid out a "divine plan." That thinking about a larger plan—shared by many Christians—became conspicuous during his years as governor, as did his belief in prayer.

Another instructive speech by the governor came on March 7, 1999, to the Second Baptist Church in Houston, the congregation of well-known preacher Ed Young. It was a rare church talk by Bush. Young introduced him by reading 2 Chronicles 7:14, which declares: "If my people, who are called by my name, humble themselves and pray and seek my face and turn from their wicked ways, then I will hear from Heaven, will forgive their sin, and will heal their land." It is a verse more suitable for a nation than a state; Ronald Reagan had used it during his presidential inauguration. Young then followed with a stream of kind words, calling the governor "humble, gracious, honest, an individual of integrity, a natural leader, a man of his word, and someone who really cares about those things that make a difference." Amid the applause that followed, he told Bush: "I mean every word of it, governor. . . . God bless you."[46]

That greeting was a harbinger of the reception Bush would receive in years to come from evangelicals, who have embraced Bush because they believe he "walks the walk." The governor made that very point in this address:

> Faith gives us purpose to right wrongs, to preserve our families, and
> to teach our children values. Faith gives us conscience to keep us

honest, even when nobody else is looking. And faith can change lives. I know. I know first-hand, because faith changed mine. I grew up in the church, but I didn't always walk the walk. . . . My relationship with God, through Christ, has given me meaning and direction. My faith has made a big difference in my personal life, and my public life as well. I make decisions every day, some are easy and some aren't so easy. . . . And I pray. I pray for guidance. I pray for patience. . . . I pray for peace. I firmly believe in the power of intercessory prayer. And I know I could not do my job without it. I have moments of doubt, moments of pride, and moments of hope. Yet, my faith helps a lot because I have a sense of calm, knowing that the Bible's admonition, "Thy will be done," is life's guide. In this hectic world, there is something incredibly reassuring in the belief that there is a divine plan that exceeds all human plans.

That last line would reappear in Bush's public statements when the governor began moving toward the White House. Bush's next remarks drew enthusiastic applause:

I believe in the separation of church and state. The church is not the state and the state is darn sure not the church. Any time the church enters into the realm of politics, the church runs the risk of losing its mission: the teachings of the Word of God. Politics is a world of give and take, a world of polls—too many polls—of human vision. The church is built on the absolute principles of the Word of God, not the word of man. But I want to make this clear: We will welcome, we *should* welcome, the presence of people of faith into the political arena. It is essential that believers enter the arena. Just as your faith helps determine how you live your life, your involvement in politics helps determine how well our democracy functions.

The governor addressed the church-state issue a number of times during this period. A few months later, now a presidential candidate, he was asked to consider where the state should stand on the teaching of evolution in schools. Bush replied:

> I believe in the alignment of authority and responsibility away from the federal government when it comes to issues of governance and schools. . . . My own personal opinion is that I believe that it's important for children to understand there's different schools of thought when it comes to the formation of the world. I have no problem explaining that there are different theories about how the world was formed. I mean, after all, religion has been around a lot longer than Darwinism. And I think it's important for people to know what people believe in—but whatever the case, here's what I believe: I believe God did create the world. And I think we're finding out more and more and more as to how it actually happened. . . .
>
> And I think over time we will find out the truth. And I have no problem explaining to children [that] there are some who believe this, there are some who believe that, and the truth of the matter is we really don't know the final answer yet.[47]

Despite the perception of some critics, Bush's public statements over the years suggest that he is in fact very sensitive to the issue of church-state separation—as his gubernatorial record demonstrates.

TUCKER AND LUCAS

As governor, Bush was more than once placed in a tough spot involving faith and public policy. He supports the death penalty, and no state carries out as many executions as Texas. A case that came before him was death-row inmate Karla Faye Tucker. After a three-day drug-induced orgy, Tucker and her boyfriend had gone on a rampage with a pickaxe in an apartment, murdering two people. Tucker later confessed to getting a sexual thrill out of each swing of the ax.

Tucker's boyfriend, also sentenced to death, died in prison of liver disease. But Tucker's attorney was vigorous in seeking clemency, and he had a compelling argument: Since her incarceration, Tucker had found Jesus. Bush felt that she seemed sincere and contrite. She had married the prison chaplain. Throughout the country, liberals took up her cause. So did Christians—not just liberal Christians. Pat Robertson, president of the Christian Broadcasting Network, inquired about clemency. An emissary from Pope John Paul II delivered a plea to spare the woman. Christians urged Bush: *Tucker is a new woman. God has forgiven her. Why can't you, Mr. Governor? Aren't you a Christian?* "She's a good Christian woman," Bush remembers being told, "surely you can spare her."[48] Even one of Bush's daughters told him at dinner that she opposed the execution.

The whole nation watched to see what this presidential prospect would do. Bush said he "sought guidance through prayer." He spoke to ministers. He called it one of his hardest decisions.[49] "I have never seen him so emotionally spent as I did in the hour before she was to die," said Wayne Slater, Austin bureau chief for the *Dallas Morning News*.[50] He decided not to grant clemency. On February 3, 1998, he signed the death warrant, and Karla Faye Tucker was executed.

"I believe decisions about the death penalty are primarily the responsibility of the judicial branch of government," Bush explained. "The process begins with a crime, an arrest, and a trial in a court of law. Only a jury can impose a death sentence in Texas." If death is the verdict, Bush noted, the case could be appealed in the courts. He pointed out that the role of the executive branch in Texas is limited; in his view the governor's role was to serve as a "fail-safe," one final review to ensure there was no doubt of the perpetrator's guilt, and that he or she had received due process under the Constitution and laws.[51]

"I don't believe my role is to replace the verdict of a jury with my own," Bush figured, "unless there are new facts or evidence of which a jury was unaware, or evidence that the trial was somehow unfair." He did not find that in this case. Quite the contrary, Tucker had again admitted her horrific crime, and even agreed that her punishment was appropriate. While the reasons for sparing Tucker offered by Christians—namely, that she could employ her new life to redirect others—were "compelling" to Bush, he said they did not erase his responsibility to enforce the laws of the state.[52]

In a news conference at the time, Bush said he concluded that "judgments about the heart and soul" of a person on death row "are best left to a higher authority."[53]

For those who worry that Bush's faith might overly influence his political actions, the Tucker case might give pause for reconsideration. Bush concluded that, even though Jesus might forgive Tucker, even though she might have been a saved and changed person, those were eternal matters between God and one of His children. A governor, however, must abide by civil law.

Indeed, Bush pushed the question further, contemplating how a governor ought to decide if, say, the death-row inmate were a Muslim. Would a different faith—particularly one that does not preach on-earth, born-again salvation—change the equation?

The ultimate proof of Bush's position came with the case of another murderer, Henry Lee Lucas. This alleged serial killer once told police he had committed more than six hundred murders, including that of his own mother. The problem was that Lucas was also a serial liar. And the case for which he had been sentenced to death was, in Bush's view, not clear. Clemency was again being sought. Lucas was hardly a regenerate soul-singing hosannas to the Good Lord. He didn't give a damn about any religion or anybody.

In reviewing the case, however, Bush and his team could not find a smoking gun. It was not, in the governor's view, "crystal clear." He again applied his test, starting with the most fundamental question: Was there any doubt over the individual's guilt in the case for which he was sentenced to death? "For the first time since I have been governor," said Bush, "the answer . . . was yes. There was real doubt. I didn't know whether Henry Lee Lucas was innocent; I also did not know that he was guilty."[54]

Bush and his staff agonized over the political prospect of sparing an apparent serial killer. Nonetheless, that was precisely what the governor did. The world was shocked. The cowboy commuted the execution of the outlaw. Because Bush wasn't completely sure that Lucas had committed the crime, he stuck to his guns.

Bush's performance, then, was consistent: He did what he believed the law asked of him—even when it meant executing a Christian and saving a devil. His faith influenced his view of fairness and right and wrong. It did not supersede his duty to review the facts of a case and make a decision based on the evidence.

COMPASSIONATE CONSERVATISM

Governor Bush attended Tarrytown United Methodist Church in Austin, which has a reputation as moderate to liberal in its theology and social concern. According to Tony Carnes of *Christianity Today*, Tarrytown's senior pastor, Jim Mayfield, preaches a "nonjudgmental brand" of Christianity. "There are those who want to focus on the primacy of Scripture," Mayfield told Carnes, "but our Methodist heritage focuses on the primacy of God's grace . . . and the primacy of God's love."[55]

Bush's personal theology seems to mix all three of those primacies—Scripture, God's grace, and God's love—but with special emphasis on the third. He subscribes to a kind of love theology, influenced by his own reading of the Bible and probably by Methodism's historical emphasis on ministering to the outcast.[56] This turn of mind is manifest in his compassionate conservatism, a concept created by Marvin Olasky, a professor at the University of Texas at Austin and editor of the influential conservative Christian magazine *World*. Though Olasky takes credit for writing the book on compassionate conservatism, he says that Bush "saw its potential, developed it, ran with it, and made it a hit."[57]

It is Bush's trademark. In his memoirs, when he laid out his vision for the country and the world, he focused on this philosophy. The closing chapter is titled "A Compassionate Conservative."

Many conservatives resent the phrase because they believe it feeds into the liberal charge that conservatives lack compassion. Bush does not believe that conservatism is wanting in compassion. The phrase merely defines him, he says. He calls it conservatism with a smile, not a frown.[58] The concept piggybacks on the work of many conservative writers and thinkers in the 1980s and 1990s. Had Jack Kemp become president, it might have defined him, though by a different name.

Bush says the philosophy outlines "a new vision" for the "proper role" of government. He envisions a state that confronts human suffering and helps the disadvantaged. In that way, his thinking is not unlike that of the War on Poverty launched in the 1960s. Yet it is different in its emphasis on enlisting the private sector: the vehicles to deliver Bush's compassionate conservative agenda are faith-based groups. Moreover, the goal goes beyond that of the War on Poverty in that the target is not merely poverty but social ills like drug and alcohol abuse, which have long been a domain of religious-based nonprofits.

Bush has long referred to these religiously affiliated institutions— ranging from soup kitchens to shelters for battered women—as "platoons" in the "armies of compassion." Because of their faith-rooted component, these groups, says Bush, can "demonstrate compassion and inspire hope in a way that government never can. And they inspire life-changing faith in a way that government never should."[59]

As Olasky notes, Bush believes that faith-based groups work "because he knows how faith in Christ led him to stop emphasizing short-term satisfaction and begin thinking about long-range responsibility."[60] He saw such religion-based reform in his own life. Ari Fleischer, later Bush's White House press secretary, has said that his boss became invested in his faith-based initiative because of his own history of drinking, where faith motivated a change.[61]

The governor's championing of the concept began auspiciously in 1995, when he backed a nonprofit Christian group called Teen Challenge in a dispute with his own Texas Commission on Alcohol and Drug Abuse, which had threatened to block its license to operate as a treatment program because of its Christian orientation. Then, at Bush's personal invitation, Chuck Colson's Prison Fellowship ministry set up a Christian prison in Texas, reportedly the first of its kind in the United States. The prison, located in Sugar Land, Texas, is described as "a radical experiment in rehabilitation." Rather than being a prison with a church inside, like many traditional facilities, this is essentially a church-prison.[62]

In the Sugar Land facility, some 150 inmates essentially live the lives of students at a committed Christian college. All week long, from dawn to dusk, they pray and participate in Bible study. They follow a "Christ-centered agenda" that seeks to employ the "life-transforming power of Jesus Christ" to move the inmates to the road of recovery. The prison, an extension of Colson's InnerChange ministry, hopes to stop recidivism. According to reports, Bush shepherded InnerChange in Texas at a time when no other state would give it a chance. Would it work? "Let's try," said Bush.[63]

The governor's enthusiasm was particularly bolstered by the testimony of one InnerChange prisoner, an inmate named James Peterson, who had changed so dramatically while in the program that he refused parole, saying he would rather stay in jail and serve his fellow brothers in Christ. "Maybe my decision to stay here will help others see that God is real—that He is truth, and He changes people," Bush quoted the inmate. "This is God's program. He's really moving in the prisons, and He's got me right in the middle of it." After the parole board recovered from its shock, it granted Peterson's request. In a memorable scene marking the program's announcement, a beaming Bush was photographed on the front page of the *Houston Chronicle* singing "Amazing Grace" with a convicted killer.[64]

Bush here again cited the thinking of his friend Pastor Tony Evans. Just as you cannot fix a crack on the wall until you first fix the foundation, Bush believes, building more prisons cannot substitute for "responsibility and order in our souls."[65]

Mike Doyle of the Cornerstone Assistance Network became a convert to Bush's faith-based vision in Texas. He was pleasantly surprised at the effectiveness of the state-church partnership. "I considered government the enemy," said Doyle, who runs a coalition of 120 churches that aid the homeless, "but God and the governor convinced me I was wrong."[66]

As governor, Bush made a move he would repeat five years later as president: He was assisted by the "charitable choice" provision of the 1996 U.S. welfare reform law, a provision that blocks government from striking religious content from faith-based groups or programs that receive federal dollars. At Bush's order, the Texas Department of Human Services included this law's protection in all contracts with private-sector providers. In doing so, according to the department's Elizabeth Darling Seale, they had "altered the whole environment of an enormous agency."[67]

The 1996 welfare reform law that made this possible was written by the Republican Congress and signed by Democratic president Bill Clinton—a presidential move that angered many liberals. Once president, Bush commended Clinton and that Congress.[68]

Compassionate conservatism is George W.'s vision. Yet the role his father played in its development should not go unmentioned. George H. W. Bush had provided an influence during his son's childhood and again during an unsure time in his adult life, prodding his son to volunteer. As a young man, he learned firsthand the power of nonprofit groups. Also influential was his father's vision of a "Thousand Points of Light"—an oft-maligned slogan which also emphasized the need to unleash the power of nonprofits, charities, and volunteers in addressing America's social ills. It was not as ambitious as his son's vision, but it reflected similar thinking. Yet again, Dad made a difference—this time inspiring a mission his son would take to the Oval Office.

A Shooting in Fort Worth

As 1999 moved along, Governor Bush witnessed an act of faith-based compassion by an entire community; it was a compassion born of a moment of barbarism.[69]

On September 15, 1999, a deranged man in a black trench coat entered a church in Fort Worth, Texas, armed with bullets and a pipe bomb. He approached a group of worshippers in the foyer awaiting choir practice, asked about a prayer meeting, and then began shooting. He headed to the sanctuary, which he sprayed with gunfire as he shouted obscenities. By the end of the incident, seven were dead and many more injured. A teenage boy stopped the slaughter when he yelled out defiantly, "You can kill me but you can't kill my faith!" Upon hearing those words, the assassin found a pew, sat down, and shot himself.[70]

The first person murdered that day was Sydney Browning, a seminary graduate and local educator who had been selected Teacher of the Year at her high school two years in a row. She was hit in the head and chest at point-blank range and died instantly. Her father, Don, has obviously never forgotten that day, nor the compassion he saw in the days that followed. "I never saw anything grip the city like that," he says today.[71]

The morning after the massacre, an impromptu prayer session was held at the pastor's house. The church was now a crime scene, filled with police, coroners, chalked lines, bullet-ridden oak walls, and blood-soaked carpets. A surprise attendee at that prayer session was Governor George W. Bush, who made the 186-mile trip from Austin. He arrived unannounced and left almost as quietly. A church of God had been converted into a Texas killing field, and the governor came to offer his personal prayers.

So overwhelming was the outpouring of grief that the shocked community was forced to hold a later memorial service at the football stadium at Texas Christian University. Sydney Browning's father was asked to speak at the service. When he arrived backstage before the event, he unexpectedly encountered the Texas governor. The two men shook hands. "Are you coming into this a believer?" Bush asked. Browning nodded. "God bless you," said Bush. "I'm praying for you." The service organizers then asked their unanticipated guest if he would like to sit at the platform with the other VIPs. The governor replied, "No, this isn't about me," and sat in the stands among the thousands.[72]

Browning spoke last. The choir director had long ago connected with this little girl through music, and he thought it fitting to finish his remarks by extemporaneously singing the first song his daughter had sung in public. "This little light of mine, I'm gonna let it shine," he began, asking the audience to join him. Browning paused to note that the last verse of the song reads: "Let it shine till Jesus comes." He told the crowd that his daughter no longer needs to sing that last line, but the rest of them do. The tribute closed with that. When the service ended, the governor approached Browning once more. "That was great," said Bush, clasping Browning's hand. "I couldn't have done it."[73]

George W. Bush then left as he had come: in a low-key manner, with no cameras. He had said nothing profound or poetic. His response was memorable only for its lack of showiness. In both visits after the shooting, Bush avoided the press, told no one he was coming, stayed, prayed, paid his respects, talked briefly to the families, and then silently drove away. This man who had spent four years as governor speaking to Texans about faith and compassion had just seen it in profusion, firsthand from an entire community.

3.

Texas Raven

"The victory over alcohol was transformative,
and it set the stage for political greatness."

—*Richard Brookhiser on Sam Houston*[1]

Books hold a certain power on George W. Bush, who has written that he is "enthralled" by history.[2] He loves to read, particularly historical biography. Asked to name his favorite book, he cites *The Raven: A Biography of Sam Houston* by Marquis James—a choice that reveals quite a bit about Bush.

Bush first read James's Pulitzer Prize–winning biography during his Texas days, prior to his presidential run. Published in 1929, the book was republished in 1981, and has been reissued several times since, in both hardcover and paperback.

James was an Oklahoman who grew up with cowboys and Cherokees. His father, a Civil War veteran, was a cousin of gunslinger Jesse James. As a young man, Marquis absorbed stories of the Wild West, particularly characters like Houston, Andrew Jackson, and less well-known figures from the period. He became fascinated by Houston after meeting Sam's son, Temple, as a boy. Temple had fled Texas; like his dad, he had saddled his horse and headed for Indian country, killing a man during his travels.[3]

Sam Houston is Texas's founding father. Born in Virginia in March 1793, he died in Texas in July 1863. He spent a good deal of his youth traversing the mountains of Tennessee. Sam and his siblings swam in Mill Creek; they fished and hunted. One morning, at age fifteen, he failed to show up for work at the family store. Weeks later, his family learned that he had fled to Indian territory to live with Cherokees. He was adopted by the chief, who gave him the name Co-lon-neh, which was Cherokee for "Raven."

As an adult, Sam Houston became both a military general and a politician. The colorful, controversial figure ran for Congress as a representative from Tennessee, winning in 1823 and 1825. In 1827 he sought the state's governorship, and won it in a landslide. After considerable political and personal turmoil, he moved to Texas. He became a member of the 1836 convention that declared Texas's independence from Mexico. When the Texas Declaration of Independence was signed in a fireproof shed, Houston was its John Hancock; soon thereafter he was elected commander in chief of the armies of Texas.

Houston's rise to the top was rapid. Taking control of the military after the fall of the Alamo, he proceeded to win a number of key battles. Later that same year, he was elected the first president of the Republic of Texas. When the republic gained statehood in 1845, Houston was elected a U.S. senator from the state. Fourteen years after that, he was elected its governor.

George W. Bush calls Sam Houston a "Texas legend,"[4] and takes obvious pride in his fellow Texan. Nearly every time he tells a reporter or a classroom about his elementary-school years, he refers to his school as "Sam Houston Elementary in Midland, Texas" and never simply "elementary school."[5] When talking to teachers, he has noted that Houston was a teacher—a vocation not dwelled upon by Houston biographers. Speaking at a magnet school in Nashville, Tennessee, Bush told an auditorium of teachers:

> Thank you for taking on a noble profession. Old Sam Houston, he used to live in Tennessee. . . . He had been the Governor of Texas. . . . And he was a famous Tennessee guy, and he was a President of the Republic of Texas. And they said, "Of all the jobs you've ever had, Sam, what was the most important one?" He said, without hesitation, "teacher."[6]

To Bush, that was the highest praise for the teaching profession. He made the point again in April 2001 when presenting the National Teacher of the Year award in the White House Rose Garden.[7]

And on January 4, 2002, he returned to the state capitol in Austin for a ceremony unveiling his portrait among the forty-six governors of Texas. As his portrait was mounted under the building's dome, alongside Houston and others, Bush commented that it was an "honor to be hanging" with Houston. (He also quipped: "It's also amazing to think that it'll be here for a long, long time. I just hope that Governor Richards doesn't mind being my neighbor for eternity.")[8]

ROOTS IN HOUSTON

It is clear that Bush relates deeply to Sam Houston, a man who has been in his consciousness from early childhood. After attending Sam Houston Elementary, Bush stepped up to San Jacinto Junior High

School—named for the spot where Houston defeated Santa Anna. The family's next move after Midland, inevitably, was Houston, Texas. Eventually, once Bush made it all the way to Austin, he lived in the same governor's mansion Houston had occupied when he became Texas governor at the end of his career.

There are a number of common threads between Houston's story and Bush's own. Like Bush, Houston was born in the East before moving west at a young age. "The West tugged like a magnet" for Houston, wrote James.[9] Though neither was born in Texas, both Houston and Bush became pure Texans. Houston, like Bush, was given his father's first name; both families had a rich history, their names redolent with renown and prestige.

Though Houston's family was educated, Sam himself was no fan of intellectuals. He harbored what his biographer dubbed "a curious prejudice" against poetry.[10] He was a patriot who loved his country and state, and took enormous pride in Texas. He spoke often of liberty and justice. Though he may (or may not) be reluctant to admit it, to a degree Bush probably also bonds with the cowboy in Houston. Whether politician, military man, or teacher, Houston was first and foremost an Old West cowboy type, riding horseback from mesa to mesa with a rifle over one arm and a flask under the other.

Bush likes cowboys—their stoic courage, sense of quiet duty, can-do nature, and rescuer mentality. When touring the country in places like Wyoming, New Mexico, and Texas, he tells crowds that it's nice to be in a place with more cowboy hats than neckties.[11] When cattle farmers in Colorado awarded him a cowboy hat, Bush thanked them: "I realize there's nobody more central to the American experience than the cowboy." In speaking to this group, he talked of terrorist "evil"—good-vs.-bad language cowboys understand.[12] Stomping around his ranch in Crawford, Texas, he frequently dons a white

Stetson, and sometimes even wears it in Washington—as on a chilly night in December 2002, when President Bush lit the Christmas tree in the nation's capital.[13]

The cowboy Sam Houston that Bush saw in James's book is an image that others have seen in him—a caricature that works both for and against him. Conservatives seem to relish it. When they later talked of President Bush as a cowboy hunting down Osama bin Laden, they did so with a smile. Others, particularly liberals, hate it; for them the idea of "Cowboy Bush" riding after Saddam Hussein was no cause for celebration.

But the links between Bush and Houston, as James's book illustrates, transcend mere Wild West symbolism.

At the pinnacle of his career, as governor in 1861, Houston staked a bold position. When the Civil War consumed the nation, Houston remained an unwavering Unionist. The majority of his Texans wanted to secede from the union. They insisted the governor take a loyalty oath to the Confederacy. "I refuse to take this oath," he said flatly.[14]

Sam had been there when Texas longed to be part of the United States. As James put it, Houston believed that "Texas was ours—we were destiny-bound to bring it under the flag."[15] In March 1861, he was removed from office because of his loyalty to the United States, and was forced to leave the state capitol. Protesters cursed his name and burned him in effigy—a cataclysmic end to an illustrious career in public service.

Sam Houston would not budge, despite the fierce protests all around him. He did what he thought was right. "The lesson Bush draws from that story," writes Richard Brookhiser, one of the few who has recognized the importance of Houston and *The Raven* to Bush, "is the fickleness of instant verdicts and the importance of doing the right thing. It is a tale of heroic principle and of virtue rewarded in the long run: the political nadir of Houston's life became a high point in the judgment of history."[16]

Once Bush became president, the world watched when he, for better or worse, applied similar conviction in the war on terror and to the invasion of Iraq—where he did what he thought was right, despite intense protests.

Yet Brookhiser is even more on the mark when he speculates that Houston's *personal* nadir may have been equally meaningful to Bush: In his mid-thirties, Houston's life went into turmoil. He resigned as governor of Tennessee and went to live with the Cherokees in what is today Arkansas. A key factor was his uncultivated belle of a wife, who deserted him only months into their marriage. He had always been a drinker. Now Sam replaced his wife by marrying the bottle, which received his total devotion. He started drinking more heavily than ever. As James put it, he "buried his sorrows in the flowing bowl," and "gave himself up to the fatal enchantress" that was alcohol.[17]

The year 1831 was his rock bottom. The Cherokees bestowed on him a new name—Oo-tse-tee Ar-dee-tah-skee, which means "Big Drunk." "When Big Drunk was in character," Marquis James narrated, "a retinue of loyal Cherokees would follow him about to forestall complications, but not always with success."[18]

The Indians tagged along with Big Drunk to the trading post he owned. In one instance, a smashed Sam became displeased with a young white clerk who worked there. Houston challenged him to a duel, but Sam's friends protested that the clerk's social station precluded him from participating in an affair of honor. An angry Houston roared: "I've always treated him as a gentleman, and I'll treat him as a gentleman now!" The two men squared off; both fired, and missed.[19]

An Englishman who encountered Houston during this wasteful period described him as leading a mysterious life, "shut up" all day in a small tavern. Washington Irving aptly described Houston as a "tall, large, well formed, fascinating man" that "God made . . . two drinks scant." Sam would have agreed.[20]

Sam Houston was a wretch—craving to be found. Fortunately, after these drunken years in the wilderness, Houston began buckling down—in a way. In 1832, he left the Cherokees and moved farther west to Texas.

Texas was a rugged place for a rugged man to settle down. The territory that today is the city of Houston was pockmarked by saloons. One resident said that of the population of six to seven hundred roughly half were unemployed, unless drinking and gambling were considered a form of employment. Drinking, said the resident, "was reduced to a system, and . . . the Texians being entirely a military people, not only fought but drank in platoons." Houston City always held a warm place in Sam's heart.[21]

Still, it was in Texas that Sam found purpose and direction beyond the bottle. Eventually, as he managed to exorcise the demon, his station improved dramatically. "The victory over alcohol," noted Richard Brookhiser, in an insightful analogy to Bush, "was transformative, and it set the stage for political greatness."[22]

Bush certainly saw drinking analogies with Houston. In early 1999, when he was considering a run for the presidency, he began meeting with potential donors and nationally known evangelicals. When he did, he gestured to a portrait of Sam Houston, and reminded them that the fellow Texan also had a drinking problem that he overcame. Then Bush noted the renewal of faith he himself had in God and how he desired to bring biblically based compassion into the national limelight.[23]

Though Houston forsook alcohol, he still embodied the Old West. He was still quite wild, especially by today's standards. He would dismally fail any political correctness test. He continued to duel, even shooting a fellow general in the stomach. (The man spent four months in bed, but recovered.)[24] Instances like this compelled the visiting Frenchman Alexis de Tocqueville, busy penning his *Democracy in America*, to assess Houston as one of those "unpleasant consequences of popular sovereignty."[25]

The Path to Salvation

But perhaps the most significant parallel between Bush and Houston has eluded observers: their shared spiritual path and faith experience. As a boy, Sam and his brothers attended church every Sunday at the stone Timber Ridge Church, which stood just a hundred yards from the family homestead. Like Bush, James said Houston had "childhood training in religion."[26] Yet his devotion ebbed and flowed as time went on and as personal crises—including the bottle—overcame him or were resolved.

All along, people prayed for Sam, for which he said he was grateful. Missionaries tried to convert him while he guzzled whiskey with Cherokees, but to little avail. Nonetheless, he encouraged their prayers. He was genuinely moved by their efforts—and, more important, he thought them effective.[27] He and Bush both put tremendous stock in the power of prayer.

Like Bush, Houston wandered spiritually, switching denominations a number of times. He left the denomination of his parents, only to return before leaving a second time. At one point in 1833–1834, he switched to Catholicism, a convert of Padre Miguel Muldoon. He was baptized into the faith, one of two or three baptisms in his lifetime.[28]

He attended Presbyterian and Catholic churches, as well as Baptist and Unitarian.

Though at times a lost soul, Houston expressed a belief that "in the affairs of men . . . there must be a conducting Providence." Much like Bush, Houston grew into this conclusion while he experienced life. "I am more satisfied of this fact," he said of his conviction that God was involved in human affairs, "when I . . . behold the changes that have taken place with myself."[29] A deep, developed faith would only come in time.

A critical spiritual moment came when Senator Houston took Communion at the E Street Baptist Church in Washington on March 6, 1851, after his remarriage. He wrestled with the matter all winter. "If the Lord spares me," he wrote his wife, "I expect to partake of the sacrament of our Lord's supper. . . . Pray for me dearest."[30]

Houston attended service weekly at the church in the nation's capital, listening keenly to the sermons while whittling with his pocketknife in the pew. At the end of the service, a happy boy or girl was awarded whatever toy or wooden cross he carved during the sermon. The Reverend Dr. Samson was surprised by Sam's knowledge of the Bible. He would have been especially impressed had he known that Sam spent each afternoon writing his own summary of the sermon, which he mailed to his wife.[31]

Houston's long quest for spiritual repose ended in the autumn of 1854, when the sixty-one-year-old humbly knelt before the altar at a chapel in Independence, Texas, and asked to be received into the church. The bell in the tower celebrated the tidings. In clerical circles, reported James, the moment was treated like a national event. On November 19, 1854, Sam was renewed in the chilly waters of Rocky Creek, baptized by the Right Reverend Rufus C. Burleson. A leading church periodical rejoiced: "The announcement of General

Houston's immersion has excited the wonder and surprise of many who have supposed that he was 'past praying for' but it is no marvel to us." The journal reported that 3,500 clergymen had been praying for him.[32]

An old friend from Texas could not resist ribbing Sam: "Well, General, I hear your sins were washed away." Houston replied: "I hope so. But if they were all washed away, the Lord help the fish down below."[33]

The general was so excited that he determined to pay half the minister's salary personally, professing that his pocketbook had been baptized, too. Like any mortal, he could not pretend to have left off sinning altogether—but now he understood the need for repentance. Soon after he waded in those waters, his horse stumbled, jolting Sam from the saddle. "God damn a stumbling horse!" he declared. To which the man traveling with Sam, John Reagan, reacted with shock. Sam paused, knelt in the road, and pleaded for forgiveness.[34]

In his lifetime Sam Houston had made a lot of money. He owned four homes, all furnished and ready to be lived in at moment's call. He had earned a solid—in some circles legendary—reputation. Yet, by his own account, he did not achieve the abundant life until that moment in the creek.

By his life's end, Sam was fully with God. In 1861, just two years before his death, he wrote a letter to his sixteen-year-old son attending military school. Don't smoke or chew, he told him, and strongly advised him: "Remember your Creator in the days of your youth . . . & my Dear boy never associate with those who . . . sneer at the teachings of the Bible."[35]

In the autumn of 1862, Houston felt weary. Since he'd left Austin, doctors had been very concerned about his condition. He was too sick to travel back to Huntsville. The physicians told his family that he would die soon. The girls wept while they sang a hymn near his bedside. Surprisingly, he regained his strength. "Yes, tell my enemies I am not dead yet," he announced.[36] On the journey back to Huntsville, he made a number of stops; the old scrapper was doing fine.

Of course, even so spiritual a rebirth could not last forever. In early July, Houston came home with a miserable cold; it was soon diagnosed as pneumonia. On July 25, he fell into what was described as a druglike sleep. The family gathered around the Reverend Doctor Samuel McKinney, who summoned a prayer. Sam slept through the night.

When morning came, his wife Margaret, at his side all night, asked for her Bible. She began to read aloud: "In my father's house are many mansions: if it were not so, I would have told you. I go to prepare a place for you." As these words left her lips, according to James, the old general stirred. Margaret dropped the book and grabbed her husband's hands. His tongue declared, "Texas—Texas!—Margaret—" and then he quit breathing. His wife paused to ask God to make their children worthy of their father. The James book ends with that plea.[37]

CONTEMPLATING THE LIFE OF HIS TEXAS FOREBEAR, Governor Bush seems to have sensed a spiritual kinship with Houston, among many other likenesses—including unforeseen similarities to come. The common ground is compelling, especially in the way both George W. Bush and Sam Houston found salvation in God rather than the bottle. Moreover, the cowboy never left Sam. Neither, certainly, did Texas. The desire for alcohol, mercifully, did leave him, with prayer and God's sustained help. And, eventually, grace found him.

4.

Campaigning for the White House

"Should it not work out, I understand that there is a force greater than myself—and it gives me comfort. . . . [There is] a higher priority in life."

—*Governor George W. Bush on his campaign for president, August 2000*[1]

One January day in 1999, just two hours before his inauguration for his second term as Texas governor, George W. Bush sat in a pew and listened to Pastor Mark Craig at the First United Methodist Church in Austin. It was a private prayer service. His family was there—Laura, Barbara and Jenna, his mother and father. Craig spoke for fifteen to twenty minutes. In the governor, what he said struck a profound chord. Bush later recalled:

Most lives have defining moments. Moments that forever change you. Moments that set you on a different course. Moments of recognition so vivid and so clear that everything later seems different. Renewing my faith, getting married, and having children top my list of those memorable moments. Mine also includes deciding to run for Governor of Texas and listening to Mark Craig's sermon.[2]

Bush, of course, had listened to many sermons in his lifetime, from staid Episcopal ministers to firebrands like Tony Evans and T. D. Jakes, the latter, says Bush, leaving him "spellbound" with his preaching. (He has prayed with Jakes, a Pentecostal minister.[3]) "I've heard powerful sermons, inspiring sermons, and a few too many boring sermons," Bush stated. "But this sermon reached out and grabbed me, and changed my life."

Though no transcript or recording exists, Bush contends that he remembers the homily nearly word for word. Speaking from the heart, Craig asked his audience to imagine what they would do if he gave them each a check for $86,400. He set conditions: The entire sum must be dispensed at that moment and spent that day. It was a use-it-or-lose-it proposition. What would you do? Craig asked. The lesson, of course, was to spend the money wisely—to be a good steward of God's resources. Yet the lesson was also to seize an opportunity.

Then Craig changed the terms. Imagine, he switched, if he gave each parishioner 86,400 seconds of time, rather than money. How would they best invest that time? Even with that change, the message was the same for Bush—seize the moment. "The sermon was a rousing call," the governor interpreted, "to make the most of every moment, discard reservations, throw caution to the wind, rise to the challenge."

The governor had been carefully contemplating a run for the

White House, but it was a move about which he felt uncertain. Now he listened as Craig described the reluctant Moses in the first pages of Exodus, uneasy over whether he was really the one to heed the call and lead the Israelites out of Egypt to the Promised Land. Moses, Bush understood, had many reasons to shirk his responsibility. The governor recounted the Bible story:

> "Who am I that I should go to Pharoah, and bring the sons of Israel out of Egypt?" Moses asks in the third chapter of Exodus. The people won't believe me, he protested. I'm not a very good speaker. "Oh, my Lord, send, I pray, some other person," Moses pleaded. But God did not, and Moses ultimately did his bidding, leading his people through forty years of wilderness and wandering, relying on God for strength and direction and inspiration.

Turning to her son, Barbara Bush said of Pastor Craig's message: "He was talking to *you*." Yes, her son agreed, the Old Testament story had spoken to him. He sensed the pastor was telling him that his re-election to back-to-back terms in Texas "was a beginning, not an end." Bush began telling friends that he had "heard the call," that God was calling him to seek the Oval Office. "Pastor Mark Craig," Bush credits, "had prodded me out of my comfortable life as Governor of Texas and toward a national campaign."

Rena Pederson, editor-at-large for the *Dallas Morning News*, was there that day. Pastor Craig "was looking right at" Bush, Pederson recalled. "You could just feel a currency in the air. I think everyone knew something happened." Later that afternoon, after the inauguration, Bush met at the governor's mansion with several evangelicals, including Richard Land. "Among the things he said to us," said Land, "was 'I believe that God wants me to be president.'"[4]

Not long after this encounter, the governor met with evangelist James Robison. "I feel like God wants me to run for president," Bush told Robison in a moment recounted by author Stephen Mansfield. "I can't explain it, but I sense my country is going to need me. Something is going to happen, and, at that time, my country is going to need me. I know it won't be easy, on me or my family, but God wants me to do it. . . . My life will never be the same."[5]

WITHIN A FEW MONTHS, GEORGE W. BUSH EMBARKED on a drive for the White House. On a number of occasions during his presidential run, he was asked about his faith. Some of these questions yielded telling insights into Bush's brand of Christianity.

In early December 1999, the governor was asked if, as a Christian, he believes that Jews who have not accepted Christ will get in to Heaven. Christ Himself, after all, said that no one comes to the Father but through Him. Bush answered:

It's really important for somebody in my position to live the word, in this case, but also understand that people communicate with God and reach God in different ways. It just doesn't have to be my way. And I think it's really important if you're trying to unite a nation that is as diverse as ours to spend more time living the example I've learned of Christ as opposed to lecturing. And I really mean that. Obviously there's the big issue between the Christian and the Jew, the Jewish person. And I am mindful of the rich traditions and history of the Jewish faith. And I am mindful of what Billy Graham one time told me: for me not to try to figure out—try to pick and choose who gets to go to heaven. . . . It is very important for people to not be haughty in their religion. And there's all kinds of admonitions in the Bible; haughtiness, rightfulness is a sin in itself. . . .

Billy Graham said, "Don't play God." I don't get to determine who goes to heaven and who goes to hell. That's not me. Governors don't do that.[6]

There are Christians who would argue with Bush's interpretation.[7] Yet, as the pages ahead will show, Bush's faith is anchored by grace, which creates in him a faith-based tolerance. On doctrinal questions such as who gets into heaven, he is much more a liberal Methodist than an inflexible fundamentalist. To be sure, his answer must have been tinged with some political sensitivity. Still, his theological sense has evolved into this more inclusive (and politically less controversial) brand of Christianity.[8]

While most of the religious exchanges in which Bush participated on the campaign trail were routine and received little publicity, there was one memorable exception: Des Moines, Iowa, on December 13, 1999. The occasion was a Republican presidential debate. The Texas governor was asked to name his favorite philosopher or thinker. He pointed to Jesus Christ.

This was no surprise to those who knew Bush. One might expect any serious Christian to cite Christ. As Richard Land, president of the Southern Baptist Convention's Ethics and Religious Liberty Commission, put it: "Most evangelicals who heard that question probably thought, 'That's exactly the way I would have answered.'"[9]

Bush's sentiment was not out of step with the American tradition. Even Thomas Jefferson, modern academe's secular saint of the American founding, hailed Christ as a philosopher. "The philosophy of Jesus," wrote Jefferson, in a description mild compared to that of his contemporaries, "is the most sublime and benevolent . . . ever offered."[10]

But that was then. Today's media and liberals were taken aback.

A mild reaction came from NBC's Tim Russert, himself a Christian, who followed up by asking Bush:

> Governor Bush, in the last debate when you talked about Jesus be-
> ing the philosopher-thinker that you most respected, many people
> applauded you. Others said, "What role would religion have in the
> Oval Office with George W. Bush?" Fifteen million atheists in this
> country, five million Jews, five million Muslims, millions more Bud-
> dhists and Hindus. Should they feel excluded [by] George W. Bush
> because of his allegiance to Jesus? . . . Would you take an expression
> like "What would Jesus do?" into the Oval Office? . . .
>
> [On] the whole issue of Jesus Christ being introduced in the
> Republican Party and into the country at large: Is it an issue that
> you think could hurt you in the general election, where non-
> Christians begin to think there's something mysterious going on
> here? . . . I think people watching, some who hear [that] your God
> is Jesus Christ, they don't have a God, or they have Yahweh or they
> have Allah. They want to know it's okay."[11]

In response, Bush replied: "It's my foundation and if it costs me votes to have answered the question that way, so be it."[12]

This had a snowball effect. Bush's single mention of Christ began to be repeated—not by Bush, but by media concerned about the implications of Bush's statement. This prompted the following ex-
change between Russert and Gary Bauer, the conservative Christian who was also running for the Republican nomination:

> *Russert:* Every Republican debate seems to have discussion about
> abortion, gay rights, Jesus Christ. Fairly or unfairly, are you con-
> cerned that many people in the country are watching that exchange

and saying, "You know, that's a little bit more about religion than it is about politics and that concerns me?"

Bauer: Well, Tim, in all due fairness, you guys brought those issues up.[13]

That was, in fact, the case. The more the media wrung its hands over the issue, the more of an issue it became. MSNBC's Brian Williams asked *Newsweek*'s Howard Fineman whether rank-and-file Republicans were unhappy with the alleged increasingly narrow direction of Bush and the GOP presidential hopefuls. "It's red meat for conservatives, the positions rather strident," said Williams, in the form of a question, "anti-gay, pro-Jesus, and anti-abortion and no gray matter in between?"[14]

Time magazine's Margaret Carlson shared that thinking. By partaking of such discussion, she said, the Republican candidates were coming off like a bunch of guys pounding beers at "happy hour"— "waving and cheering and stomping the most simple-minded statements. And this comes across as, you know, intolerant." Carlson assured: "And they're [the Republican candidates] not right on the issues that people care about. They've got to play outside that [debate] room. And they're not going to with that stuff."[15]

Given his convictions and experience, it is hard to imagine Bush honestly answering any other way. Yet, as an article in the *New York Times* contended, "some saw it as a blatant bid for the evangelical vote."[16] The *Times* needed look no further than its own pages: In an op-ed titled "Playing the Jesus Card," columnist Maureen Dowd chalked up Bush's reference to sheer political opportunism. Politicians like Bush, said Dowd, apparently estimate that they can't win the presidency without dragging in religion. She quoted H. L. Mencken, who wrote that religion "is used as a club and a cloak by both politicians and moralists, all of them lusting for power and most of them palpable frauds." She said that Bush had "finally scored some debate points" by citing Jesus. "This is the era of niche marketing," explained Dowd, "and Jesus is a niche. Why not use the son of God to help the son of Bush appeal to voters? W. is checking Jesus's numbers, and Jesus is polling well in Iowa. Christ, the new wedge issue." Rather than being sincere about his faith and heart, to Dowd it seemed that Bush had been a scoundrel. "It raises the question," Dowd preached, of whether the governor wanted Jesus as his "personal Savior or political savior. Genuinely religious people are humbled by religion and are guided by it on the inside. They don't need to wear Jesus on the outside as a designer label."[17]

Much of the scorn reflected the bias of the journalistic community. Among reporters at major media outlets, only 11 percent attend church weekly—far lower than the public as a whole. Estimates are that one-third to one-half of the public attends a church, mosque, or synagogue weekly.[18] Thus, it is, in fact, probably unusual for media figures to encounter serious religious conversation in their daily lives, whereas tens of millions of Americans hear such at least once a week.

The media's negative take on Bush's statement was to be expected. Prior to Bush's remark, the Center for Media and Public Affairs, Robert Lichter's nonpartisan watchdog, did a major study on media coverage of religion. Out of the 3,144 discussions of religion it coded, 93 percent contained no "spiritual dimension." The focus was on hard news. A story on the Catholic church is far more likely to focus on pedophile priests than the seven sacraments. Stories like "how God changed my life" are almost nonexistent. Further, concluded the study, "theological referents were disproportionately connected to non-Christian religions with a small membership in this country."[19]

A 2003 survey of top newspapers by the University of Rochester found that stories about religion itself "infrequently address religion's beliefs and values."[20]

The negative reaction was not limited to the American media. Overseas, the response was derision. Noting that in Britain "nothing opens a politician to ridicule like religion," Michael Gove wrote in the London *Times* that when Bush declared Christ his philosopher, "the scorn on this side of the Atlantic could not have been greater if he'd said Homer Simpson."[21] That European characterization of Bush would not go away. A *Time* magazine piece reported that the common European perception of Bush, particularly that of the European press, was that he was "a shallow, arrogant, gun-loving, abortion-hating, Christian fundamentalist Texan buffoon."[22]

In a way, many liberals who objected to Bush's citing Christ as his preferred philosopher were boxed in by their position: liberals champion free speech, and yet they could not contain their distaste for what Bush had said. "He ought to be able to explain why he picked Jesus," conceded free-speech enthusiast Eliot Mincberg, vice president for People for the American Way. "We did not object to the fact that Bush mentioned Jesus, but the fact that that was the only person Bush referred to and he said he just couldn't explain it."[23]

Mincberg was bothered that Bush picked Christ alone as his favorite philosopher. He was also unsatisfied by Bush's follow-up. When asked what he meant by saying that Christ was his preferred philosopher because Christ changed his heart, Bush said, "Well, if they [the public] don't know, it's going to be hard to explain. When you turn your heart and your life over to Christ, when you accept Christ as a Savior, it changes your heart and changes your life, and that's what happened to me."

To Mincberg that was unacceptable, as it was to Maureen Dowd, who wrote of Bush's explanation: "Translation: You're either in the Christ club or out of it, on the J.C. team or off." This, said an angry Dowd, was an "exclusionary attitude, so offensive to those with different beliefs."[24] Perhaps his answer could have been more effective. Of course, had Bush fully elaborated, he might just as likely have been assailed for trying to proselytize.

Some found other aspects of Bush's position bothersome: "It makes me uncomfortable," said Abraham Foxman, national director of the Anti-Defamation League. Bush's statement about Christ, said Foxman, in a statement offered in support of tolerance, "makes a lot of us uncomfortable." While he said that he respected Bush's right to espouse his religious beliefs, Foxman noted: "I felt left out, and I think a lot of Americans felt left out." He said that Bush's choice of Christ left out "Jews, Muslims, Buddhists and Hindus."[25]

All religious faiths make exclusionary claims that leave out other faiths. A Muslim's choice of Muhammad would leave out Jews, Buddhists, Hindus, and Christians. The key is whether Bush could choose Jesus, as have previous presidents, but still respect people of other faiths and represent them as their president.

Bush's Christian declaration had clearly started something. To the media elite, it seemed to have launched not an exploration of deeper, transcendent issues, nor the influence of faith in a man's life, but rather a regrettable simplification of the political debate; it had lowered, rather than elevated, the public discourse. With that one mention of Christ, Bush had rolled a grenade into the coffee room of the press corps. And yet this was just the tip of the iceberg: he would go on to mention Christ many times as his public career flourished, and each time the critics' sore spot got redder.

The Presidential Campaign

For George W. Bush, 1999 had begun with the sermon by Mark Craig that had prodded him toward 1600 Pennsylvania Avenue. The year ended with another moment of striking religious symbolism—the Christ-philosopher-thinker episode on the campaign trail. The next year brought the presidential primaries, and the general election itself. Bush's statements and actions during this period illuminated his faith and its influence on his political positions, on him as a person, and, potentially, on him as a president.

As the governor moved outside Texas to pursue the presidency, he began pushing his faith-based, compassionate conservative agenda at the national level. In July 1999, speaking to a racially diverse crowd in Indianapolis, the early front-runner unveiled a series of policies to rally religious and community groups in the fight against social problems. He proposed $8 billion in tax incentives to encourage charitable giving. He was practicing what he was preaching: that year, Bush donated 16 percent of his income (or $514,000) to charity—beyond the 10 percent that Christians are expected to tithe.[26]

In Indianapolis, he said that he hoped his faith-based proposals would someday call forth the nation's armies of compassion. In announcing his plan, he spoke directly to his Republican cohorts: "I bring a message to my own party. We must apply our conservative and free-market ideas to the job of helping real human beings, because any ideology, no matter how right in theory, is sterile without that goal."[27] He chose Indianapolis for the announcement because of the influence of one of his top advisers, the creative Indianapolis mayor Stephen Goldsmith, who led a revolution in championing private-sector initiatives at the state and local levels throughout the 1980s and 1990s.

The issue of government support of faith-based programs brought allegations that Bush was not separating church and state. The candidate addressed the matter:

> We must maintain the balance of church and state. I think that's a really important principle. . . . I've heard from a lot of very important leaders . . . that are deeply concerned about my position. . . . It makes them nervous when they hear me say, "And I intend to encourage faith-based institutions to perform their commonplace miracles of renewal." So it sounds like to them that I want government to fund religious institutions. And I argue the case: What I'm asking for is government to empower people to make decisions or to fund the programs within certain institutions of faith. And I argue that's a difference. . . . We have a different application of funding programs and people as opposed to funding church.[28]

Bush argued that the state is constitutionally permitted to fund certain faith-based programs as long as it does not favor a particular denomination or church.

The campaign trail shed light on more personal aspects of Bush's faith. In two August 2000 interviews, the governor referred to himself as a "lowly sinner" in need of redemption. He said that it was an "important admission" for someone running for office. "It's a humbling experience to make that admission," he insisted. He said that such an acknowledgment drove him to seek redemption in Christ. "Without making that admission," says Bush, "I don't think there's such a thing as redemption."[29]

Bush had learned humility at home. His father's mother had drilled the words *don't brag* into her son's mindset, and George W. has said that he respects his father's modesty and has tried to match it in his own life, public and private.[30] His humility is also an outgrowth of his "Amazing Grace" theology. "I was humbled to learn that God sent His Son to die for a sinner like me," said the governor. "I was comforted to know that through the Son, I could find God's amazing grace, a grace that crosses every border, every barrier and is open to everyone." He says it is "through the love of Christ's life" that he can understand "the life-changing powers of faith." The Christian faith, Bush says flatly, "teaches humility."[31]

Faith-based humility remains prominent on Brian Berry's radar screen. Having observed Bush closely for ten years, Berry was eager to "set the record straight" on the president: "I'm very upset with the caricature by the media." Asked what upset him most, he jumped: "The man is humble. He is very humble. That image of him does not get represented by the media."[32] Asked from where the humility comes, he noted that Bush "grew up in the shadow of stars," around congressmen, vice presidents, even presidents. He also cited the man's faith: "A heavy influence. It's heavily biblical based."[33]

Reporters who talked to the presidential candidate about his faith were struck by its lack of self-righteousness. Journalist Joe Klein, a liberal, observed after several discussions with Bush that the governor "never displayed the vaguest hint of dogmatism. . . . Quite the contrary: his faith was humble and, well, soft. . . . He used words like love and heart more than any other presidential candidate I've ever seen."[34]

Humility aside, the presidential campaign revealed other aspects of how Bush's faith affected his personality, policy positions, and even his performance. This was particularly true of the Republican convention in Philadelphia in August 2000.

The convention reflected Bush's embrace of diversity. The event was his show entirely. As political commentator Mark Shields put it,

"This was a Bush convention, not a Republican convention." The *Washington Post's* Haynes Johnson called it "a very successful convention" that "was almost letter perfect." Presidential historian Michael Beschloss echoed the sentiment: "This was an almost perfect convention for George W."[35]

If anything, the convention went overboard in its attempt to achieve political correctness. The color, creed, or gender of a speaker seemed to trump his or her statement or position on the issues. Yet much of this Bush mosaic was genuine. The governor had long worked with African-Americans and Hispanics. Condoleezza Rice and Colin Powell spoke because of their standing with Bush, who later as president made them, respectively, the first black woman national security adviser and first black secretary of state. One of the Hispanics who spoke was none other than Jeb Bush's own son. The black pastors who spoke at the convention knew Bush because he visited their churches; likewise, he had long listened to black ministers in Texas.

The Republican convention also signaled Bush's faith-based acceptance of religious diversity. The invocation one evening was provided by a Mormon—San Francisco 49ers quarterback Steve Young—who is a direct descendant of Brigham Young. Many Christians consider Mormonism a kind of cult, but Bush gave no inkling that he shared this view. During the four days of the convention, delegates heard prayers and speeches from clergy representing the Jewish faith, Catholicism, Greek Orthodox Christianity, and various Protestant traditions. In his acceptance speech at the convention, Bush declared, "I believe in tolerance, not in spite of my faith, but because of it. I believe in a God who calls us not to judge our neighbors, but to love them."[36]

That address was the most significant of his life to that point. He shared the story of Mary Jo Copeland, whose Minneapolis ministry dishes out a thousand meals a week to the homeless. Copeland advises her hungry to "look after your feet" because they "must carry you a long way in this world, and then all the way to God." Citing this gospel, Bush emphasized the deeper change that must take place before the downtrodden truly step up. While government can feed the body, he said, it cannot feed the soul. That, said Bush, is where faith-based groups come in, and why America must support them.[37]

Bush's acceptance speech in Philadelphia, broadcast on national television, was his highest-profile appearance to date. His capabilities as a speaker had been dismissed. His upcoming address was a nerve-racking concern to his party and supporters. Yet by all accounts his performance exceeded expectations.

Bush has frequently surprised observers with his knack for unexpectedly rising to the occasion at key moments throughout his presidential path. The next such occurrence came in the October 11, 2000, presidential debate at Wake Forest University. MSNBC's Chris Matthews dubbed Bush's debate performance "totally presidential," and his handling of foreign policy particularly impressed the media. The *Boston Globe*'s Mike Barnacle said Bush was "superb on foreign policy." Journalist Jonathan Alter said Bush showed he was "clearly not a dope" and demonstrated an impressive ability to "think in time" about foreign policy, rather than just serve canned answers. "George Bush had a terrific night on foreign policy," agreed NBC's Andrea Mitchell. "He certainly indicated he can hold his weight on foreign policy."[38]

Bush's responses may have appeared especially thoughtful for a specific reason: he has said that when he pauses briefly before speaking at major moments, he is actually praying—asking for God's assistance in a pivotal situation.

Asked how his faith manifests itself in his life, during the campaign Bush also indicated that it gave him "a certain confidence about my life." Pointing out that his happiness does not depend on material success or electoral success, he conceded that he would like to be president, "But should it not work out, I understand that there is a force greater than myself—and it gives me comfort."[39] When his campaign seemed to be dragging, he told *Newsweek*: "If this doesn't work out, I've got a life."[40] He had said much the same a few months earlier, telling the *Washington Post*: "[I]f it doesn't work, that's just the way it goes, and I'll come back home and my wife'll love me, the dog'll love me, the cats will play like they don't but they really will."[41] He says that knowing there is a God helps him understand that there is "a higher priority in life, ultimately, than the priorities I may have set before me."[42]

This stood in marked contrast to the man he ran against. Vice President Al Gore was aware of Bush's inner contentment, but acknowledged that he did not feel the same way about potentially losing the presidential race. "I'll do anything to win," Gore said. "If he wins or loses," he said of Bush, "life goes on. I'll do anything to win."[43]

Bush feels that his Christian faith provides a unique reassurance because of Christ's sacrifice. "You know, people search for something good in times of darkness, and our faith provides that," he says. "That's a wonderful thing about Christianity. There is spiritual reassurance."[44]

Brian Berry had seen this in Bush as early as 1993. "He knows who he is," said Berry. "Always has. I saw that back in the first governor's race." Asked if he believed that that confidence was rooted in Bush's faith, Berry replied: "I think it is. If he knows who he is, and that he is here for a purpose and is living that purpose, that gives him a confidence—an unflappable component to weather any hurricane. It's not arrogance. It's a sureness that the purpose is here and now."[45]

Confidence also aided Bush's decision-making. The governor referred to his faith as a "shiftless foundation" that "frees me to put the problem of the moment in proper perspective . . . frees me to make decisions that others might not like. Frees me to try to do the right thing, even though it may not poll well."[46]

His faith shields him. To Bush, God is that shield spoken of in "Amazing Grace": "He will my shield and portion be, as long as life endures."

5.

"So Help Me God"

"Unity is within our reach, because we are guided
by a power larger than ourselves, Who creates us
equal in His image."

—*George W. Bush, inaugural address,*
January 2001

On the morning of January 20, 2001, Blair House was filled with
Bushes. The home of soon-to-be presidents during their transition to the White House, Blair House on this morning hosted both
a former president and a president-elect. The families of the two
George Bushes scurried around the house, preparing for a prayer service at St. John's Church, as they had done the morning of January
20, 1989. George W. and Laura had attended St. John's, an Episcopal
church located across Lafayette Park from the White House, while
they lived in Washington in 1987 and 1988; they had found the
Methodist church too political, its liberal minister fond of giving sermons that criticized Bush's father. Now, at St. John's, they met up

with the family of Vice President-elect Dick Cheney and his wife Lynn, both also Methodists. The Reverend Luis Leon's sermon was described as short but sweet—sympathetic to the frenetic day ahead.[1]

After a year of rigorous campaigning for the presidency, and two years after his Austin epiphany with Pastor Craig, George W. Bush was inaugurated again—this time swearing an oath that would make him the forty-third president of the United States. That January 20, the man from Midland stood before a nation ripped apart by the narrowest, most divisive presidential election in modern times. He placed his hand on the same Bible his mother had held when his father was sworn in as president.[2]

In just six years, after never before holding public office, the fifty-four-year-old had twice been chosen governor of the nation's largest state, and then elected president of the world's most powerful country. Between 1994 and 2000, he had won three major elections.

George W. had received two surprise endorsements for the White House. One came from Texas billionaire H. Ross Perot, a longtime Bush-family adversary. It had always been assumed that Perot's political opposition to the Bushes stemmed from personal animosity. Perot "had been instrumental in defeating my dad in 1992," as George W. remembered.[3] He had even endorsed Ann Richards in 1994. Yet he announced to a surprise viewing audience on CNN's *Larry King Live* that he was voting for the son of the man he helped unseat in the 1992 presidential election.

The other big surprise came from Billy Graham. The reverend rarely endorsed a candidate; he saw his duty as ministering to presidents, not advocating their campaigns. Like Perot, however, he dreaded a Gore presidency. "I have been praying for this crucial election," said the Bible man on the eve of the vote. "I've been praying that God's will shall be done. I don't endorse candidates. But I've come as close to it, I guess, now as any time in my life, because I think it's extremely important." Though frail, Graham spoke forcefully: "This is a crucial election in the history of America." As he stood next to Bush, he grinned and noted that he had cast an absentee ballot in North Carolina:

> I'll just let you guess who I voted for. And my family the same way. And we believe there's going to be a tremendous victory and change by Tuesday night in the direction of the country—putting it in good hands. I believe in the integrity of this man. I've known him as a boy. I've known him as a young man. And we're very proud of him.[4]

Graham then turned his attention to Laura Bush. "It's worth getting him into the White House to get her in the White House," he said, smiling. "If they, by God's will, win, I'm going to do everything in my power to help them make a successful presidency."

Bush's eyes welled with tears at the tribute from the man who had planted that mustard seed in his heart. He reciprocated by calling Graham a close friend, a great American, and a "major influence in my life."

Once the Florida vote was resolved, and the governor was named president-elect, Bush's first order of business was to try to heal the nation after the disastrous election. In November, both he and Gore had earned over 50 million votes—each grabbing more ballots than Bill Clinton in 1992 and 1996.[5] Gore outpaced Bush by 540,000 votes. The key in the vote total was California. Curiously, a Zogby poll actually showed Bush in a dead heat (43 percent to 43 percent) with Gore in California on the morning of the election. Whether the voting there was affected by the premature call in Florida is impossible to calculate, but in the end Bush lost California by 1.2 million votes, or 54 percent to 42 percent. Zogby was one of the only polling organizations that predicted Gore would win the overall popular vote, and yet Zogby was off by a huge 12 percent in California.

As it turned out, there were California voters who did what Bob Glass did in Florida. Glass is a Southern Baptist who lives in the Florida panhandle, which places him in the country's central time zone, as opposed to the rest of the state, which falls an hour behind in the eastern time zone. This is the Pensacola Bible Belt area, as well as an area flush with military installations. Bush's supporters in the region outnumbered Gore's by 2 to 1.[6]

After work, Glass raced to get to his polling place. Then he heard on the radio that the TV networks had called Florida and its twenty-five electoral votes for Gore. Glass knew that the networks would not make a premature call if the numbers, predicated on sample sizing, forecast a Gore victory. So he turned the car around and decided not to cast his vote. "What's the use?" he reasonably concluded, throwing his hands in the air. "I mean, if Gore's already won the state, there's no use in voting for Bush. I was so infuriated. I was distraught. And I just went home."[7] Glass shared Bush's spiritual and moral values—key reasons he wanted to vote for the governor. Now it didn't matter—he thought.

According to Bill Sammon, Glass was among 187,000 registered voters in the Florida central time zone who did not vote in the election. As Yale's John R. Lott Jr. concluded: "By prematurely declaring Gore the winner shortly before the polls had closed in Florida's conservative western Panhandle, the media ended up suppressing the Republican vote."[8] For Bush, the media made a grave mistake he had to overcome. But what about California? How many California voters went home like Bob Glass?

The other great unpredictable that swung the overall vote total in Gore's direction was the African-American vote. Gore had energized the black vote unlike any politician in recent memory. White voters favored Bush by a wide margin, but nothing compared to the solid bloc of support black voters offered Gore.

In Florida, blacks went for Gore by 93 percent to 7 percent. Even in Texas, where Bush as governor once garnered 25 percent of black votes, he somehow gained only 5 percent. While Bush got more white votes in Illinois than Gore, the vice president's 92 percent to 7 percent advantage gave him Illinois by a staggering 12 percent. The same was true in Maryland, Michigan, and Pennsylvania. In Maryland, Bush won among white voters 51 percent to 46 percent. However, the number of black votes was so large that Gore took Maryland handily with a 57 percent majority. (Women and Hispanics voted Republican in far stronger proportions than in any recent presidential contest. In 1996, according to a Bush spokeswoman, the Democrats' margin of victory among Hispanics was seven-to-two, whereas it was only two-to-one in 2000.)[9]

Blacks have historically voted Democrat by huge margins. In the 2000 contest, however, they voted in much larger percentages than usual. It was this black turnout that pollsters had not foreseen. Whatever Gore had said or did (Republicans accused him of scare tactics in trying to attract the black vote), it worked.

These factors help explain the big mystery: how so many polls could be so wrong in predicting that Bush would win the popular vote. Polling has become a fairly exact science. Most pollsters foresaw an easy Bush win on Election Day. As the candidate flew across the country, his campaign chief, Karl Rove—visiting Florida, ironically, on the final day of the sixteen-month campaign—confidently forecast an electoral-college sweep of close to 320 votes for his candidate, and a popular-vote margin of 51 percent to 45 percent.[10]

In the end, Gore took 48.4 percent of the popular vote. Bush took 47.9 percent.[11] Unfortunately for Bush, elections are not judged by territory. He won thirty states—the so-called "red states"—compared to Gore's twenty "blue states"; thus, Bush won 60 percent of states compared to Gore's 40 percent. The population of counties won by Bush was 143 million people compared to 127 million for Gore. Bush cornered 2.43 million square miles of the nation's territory; Gore secured 580,000—meaning Bush grabbed 81 percent of the nation's landscape, while Gore took less than 20 percent. After the election, USA Today published a map of counties won by Bush and Gore. The difference is even more marked than the state gap. If Al Gore had become president, he could have literally flown from the White House to the West Coast without passing over a county he had won.[12]

In winning Florida, Bush barely won the electoral college, taking 271 electoral votes against Gore's 266.[13] The vote was nearly dead even, and voter turnout was relatively high at 50 percent–plus. The country was almost perfectly split.

It was ironic that the governor ran as a "unifier" who could bring people together, which was a trait he displayed in Texas. Speaking of Vice President Gore just days before the election, Bush told a crowd in Burbank, California: "My opponent cannot bring America together because he practices the politics of division. We will not divide and conquer. We will inspire and unite." His promise was bolstered by the fact that he spoke these words alongside Senator John McCain (R-AZ), with whom he had fought a nasty Republican primary battle.[14] Surely Bush had no idea of how important this characteristic would prove once he became president.

A great divide faced the country. A month earlier, the Reverend Jesse Jackson had promised a "civil rights explosion" if the U.S. Supreme Court voted in favor of Bush's victory in Florida. He likened the court ruling to the Dred Scott case and earlier civil rights demonstrations in Selma and Birmingham, Alabama. "All that we bled for and suffered for the last 25 years is now in the balance here today," said Reverend Jackson of black Americans and the impending court decision. "The case is up there with the Dred Scott level of case; did the black man have a right the white was bound to respect." If the court ruled for Bush, Jackson predicted that African-Americans would "not surrender to this tyranny. We will fight back."[15]

The reverend's words hardly helped; they were not what Bush wanted to hear. The governor had reached out to minorities to such an extent in Texas that, for a Republican, he had gained unprecedented support from African-Americans and Hispanics. He was the orchestrator of the glaringly multicultural 2000 Republican convention—"the most inclusive Republican Convention in memory," according to Time.[16]

Bush saw his inaugural address as an opportunity to reemphasize his earlier calls for unity. "Unity," he said early in his speech, "is within our reach, because we are guided by a power larger than ourselves, Who creates us equal in His image." He spoke of the need for civility, courage, compassion, and character. For some, this new tone worked. Among the attendees, John Evans, a student from Gettysburg College, said it was "the first speech in a while that made me feel good about being an American." A thirty-four-year-old air-force major named Matthew McKenzie asserted: "I think George W. will do a great job. He's definitely a man of character and faith."[17]

A few blocks away, civility was not the word on Fourteenth and K Streets, where protesters blocked the way toward the inaugural parade route down Pennsylvania Avenue. Nearby, Jed Dodd, a union organizer from Philadelphia, complained of the new president: "I don't even think he won Florida. I came down here to show my outrage."[18]

Near the grandstand, scattered among the spattering cold rain, were hard-liners who floated black balloons and hoisted placards with phrases such as DUBIOUS GEORGE, HAIL TO THE THIEF, and BUSH-WHACKED BY THE SUPREMES. One of the dissenters, Shelly Levine of Washington, D.C., braved the cold to claim: "Let Bush see that more than half the people here don't believe in him."[19]

A five-hour drive away, at a protest in Pittsburgh, a group of one hundred paused for a moment of silence "for the death of democracy" at the moment Bush placed his hand on the Bible. He was dubbed "King George" and "President Death." "The presidency is in the process of being stolen," explained one organizer, Jeanne K. Clark, president of the local chapter of the National Organization for Women.[20] Though Bush had reached out to Gore supporters, many were too angry to shake hands.

The enemy camps were prominent in the inaugural grandstand. Sitting behind Bush was Gore and President Bill Clinton, who was gracious, even enthusiastic. Speaker of the House Newt Gingrich sat in the background, as did James A. Baker III, the close friend and former secretary of state to Bush's father, who had been tapped by Bush to manage the legal and constitutional aspects of the election controversy. Conspicuous was the beaming countenance of George H. W., who at one point (caught in a photograph published around the country) could be seen peering at Bill Clinton, the man who had taken the White House away from him, as Clinton watched Bush's son take the oath.

There had been speculation that George W. pursued the presidency in part to avenge his father's loss in 1992, a charge that he disputes. Frank Bruni explored the notion in a *New York Times* piece titled "Senior Bush's Loss Set Course for Son's Candidacy." While we may never know, there is no question that the loss was painful to the son, particularly coming as it did at the hands of Bill Clinton. The Bush family places a premium on character and integrity; it burned to lose to a man they saw as seriously wanting in those areas. As Bush put it, he hated "to see a good man get whipped."[21]

The senior Bush, a man not prone to sweeping statements about divine intervention, came to see God's hand in his own defeat. "You ever heard the expression, 'The Lord works in mysterious ways?'" George H. W. Bush would say later. "We had that [happen] in our family all the time, even with some bad things. . . . And if I'd had won that election in 1992, my oldest son would not be president of the United States of America." With his voice crackling with emotion, the proud father concluded: "So, what more can a dad ask? I think the Lord works in mysterious ways."[22]

In George W. Bush's inaugural address, he talked of healing at home, and of his vision of foreign policy. His words would take on new meaning after September 11:

> The enemies of liberty and our country should make no mistake, America remains engaged in the world, by history and by choice, shaping a balance of power that favors freedom. We will defend our allies and our interests. We will show purpose. . . . We will meet aggression and bad faith with resolve and strength.

Bush also talked about faith-based groups, and defined compassion as the work of a nation, not just a government. He said that "some needs and hurts are so deep they will only respond to a mentor's touch or a pastor's prayer." He emphasized that this could be achieved through multiple faiths, and interjected one of his favorite stories—the account of the Good Samaritan. He made a "pledge" in those first presidential minutes: "When we see that wounded traveler on the road to Jericho, we will not pass to the other side."

He ended with a story about the American founders. After signing the Declaration of Independence, Virginian John Page wrote to Thomas Jefferson: "We know the race is not to the swift nor the Battle to the Strong. Do you not think an Angel rides in the Whirlwind and directs this Storm?" To George W. Bush, the answer was certain. And for the first of many times as president, he told the nation:

> Much time has passed since Jefferson arrived for his inauguration. The years and changes accumulate. But the themes of this day he would know: our nation's grand story of courage, and its simple dream of dignity.
>
> We are not this story's author, who fills time and eternity with His purpose. Yet His purpose is achieved in our duty; and our duty is fulfilled in service to one another. Never tiring, never yielding, never finishing, we renew that purpose today: to make our country more just and generous; to affirm the dignity of our lives and every life. This work continues. This story goes on. And an Angel still rides in the whirlwind and directs this storm. God bless you all, and God bless America.[23]

With that, the new president walked over, kissed his smiling mother, and embraced his father. Once again, his oratorical performance surpassed expectations. As he left the podium, Howard Fineman allowed that he was "continually struck," even "astonished" at how Bush "rises to the occasion" during such key moments.[24]

The invocation at the ceremony had been provided by Billy Graham's son Franklin, who stood for his ailing father; now the benediction was done by Reverend Kirbyjon Caldwell of the Windsor Village United Methodist Church, the African-American congregation in Houston that Bush had addressed as governor. Caldwell, who described himself as politically independent but a "spiritual supporter" of his Texas comrade, had also spoken at the Republican convention just before Bush accepted his party's presidential nomination. Reverend Caldwell urged forgiveness: "Almighty God, the supply and supplier of peace, prudent policy, and non-partisanship, we bless your holy and righteous name. Thank you, O God, for blessing us with forgiveness, with faith, and with favor."[25]

After the ceremony, Bush made his goodbyes and headed to the White House. As the first car in his presidential motorcade drove slowly down Constitution Avenue, it was greeted by a flame engulfing an American flag. The woman who ignited the fire was whisked away by Capitol police. Just then, an enraged demonstrator dove from a light pole into the crowd below.[26]

While there were such protests, others heeded Bush's call. *Time* magazine wrote of the new president: "Even Democrats now say privately that Bush and his soft serums may be better suited [than Gore] to cure the disease that afflicts the capital."[27] The perception of Bush as a unifier was a key reason *Time* gave in naming him its 2000 Person of the Year.[28] Richard Cohen, the liberal columnist for the *Washington Post*, who voted for Gore, wrote: "I now think that under current circumstances he [Gore] would not be the right man for the presidency. If I could, I would withdraw my vote." He said that Bush's claim to be a unifier rather than a divider was not just campaign talk—"in Bush's case it appears to be true." Gore, on the other hand, wrote Cohen, had "little" such ability.[29]

Despite the Florida controversy, George W. Bush believed he was now on the job for a reason. He awaited what the story's author would write in the pages ahead.

6.

Faith and the Presidency

"True faith is never isolated from the rest of life,
and faith without works is dead."

—*President George W. Bush*[1]

"Mr. President, why do you refuse to respect the
wall between the church and state? . . . You are a
secular official. And not a missionary."

—*White House reporter Helen Thomas to
President Bush, February 2001*[2]

From day one, George W. Bush integrated his faith into his presidency. His first official act was to make Inaugural Day a National Day of Prayer and Thanksgiving, "knowing that I cannot succeed in this task without the favor of God and the prayers of the people." In the proclamation, he asked Americans to "bow our heads in humility" before the God that "calls us not to judge our neighbors, but to love them, to ask His guidance upon our Nation and its leaders in every level of government."[3]

The second day of Bush's presidency, Sunday, January 21, began with a special service at the National Cathedral, which featured a cornucopia of faiths: Jewish, Eastern Orthodox Christian, Catholic, and other denominations. Kirbyjon Caldwell again delivered a prayer, and Franklin Graham preached. Most appropriately, Pastor Mark Craig, whose sermon in Austin two years earlier had prompted Bush to seek the presidency, read the New Testament's 1 John 4:7–8: "Dear friends, let us love one another, because love comes from God. Whoever loves is a child of God and knows God. Whoever does not love does not know God, for God is love."[4]

These weekend activities were a fitting start for a presidency that had its roots in faith. Yet some observers seemed eager from the start to call Bush's a "faith-based presidency," to claim that Bush has pursued a "religious renovation" of government, when in fact Bush's religiousness comes quite close to what the founders envisioned: a government whose leaders were deeply grounded in faith, but also mindful of the need to separate church and state.

George W. Bush practices a nonjudgmental brand of Christianity that prompts him simultaneously to concede that "men and women can be good without faith," and to assert that all believers need not be Christians. Still, he places an overwhleming faith in the power of faith: As he has said frequently, "True faith is never isolated from the rest of life, and faith without works is dead. . . . [It] proves itself through actions and sacrifice, through acts of kindness and caring for those in need."[5]

Bush's spirituality affects his presidency in both tangible and intangible ways—from specific policy positions to a subtle but critical influence on Bush's personality and character traits. In practical terms, however, it is not easy to separate the two. Most of the intangibles have basic Judeo-Christian roots. Some, however, are more explicitly Christian. Though forgiveness is a virtue shared by many faiths, it is especially central to Christianity, grounded in the example of Christ's sacrifice. Bush has placed special emphasis on both forgiveness and hope. Hope, he says, is eternal, and it is eternal because of what Christ offered on the cross. The Christian faith, said the new president, "finds hope and comfort in a cross."[6]

Among the intangibles, his faith-based humility has been evident in his behind-the-scenes actions as president. This was clear in the first foreign-policy crisis of the Bush presidency, which occurred on April 1, 2001, when China detained twenty-four American military personnel who landed their damaged spy plane in Chinese territory. These troops were in a desperate situation, and so was the freshman president. Bush asked U.S. officials to be sure to get Bibles to any of the twenty-four who wanted them.[7]

The Chinese government insisted on an American apology, appearing eager to humiliate the new president in order to secure some sort of realpolitik gain. The media spotlight on Bush was intense, and he did not have a lot of options. Foreign-policy analysts hoped the crisis would die without any apology or other unpleasant actions, and that no U.S. sanctions would result.[8] Yet the Bush administration refused to apologize, particularly because the actions of the Chinese pilot who brushed the airplane had jeopardized the lives of twenty-four Americans. Perhaps it was *China*, many believed, that should be making amends.

Just when it looked like there was no hope, the crisis subsided. On April 11, in a brief, early-morning statement, Bush shocked the world by announcing that the twenty-four crew members were coming home. There would be no hostage crisis for the new presidency.

Senator Joe Biden, the ranking Democrat on the Senate Foreign Relations Committee, gave Bush "high marks" for his handling of the situation, and insightfully noted that the president had carefully avoided using the words *hostage* and *crisis* throughout the affair. The president's handling of the fiasco was widely commended by former Clinton administration members like Nancy Soderberg, Sandy Berger, Jamie Rubin, David Gergen, and James Woolsey.[9] In acknowledging this major win, Bush ordered his jubilant staff to refrain from "high fives" and to be "humble" about this "victory." There would be no gloating, he made clear, when American lives were at stake.[10]

LIFE ISSUES

The spy-plane incident was the first foreign-policy crisis of the young presidency. Before that, however, George W. Bush's faith had already directly influenced major policy changes—particularly on the issue of abortion.

During the campaign, Bush had said what pro-lifers wanted to hear. As NBC's Tom Brokaw rightly noted, the largest ovation in Bush's Republican convention speech came when he stressed the need to protect "the unborn." When he was president-elect, Bush held a private talk with Colin Powell, whose pro-choice position was a matter of record, several weeks before naming him secretary of state. He told Powell that as secretary of state he would be expected to purge any vestiges of the Clinton State Department's program to promote global abortion rights. Powell told Bush that he understood and would follow his lead.[11]

The change on abortion was immediate. On his first day in office,

Bush authorized a ban on all U.S. funding of international abortion rights groups, reversing President Clinton's previous executive order. He appointed prominent pro-lifers to key cabinet posts, including John Ashcroft as attorney general and Tommy Thompson as secretary of health and human services.

A silent storm of pro-life actions by Bush would follow in the months and years to come. On August 5, 2002, for example, he signed the Born Alive Infants Protection Act. Passed by the Senate the previous month, the act provides for the protection of a child who survives an abortion. In so doing, it affirmed the right to life of newborns. If a child managed to survive an abortion, it would now need to be protected rather than destroyed by a doctor or nurse, regardless of whether its birth was intended or desired.

Most Americans were unaware of the fact that for decades infants who survived abortions were left to die once outside their mother; a situation that had occurred countless times since abortion became legal in 1973, it now became illegal with one stroke at Bush's pen.

Conservatives hailed the move. Kenneth L. Connor, president of the Family Research Council, called the act "a watershed" in the effort to roll back "the abortion-on-demand regime" created by the 1973 Roe v. Wade decision. Professor Hadley Arkes, a Vaughan Fellow in the Madison Program at Princeton University and a chief player in the Born Alive Act, deemed Bush's affirmation a "landmark" action. With the president's signature, he said, no one would be able to deny the humanity of an abortion survivor.[12]

Other moves followed. In January 2003, Bush signed the Sanctity of Life bill. Two months later, in an especially significant move, he chose not to veto the Republican Senate's March 2003 passage of a ban on partial-birth abortion, which President Clinton had repeatedly blocked. For the two years prior to that ban, the Bush Justice

Department had been lending its support to local efforts to prohibit partial-birth abortion at the state level.

Eventually, in November 2003, he signed the partial-birth abortion ban that was passed by Congress, fulfilling his earlier promise: "When Congress sends me a bill against partial-birth abortions, I will sign it into law."[13] Following the signing ceremony, he met in the Oval Office with a gathering of evangelical pro-life leaders: Janet Parshall, Southern Baptist Convention (SBC) President Jack Graham, former SBC President Adrian Rogers, American Center for Law and Justice Chief Counsel Jay Sekulow, National Religious Broadcasters President Frank Wright, National Association of Evangelicals President Ted Haggard, President of the Ethics & Religious Liberty Commission Richard Land, and Moral Majority founder Jerry Falwell. The meeting, described as a time of "joyous fellowship," concluded with Bush asking his allies to join hands with him in praying to God to bless both the nation and their efforts to preserve life. Falwell called it "an astounding moment" for him personally. "Standing there in the Oval Office," he reported, "I felt suddenly humbled to be in the presence of a man—our president—who takes his faith very seriously and who seeks the prayers of his friends as he leads our nation." Falwell turned to Bush and told him that he, the others in the room, and the 80 million believers nationwide who he said they represented, considered Bush "a man of God." Bush turned to Falwell and replied, "I'll try to live up to it."[14]

A few months later, at the Solemn Mass for Life at the Basilica of the National Shrine of the Immaculate Conception in Washington, D.C.—the largest Catholic chapel in the United States—a packed throng of anguished Catholic faithful, kneeling in prayer after taking Holy Communion, listened intently while the presiding bishop closed the mass with a surprise message from the president.

When the Bush letter acknowledged his ban of partial-birth abortion, the solemnity was interrupted with a burst of loud applause, exceeded in duration only by the clapping that followed the sign-off at the letter's end.[15]

Banning partial-birth abortion was an easy decision for Bush—the procedure was an evil whose time had come to an end. A more difficult moral dilemma had confronted him during his first summer in the White House, when he had been obliged to decide whether to permit federal funding of embryonic stem-cell research (ESCR). It was another area in which Bush clearly stood out from his predecessor.

ESCR seemed the ultimate life issue—in both directions. Supporters wanted to use stem cells from human embryos to do research they believed would ultimately extend and improve lives. They argued that stem cells could produce advances in curing cruel diseases like Alzheimer's. Nancy Reagan, whose husband was dying from the disease, appealed to Bush to allow the research, as did former Reagan Chief of Staff Ken Duberstein, wheelchair-bound actor Christopher Reeve, and actress Mary Tyler Moore.

President Clinton, or a President Gore, would surely have deemed the decision simple, and chosen to authorize the research. George W. Bush, according to his press office, was torn. He felt these embryos were, if not lives themselves, at least potential lives—lives at the earliest stage of development. He was appalled at the prospect of "embryo farms" or "parts farms"—the start of a slippery slope into a Brave New World in which some "humans" might one day be raised solely for their parts, exploited by those lucky enough not to be born or "harvested" in such fashion.

The country waited while Bush pondered the question. At 9:00 P.M. on August 9, 2001, he announced his decision in a nationally televised speech—Bush's first prime-time address to the nation, a gesture that underscored the issue's importance. He resolved to halt federal funding of research on future or newly created embryos. Conservative Christians were thrilled with that aspect of the decision. Yet he also elected to permit continued research on the existing sixty stem-cell lines that had already been extracted for research—a decision that alarmed some, though not all, conservatives.

Bush's speech was hailed for its balance and thoughtfulness. It was educational, carefully laying out the issue and fairly representing where each side stood and why. Though authoritative, it was not condescending.

Leading Christian conservatives were split in their reactions. The morning before the announcement, Dr. James Dobson, president of Focus on the Family, featured a bioethicist on his radio show, who said that this would be Bush's "Lincolnian moment." Many social conservatives perceived political-moral dimensions to the question, akin to the devaluing of human beings inherent in slavery.

After the speech, Dobson appeared on CNN's *Larry King Live* to offer his reaction. Dobson proclaimed himself pleased with the decision, and said that Bush had not only reached "a good solution" but had "amazingly" satisfied both sides of the debate.[16] He was joined by other Christian conservatives, including Greg Koukl, director of the Los Angeles–based ministry Stand to Reason.

Yet for each of these approving conservatives, there was a conservative Christian dissenter. The Family Research Council announced that it "deeply regretted" Bush's verdict, calling a press conference with a host of displeased conservative Christians. Among them, Andrea Lafferty of the Traditional Values Coalition called the move "genetic cannibalism, not scientific advancement." Bay Buchanan feared that Bush had dangerously "opened the door" by allowing more research on already existing stem cells. The consensus among these dissenters was that it was wrong to continue to use any material drawn from onetime human embryos, just as, some argued, it would be wrong to use any material or research from Jewish corpses murdered and dissected by Dr. Joseph Mengele and the Nazis.[17]

This was the thinking of Alan Keyes, who called the existing stem-cell lines "fruit from a poisoned tree," and said: "The ends don't justify the means." Keyes's point was that any good that may come from destroying embryos does not justify their destruction.[18]

Such conservative Christians showed disappointment with Bush, yet few showed any anger. They believed that Bush had made a conscientious effort but simply came to a flawed conclusion. They forgave him because they felt he was generally in agreement with them on life issues, especially abortion. "I don't doubt for a moment his pro-life intentions," said Ken Connor, "but we think he has made a mistake."[19]

The ESCR issue did not go away, and it's unlikely to in the future. Indeed, only eight months later, on April 10, 2002, Bush made another judgment on the matter that merits attention. It was one of the weightiest, most nuanced statements of Bush's entire presidency, and one of the most neglected. Speaking from the East Room of the White House, he called on the Senate to back a ban on human cloning. He said:

> As we seek to improve human life, we must always preserve human dignity. . . . Advances in biomedical technology must never come at the expense of human conscience. As we seek what is possible, we must always ask what is right, and we must not forget that even the most noble ends do not justify any means. Science has set

before us decisions of immense consequence. We can pursue medical research with a clear sense of moral purpose or we can travel without an ethical compass into a world we could live to regret. . . . How we answer the question of human cloning will place us on one path or the other.

Human cloning is deeply troubling to me. . . . Life is a creation, not a commodity. Our children are gifts to be loved and protected, not products to be designed and manufactured. Allowing cloning would be taking a significant step toward a society in which human beings are grown for spare body parts, and children are engineered to custom specifications; and that's not acceptable.[20]

Bush's strong position on cloning—indeed, his willingness to take such a position at all, and to frame it in such terms—highlighted the president's tendency to judge such ethical challenges from a deeply moral, and spiritual, position.

FAITH-BASED INITIATIVES—COMPASSIONATE CONSERVATIVE PRESIDENCY

The change in abortion policy was not the only immediate action in which Bush's faith contributed to a significant policy shift from the previous administration. It was not coincidental that one of the first major acts of Bush's presidency was to sign an executive order (his first) creating a White House Office of Faith-based and Community Initiatives. The goal of the office is to ensure that local community "helpers and healers"—who operate within faith-based or religiously affiliated organizations and institutions—can receive federal money while facing fewer bureaucratic obstacles.[21]

Bush also created a Compassion Capital Fund that aims to match private giving with federal money. He recommended allowing taxpayers to deduct charitable contributions, which he hopes will spark a boon in charitable giving. He also sought to implement and expand the "charitable choice" policy, which ensures that faith-based groups are not denied federal contracts because they are faith-based.[22] All of this fulfilled the plan he offered in Indianapolis as a presidential candidate in 1999.

The policy of the Office of Faith-based and Community Initiatives is that faith-based organizations that receive federal funding cannot engage in direct proselytizing. The goal of these groups must be to use the government funds they receive for the purpose of assisting the needy, not to convert the needy to a particular faith.

Even with such provisions in place, however, not everyone shared Bush's enthusiasm for his new office. In the president's first press conference, on February 22, 2001, he was lectured by veteran White House reporter Helen Thomas. Thomas seemed eager to accuse Bush of creating not an Office of Faith-based and Community Initiatives, but rather an Office of Christian Apologetics and Crusading:

Thomas: Mr. President, why do you refuse to respect the wall between the church and state? And you know that the mixing of religion and government for centuries has led to slaughter. I mean, the very fact that our country has stood in good stead by having the separation—why do you break it down?

Bush: Helen, I strongly respect the separation of church and state—

Thomas: Well, you wouldn't have a religious office in the White House if you did.

Bush: I didn't get to finish my answer, in all due respect. I believe that so long as there's a secular alternative available we ought to allow individuals . . . to be able to choose a faith-based program. . . . Some of the most compassionate missions of help and aid come out of faith-based programs. And I strongly support the faith-based initiative that we're proposing, because I don't believe it violates the line between the separation of church and state, and I believe it's going to make America a better place.

Thomas: Well, you are a secular official.

Bush: I agree. I am a secular official.

Thomas: And not a missionary.[23]

Bush let Thomas have the last word. He called on the next questioner.

The Texan had brought his compassionate conservative agenda to the White House. To the uninitiated, he explained the link between that agenda and his faith: "Faith teaches us that God has a special concern for the poor. . . . Faith proves itself through actions and sacrifice, through acts of kindness and caring for those in need." He cited Christ's admonition to care "for the least of these."[24] An effective war on poverty must deploy "the weapons of the spirit," he said.[25] Quoting Martin Luther King Jr., Bush said that churches are not the servant of the state but, rather, "the conscience of the state."[26]

At Notre Dame University in May 2001, Bush said he was committed to government support of faith-based groups for both "practical reasons"—because the groups are effective—and "moral reasons."

He cited his duty as a person of faith: "The same God who endows us with individual rights also calls us to social obligations."[27]

Not all of Bush's compassionate conservatism, however, is private-sector driven. The president has insisted that, "Government has an important role. It will never be replaced by charities." As evidence of that role, at Notre Dame he boasted that his administration would increase funding for "major social welfare and poverty programs" by 8 percent.[28]

This later manifested itself in his signing of Congress's Medicare Drug Plan, which was opposed by a number of conservatives. Bush called the plan "historic legislation" to strengthen and "modernize" Medicare. For the first time in Medicare's thirty-eight-year history, it would provide for senior citizens to receive prescription drug coverage.[29]

The apotheosis of Bush's faith-based crusade, however, was a December 2002 address in Philadelphia, an event he considered a hallmark of his presidency. He was there to sign another faith-related executive order, one that directs all federal agencies to give equal treatment when providing social service grants.[30] The order demands that faith-based organizations should not be held to a different standard—or denied a government grant—because they are faith-based. "The days of discriminating against religious groups because they are religious are coming to an end," insisted Bush, to roaring approval.[31]

Bush singled out several federal agencies that he claimed had a history of discriminating against faith-based groups. Specifically, he ordered that the Federal Emergency and Management Agency (FEMA) revise its policy on emergency relief, which denied funding to religious organizations seeking to offer assistance after natural disasters. He also singled out the departments of Housing and Urban

Development (HUD) and Health and Human Services (HHS), announcing that the federal government would be producing a guidebook explaining how faith-based groups can apply for government grants.

The Philadelphia crowd was so energized that at times it sounded like Bush was preaching at a revival. When he complained that for too long too many in government have argued that there is no room for faith in the public square, Bush was interrupted by an audience member who shouted, "Preach on, brother!" while others cheered. At one point, Bush told the crowd of compassion warriors that he was "incredibly grateful" for what they did. "There is a saying," he continued, "that nobody can teach you how to be a good servant of God. You have to learn it on the job. And you are doing that job so incredibly well." Just then, one attendee audibly interrupted, "And you are, too!" Raucous applause followed. A presidential policy speech had turned into a love-in.

Not everyone was so enamored with Bush's faith-based agenda. Vermont Governor Howard Dean—then the front-runner for the Democratic nomination for the presidency—promised that if he became president: "I would undo every single one of the president's [faith-based] initiatives."[32]

COMPASSIONATE CONSERVATISM ABROAD

One of the single most striking echoes of Bush's compassionate conservatism was his African AIDS initiative. Foreseen by no one, it appeared dramatically in his January 2003 State of the Union address, a speech in which he also pushed a number of other compassion-based policies, such as federal assistance for prisons, shelters for battered women, and senior-citizens homes.

The AIDS announcement, however, was stunning. "As our nation moves troops and builds alliances to make our world safer," Bush began, "we must also remember our calling, as a blessed country, to make this world better." He continued: "Today, on the continent of Africa, nearly thirty million people have the AIDS virus—including three million children under the age of fifteen. . . . Yet across that continent, only fifty thousand AIDS victims—only fifty thousand—are receiving the medicine they need." He noted that there were entire nations in Africa in which more than one-third of adults carry the infection.[33]

Speaking of how the United States could help these Africans, he claimed that "seldom has history offered a greater opportunity to do so much for so many." He proposed the Emergency Plan for AIDS Relief, which he called a "work of mercy" to provide "humane care" for the millions afflicted. He asked Congress for $15 billion over the next five years, including $10 billion in "new" money. This was no small sum, especially during a time of recession and record budget deficits. It meant billions in taxpayer dollars for drugs, treatment, and prevention.

Writing in the *Washington Post,* Michael Kelly said that until Bush's remarks the response by the United States to the African AIDS "holocaust" had been "scandalous." Bush's proposal, he said, was a "rare and wonderful thing." "History will judge whether a world led by America stood by and let transpire one of the greatest destructions of human life of all time," assessed Kelly, "or performed one of the greatest rescues of human life of all time." The president, he maintained, had opened the door to the latter possibility.[34]

There was little criticism of the humanity of Bush's AIDS proposal. Disapproval came almost exclusively on the issue of cost.

Bush followed this announcement with a sustained commitment

to the cause. A few months later, on April 29, he issued a major statement in the East Room, in which he assembled the press, the secretary
of state, and others, and urged Congress to "act quickly" on his "emergency plan." He tried to enlist the world in this "great effort," calling
the AIDS "tragedy" the "responsibility of every nation." Bush called
AIDS a "dignity of life" issue. "We believe everyone has the right to
life," said Bush, "including children in the cities and villages of Africa
and the Caribbean." This "urgent work," he said, was a "moral imper-
ative" on which "time is not on our side."[35] "This cause is rooted in the
simplest of moral duties," he lectured the press assembled. "When
we see this kind of preventable suffering . . . we must act. When we see
the wounded traveler on the road to Jericho, we will not, America will
not, pass to the other side of the road."[36] (He later spoke of his country's "responsibility to fight AIDS"; this was "history's call to America.
I accept the call and will continue to lead in that direction."[37])

Just four weeks later, on May 27, he signed his $15 billion plan
into law; in only four months his announcement had become reality.
Few things have happened so quickly in American politics—not even
Marshall Plan aid had come as rapidly. When he signed the bill Bush
challenged Europe to match the U.S. commitment without delay.
The following week, at the Group of Eight summit for the world's
wealthiest nations, he pleaded for help in this "moral" obligation.[38]
In late June, he continued the cause in a speech at the Washington
Hilton.[39] Then, in July, he made a major trip to Africa, where he
again spoke out on AIDS. George W. Bush's compassionate conservatism, once the province of Texas politics, now had global borders.

Actually, that had always been the plan. "My vision of compassionate conservatism also requires America to assert its leadership in
the world," Governor Bush had said. "We are the world's only
remaining superpower, and we must use our power in a strong but

compassionate way to help keep the peace and encourage the spread of freedom."[40]

Bush's penchant to expand federal programs and create new ones has led the Weekly Standard's Fred Barnes to dub the president a "big government conservative."[41] Another leading conservative, National Review's Rich Lowry, pleads with liberals that there is much about Bush they ought to welcome. Listing some of the initiatives described above, Lowry writes, "This is the kind of Bible-thumping any bleeding heart should love."[42] Given how many critics have characterized Bush as a panderer to the religious right, it is intriguing to note just how many of his faith-grounded policies should also appeal to the religious left.

FAITH-BASED LOVE AND TOLERANCE

Central to Bush's policy initiatives is his incessant emphasis on faith and love—a matter that colors his public statements far more frequently than with most presidents. Bush has drawn parallels between the love of God and the love of a parent, and the unconditional love extended by each. He sees unconditional love as "the greatest gift" offered by God—particularly the Christian gospel[43]—and a parent.[44]

In his 2001 remarks on Easter, President Bush called God's love a "boundless love."[45] In his 2001 Christmas statement, he said that Christians celebrate God's love revealed to the world through Christ: "The message of Jesus is one that all Americans can embrace this holiday season—to love one another."[46] The following Easter, he said that Christ's death "stands out in history as the perfect example of unconditional love."[47] The next year, he observed that for Christians, the life and death of Jesus are "the ultimate expressions of love," and spoke of "Christ's example of love" through the sacrifice on the cross.[48] Though these descriptions came during Christian holidays,

Bush has made similar remarks on other occasions. He told a group of firefighters in October 2001 that "Scripture teaches" that "there is no greater love than to lay down one's life for another"—a reference to Christ's sacrifice.[49]

Bush has also called attention to the parallels between God's love and a father's love. Speaking to the Fourth National Summit on Fatherhood, he affirmed that children look to their fathers to provide protection, discipline, care, guidance, "and most importantly, unconditional love." "And," he continued, "many of us believe a father's love, like a mother's love, even imperfectly, mirrors divine love."[50]

It is this exhortation to love that teaches Bush to tolerate those who are different from him. Writing in *Time*, Joe Klein has observed that there has been "a great deal of nonsense written about Bush's religious convictions, much of it emanating from Europe—a continent where God has been relegated to the back pews—and from secular intellectuals at home." Klein notes that there is "scant evidence" that Bush is a "hard-edged religious determinist."[51] The greatest misperception of Bush's faith is that it makes him intolerant. This is not a man yearning to drown witches in the Potomac River.

How does George W. Bush's faith teach tolerance? He answers, "Once we have recognized God's image in ourselves, we must recognize it in every human being." Because every person is made in the image of God, he has said, believer and nonbeliever alike are all due respect and dignity by those who believe in God. "The promise of faith," he says, "is the presence of grace."[52] Bush claims, "In Scripture, God commands us to reach out to those who are different."[53] And it instructs Christians to love all others: "Faith teaches us to respect those with whom we disagree. It teaches us to tolerate one another. And it teaches us that the proper way to treat human beings created in the divine image is with civility."[54]

Bush's own tolerance in some policy areas has caused him to be at odds with Christian conservatives. On homosexuality, for example, he retained the Clinton administration's Office of AIDS Policy, and appointed an openly gay man to run it. He named a second openly gay individual to the Advisory Commission on the Arts, and chose not to repeal the homosexual spousal benefits for federal employees begun by Clinton. And he did not object when some cabinet secretaries participated in Gay Pride events with their departments,[55] even though such openness toward gays brought him occasional ire from cultural conservatives.

Nevertheless, Bush is on record as believing that homosexuality is a sin. His reading of the Bible appears to tell him three key things on the issue: (1) the act of homosexuality is a sin; (2) all humans commit sin; and (3) people must be tolerant of differences. This was evident in a July 2003 remark he made on gay marriage. Asked during a press conference if homosexuality is immoral, he replied, "I am mindful that we're all sinners, and I caution those who may try to take the speck out of their neighbor's eye when they got a log in their own." These were Christ's words in the New Testament. Bush continued: "I think it's very important for our society to respect each individual, to welcome those with good hearts, to be a welcoming country." At the same time, he affirmed his belief that the concept of marriage should be reserved to the union of a man and a woman.[56]

Religious Tolerance

Religious tolerance has long been a Bush priority. In his memoir, he stressed the importance of a leader respecting the faith of others. He often speaks emotionally of an ecumenical experience he had in a visit to Israel in 1998, when he toured the Old City, the Western Wall, the Church of the Holy Sepulcher, and made a pilgrimage to the Sea of Galilee, where he stood on the hill where Christ gave the Sermon on the Mount. His delegation included Methodists, Catholics, a Mormon, and Jews. They all read and sang their favorite hymns and verses. Bush read "Amazing Grace." They held hands together. It was a sentimental but authentic experience; Bush loved it.[57]

Once he won the presidency, Bush's tolerance of other faiths seemed to intensify. It was fitting that in his first Prayer Breakfast, held only a week and a half after his inauguration, Bush told his predominantly Christian audience: "America's Constitution forbids a religious test for office, and that's the way it should be. An American President serves people of every faith and serves some of no faith at all."[58]

Michael Coulter, professor of political science at Grove City College, calls Bush "a Catholic president" in the sense that he has been so open to, and warmly received by, Catholics. Catholic voters have supported Bush more than any modern Republican presidential candidate. He is with them on many issues, particularly life issues. His support of faith-based programs is in lock step with Catholic efforts and even Catholic doctrines like the principle of subsidiarity. The only notable disagreement between Bush and Rome was over the use of military force in Iraq. Even there, he had a solid majority of support from the Catholic laity in the United States.

Bush has immense respect for Pope John Paul II, whom he has called a "great world leader," a "rare man," and a "hero of history."[59] In a July 2001 news conference in Rome with the Italian prime minister, Bush spoke effusively of this "extraordinary man" and his "profound impact on the world." "I'm not poetic enough to describe what it's like to be in his presence," said the president of the pope.[60] In a speech in Warsaw, Bush told the Polish people that communism in their land had been "humbled" by two forces—a massive citizens' movement and "the iron purpose and moral vision of a single man: Pope John Paul II."[61] In June 2004, Bush presented the Pope with America's highest honor—the Presidential Medal of Freedom.

Bush values the pope's opinion, which may have been a factor in one aspect of the Iraq situation: on March 5, 2003, Bush met with a cardinal representing John Paul II, who said that the pope believed that invading Iraq without UN approval would be "illegal." The Bush administration disagreed, thinking it had an airtight legal case. Nonetheless, the next day, news organizations reported that the administration was trying to reach a compromise with UN Security Council members on a short deadline before force was used in Iraq. Of course, the United States had already been working this diplomatic angle. Did the pope's message make a difference? It was certainly not a hindrance.

Bush has also made warm overtures to the Jewish faith. In his first presidential radio address on Easter, he was careful to note that Easter weekend also marks the close of Passover, which he then briefly explained. He closed the radio address with an ecumenical message: "In the end, even death itself will be defeated. And that is the shared belief of many faiths, and that is the promise of Easter morning."[62] He had honored Easter (a Christian day) in a way that included other faiths.

Bush has marked Jewish religious days in other ways. In his first year in office, he observed eight separate Jewish events, including Passover, Rosh Hashanah, Yom Kippur, and Hanukkah.[63] By comparison, he observed only two Christian holidays—Easter and Christmas. (He observed two Muslim holy days that first year, and also marked the celebration of Kwanzaa, which he continues to note.) Approaching the end of his first year, for the first time in American history, Bush lit a Hanukkah menorah at the White House residence as a symbol that the White House is "the people's house" and that it belongs to people of all faiths.[64] Bush emphasizes, "It is very important for all of us to reject anti-Semitism wherever it is found."[65]

Bush has been so open to the Jewish faith that a bizarre axis of the extreme left and far right, in a rare union, have jointly charged that a Jewish-neoconservative conspiracy was surreptitiously pulling Bush into war against Iraq. This conspiracy was allegedly orchestrated internally by advisers Paul Wolfowitz, Richard Perle, and Douglas J. Feith, and externally by influential columnists Charles Krauthammer, William Kristol, and Martin Peretz. Such speculation was not surprising when it came from longtime arch-conservative Patrick J. Buchanan. What was unusual was to see it emanating from liberal journals like the *Washington Monthly*, *Salon*, and *The Nation*.[66] The belief on the left was so pronounced, particularly from liberal academics, that David Horowitz, the former 1960s Communist radical turned conservative, began hosting seminars in his magazine examining the "new anti-Semitic left."[67] What had once been the province of the John Birch Society had slithered its way into the ivory tower.

Bush has had a number of Jewish spokespersons and advisers, including Ari Fleischer as press secretary, John Bolton at the State Department, and Elliott Abrams at the NSC. Among them, some of these ethnic Jews are devoted to Judaism, Abrams among them.

Another Jew on Bush's team was speechwriter David Frum, who has offered a number of assessments of his former boss's faith. To Frum, the view that Bush's intense Christian faith somehow biases him against non-Christians is "both unjust and unintelligent." Speaking from personal experience, he insists that the most religious members of the Bush administration tended to be the most friendly to Jews as individuals and to Israel as a Jewish state. American Jews wary of Bush because of his faith are, by Frum's estimation, "making a catastrophic political error."[68]

Indeed, Bush and his administration have been anything but hostile to the nation of Israel. During one White House press conference with the president, Israeli prime minister Ariel Sharon shouted at the press corps that George W. Bush is the best friend Israel has ever had.[69]

In many of his public prayers during times of tragedy, Bush has pointedly chosen texts that are not explicitly Christian—often reaching for the Old Testament rather than the New. On the Saturday morning in February 2003 when Mission Control in Houston lost contact with the space shuttle Columbia, as the ship disintegrated as it reentered earth's atmosphere, Bush offered a short, poignant statement that concluded with words from the Old Testament:

> Yet farther than we can see there is comfort and hope. In the words of the prophet Isaiah, "Lift your eyes and look to the heavens. Who created all these? He who brings out the starry hosts one by one and calls them each by name. Because of his great power and mighty strength, not one of them is missing."
>
> The same Creator who names the stars also knows the names of the seven souls we mourn today. The crew of the shuttle Columbia did not return safely to Earth; yet we can pray that all are safely home.
>
> May God bless the grieving families, and may God continue to bless America.[70]

Bush's tribute was reminiscent of Ronald Reagan's words a decade and a half earlier when the space shuttle Challenger exploded. Those who died, said Reagan, had "slipped the surly bonds of earth to touch the face of God." This time, too, the Christian president craved to invoke God, and he reached for the Old Testament to find a prayer that would be meaningful to more than those who shared his personal faith.

Within the Christian community, too, Bush has branched out. His audiences are not confined to evangelicals. He was the keynote speaker at the first National Hispanic Prayer Breakfast in May 2002. Bush interchangeably spoke English and Spanish at the event, to the delight of his audience. He spoke of "faith in Dios" and preached the importance of knowing that America is a nation of many faiths. "We have never imposed any religion, and that's really important to remember," he said. "We welcome all religions in America, all religions. We honor diversity. . . . We respect people's deep convictions."[71]

He thrilled that "a *revolucion espiritual* is taking place amongst *los jovenes Hispanos aqui*"—that is, among Hispanic youth. "That's good," said Bush, to loud applause. "Really good news." He thanked his audience for leading the effort to bring God to Hispanic youth, which he called "an important contribution to our country." One Hispanic youth leader told Bush that this spiritual revival was impacting youth most of all "because they do not set limits on God. God is doing something so big with the youth of this nation." Bush loved that statement. "Those are mighty powerful words for a president to hear," he replied. He claimed that there was "nothing more powerful in helping change the country" than "faith in Dios."

Bush also displayed his tolerance of people with *no* spiritual beliefs. "We know that men and women can be good without faith," Bush told the prayer breakfast audience, in a line he uses often. "We know that." This is another of Bush's beliefs that has been disputed by some religionists, including Calvinists, who believe that man is inherently depraved, that only God is good, and that man cannot be good without God.

Nonetheless, Bush makes such statements constantly. At the National Prayer Breakfast, which carries a strong Christian evangelical flavor, Bush affirmed: "Every religion is welcomed in our country; all are practiced here. Many of our good citizens profess no religion at all. Our country has never had an official faith." In a gesture that may have surprised some secular liberals, he told that same group: "Respect for the dignity of others can be found outside of religion, just as intolerance is sometimes found within it."[72]

These statements contrast with the assertion by Barry Lynn, executive director of Americans United for Separation of Church and State, who claims that, "The tone set by Bush is, 'I am a Christian; I'm going to tell you about it on a regular basis.' It eventually gets very exclusionary."[73] Bush's own public record suggests that his Christian faith has rendered him anything but.

Should a Christian like Bush censor himself from speaking of his Lord only as "God," and purge the name *Jesus Christ* from his public lips? Christians might assert that such a practice is precisely what Bush's faith commands him *not* to do. A common complaint of Bush-supporting Christians is that if George W. Bush is expected to be tolerant of other faiths and how they are expressed, then others ought to be expected to be tolerant of his faith and how he expresses it.

Racism and Slavery

Bush contends that the greatest misconception about him is that he is not racially sensitive.[74] He says that his faith, and his own experience, have taught him tolerance of other races. At home, he was

taught that all people are equal and are children of a loving God, regardless of their skin color. Once, he remembers, as a young boy he
came home and repeated a racial slur he'd heard at school. His
mother responded by first washing his mouth with soap and then giving him a lecture.[75] As an adult, Bush invokes the commandment
"love thy neighbor as thyself" as a simple decree from God to accept
all races. He says that the notion of equality is not a "theory of
philosophers" but rather "the design of our Creator."[76]

One of Bush's most remarkable presidential statements on race
was his speech in Senegal, Africa, in July 2003.[77] As slavery persisted
in eighteenth- and nineteenth-century America, Bush lamented, his
fellow Christian Americans "became blind to the clearest commands
of their faith and added hypocrisy to injustice." This was particularly
hypocritical because, said Bush, the Christian faith clearly commands
that slavery is unjust. Mercifully, "the purposes of God" ultimately
ensured that the pernicious institution of slavery came to an end.

In America, said Bush, enslaved Africans related to the story of
the exodus from Egypt. In Christianity, they discovered a "suffering
Savior" whom they found to be "more like themselves than their
masters." The rights of African-Americans were not the gift of those
who had authority; rather, "those rights were granted by the Author
of Life." He quoted early black American author Phyllis Wheatley,
who, as a child, in 1761, was dragged from her West African home:
"In every human breast, God has implanted a principle which we call
love of freedom." While condemning white Christian Americans
who did nothing to stop slavery, Bush commended those who "clearly
saw this sin and called it by name," and did something. He stated:

> We can fairly judge the past by the standards of President John
> Adams, who called slavery "an evil of colossal magnitude." We can

discern eternal standards in the deeds of William Wilberforce and John Quincy Adams, and Harriet Beecher Stowe, and Abraham Lincoln. These men and women, black and white, burned with a zeal for freedom, and they left behind a different and better nation. Their moral vision caused Americans to examine our hearts, to correct our Constitution, and to teach our children the dignity and equality of every person of every race. By a plan known only to Providence, the stolen sons and daughters of Africa helped to awaken the conscience of America.

This speech was among the most forceful, scathing antislavery statements ever delivered by a president. The Texan closed his remarks by calling slavery "evil," and one of the "greatest crimes in history." Although they frequently object to Bush incorporating his faith into his public life, liberal secularists everywhere made no complaint about Bush's choice to integrate his religious views in this instance; nor did they question his certainty about God's intervention. They also did not protest his identification of this "sin," nor his perception of evil within the behavior of the slave holders.

RELIGIOUS FREEDOM WORLDWIDE

Bush's faith has influenced not only his domestic policy but also his foreign policy. His close friend Don Evans explained the connection to *Christianity Today*: "It's love your neighbor like yourself. The neighbors happen to be everyone on the planet." Jay Lefkowitz, deputy assistant to the president, said that Bush begins every discussion of a particular action in foreign policy by asking, "What is the right thing to do?" Lefkowitz translates that as meaning, "What is the morally correct thing to do?"[78]

The extent to which Bush's faith affects his foreign policy, of course, can be overstated. Some have called his foreign policy "faith-based." Others have suggested that faith is the driving force in his foreign policy.[79] The reality is that the Bush doctrine in international affairs was molded almost exclusively by September 11. The threat of terrorism and weapons of mass destruction—by rogue regimes and possibly by terrorists themselves—are the twin signposts that have guided his foreign policy. Nonetheless, his faith is a major factor.

A key way his faith influences his foreign policy is seen in his emphasis on the importance of freedom. Bush views freedom as God's gift to all people. "I have said many times," he reminded journalists in the Roosevelt Room, "that freedom . . . is the Almighty God's gift to each and every individual. I firmly believe that."[80] He believes in Jefferson's inalienable rights—life, liberty, and the pursuit of happiness—and the First Amendment freedoms, the first of which is freedom of religion. He believes that genuine freedom must include religious freedom, which he views as the most liberating liberty of all. Because all people everywhere, in his view, are children of God, they all deserve religious freedom.

Bush laid this out early in his presidency. On May 3, 2001, in a remarkable address to the American Jewish Committee, he noted that the Middle East is the birthplace of three great religions: Judaism, Christianity, and Islam. He then asserted that "lasting peace" in the region must respect all faiths—a matter of pure common sense, as he pointed out. Yet, along with common sense, he urged that a "*moral sense*" (his emphasis) be applied to the region—a moral sense based on "the deep American commitment to freedom of religion."[81] He then infused two personal concepts: his view of the importance of faith, and his faith-centered view of the importance of tolerance of all faiths. For that, he relied on a rarely cited quote from the nation's first president. In his letter to the Touro Synagogue in Newport, Rhode Island, George Washington decried bigotry toward other faiths. Bush said of Washington:

> He argued for an attitude beyond mere tolerance—a respect for the inherent and equal right of everyone to worship God as they think best. . . . Over the years, Washington's rejection of religious bigotry has matured from a foundation of our domestic politics into a guiding doctrine of our foreign policy.

That was quite a claim. Yes, American foreign policy has been guided by many principles since its inception. It seems a stretch, however, to suggest that rejection of religious bigotry has been a guiding doctrine of U.S. foreign policy. Of course, the United States certainly rejects religious bigotry, and some presidents have given voice to that concern—most prominently, Ronald Reagan in his 1988 trip to Moscow. Yet it is difficult to make a case that a rejection of religious bigotry has been a major, consistent force within U.S. foreign policy. And yet Bush was clearly signaling that a rejection of religious bigotry is a guiding doctrine of *his* foreign policy—a conclusion supported by other statements he would later make.

Thanking the American Jewish Committee for promoting religious tolerance and religious liberty worldwide, Bush hailed it as one of the first groups to support the International Religious Freedom Act of 1998.

He then relayed a progress report on religious liberty. He named nations that had improved—Morocco, Tunisia, Jordan, and Bahrain. But there were certain regimes, Bush said, whose disrespect for freedom of worship was seriously disturbing. At the top of his list—two years before the invasion—was Iraq, which, in his words, "murders dissident religious figures." He then singled out Iran, Burma, Cuba, China, and Afghanistan. Speaking four months before planes crashed into the Twin Towers, and seven months before he removed Afghanistan's Taliban government, Bush focused on the Taliban, which had "horrified the world with its disdain for fundamental human freedoms."

He concluded by declaring it no accident that freedom of religion is one of the central freedoms in the Bill of Rights. "It is the first freedom of the human soul," he asserted, "the right to speak the words that God places in our mouths. We must stand for that freedom in our country. We must speak for that freedom in the world."

Bush's sentiments on this day were not isolated. Two months later, on July 12, 2001, he formally issued Proclamation 7455, marking Captive Nations Week. The first two sentences in the proclamation read: "The twenty-first century must become the 'Century of Democracy.' Democracy and freedom have taken root across the globe, and the United States will continue to stand for greater consolidation of pluralism and religious freedom." Among a short list of five nations, he again criticized the regimes in Iraq and Afghanistan for their religious repression.[82]

Both of these statements—the July 2001 Captive Nations proclamation and the May 2001 speech to the American Jewish Committee—must be remembered in light of what would shortly happen in Afghanistan and, later, in Iraq.

7.
"Evildoers"

"This will be a monumental struggle of good
versus evil, but good will prevail."

—*President George Bush,*
September 12, 2001[1]

George W. Bush's first months in office featured a string of faith-
based actions. Incorporating his spiritual views into his policies, the new president urged religious freedom for the world's
dungeons of disbelief and promoted the work of America's faith-
based organizations. He spoke not only of integrating faith but of tol-
erating other faiths. And then, ironically, before the end of that first
year the Bush presidency was instantly transformed by an act of horrific religious intolerance—religious hatred—committed by a group
of religious extremists.

Monday, September 10, 2001, had been a normal presidential
day. The president's agenda continued to be chiefly domestic. His
weekly radio address had focused on education. In his meeting with

the Senate minority leader the previous week, the discussion was domestic: the capital-gains tax, federal spending, the Social Security surplus, immigration policy.

On Monday morning, he had received Australian prime minister John Howard. They met, issued joint statements, made two ceremonial stops, then staged a very brief 11:20 A.M. press conference at the West Colonnade of the White House. The exchange with reporters was again largely domestic. Later that afternoon, the president jetted to Florida for the night.

Despite the visit from Australia's head of state, there was still little talk of international issues. Foreign policy was not on the radar, certainly not Middle Eastern terrorism. There was little hint that a storm cloud was stirring, in the form of nineteen ready and willing fanatical suicide bombers.

Tired, the president turned in at 9:30 P.M. As was often the case, he read about history. As fate would have it, at that moment—on the eve of the nightmare that was September 11—he was contemplating another momentous turning point in American history.

He dug into Jay Winik's chronicle of Civil War history *April 1865: The Month That Saved America.* When he flipped open the book's jacket, a set of prophetic words jumped out at him: "April 1865 was a month that could have unraveled the nation. Instead, it saved it." The president didn't know it yet, but in just twenty-four hours, that line might be rewritten: "September 11, 2001, was a day that could have unraveled the nation. Instead, it saved it."[2]

On the night of September 10, however, President Bush was riveted by Winik's work of history, and what it said about President Abraham Lincoln and the crisis he confronted.[3] In the opening pages, Winik's almost eerie words leaped out at him: "Never before or since in the life of this nation has the country been so tested."[4] On that

September 10 evening, Bush could nod in agreement. The next time he opened Winik's book, however, the story had changed forever. "For historians," Winik wrote,

it is axiomatic that there are dates on which history turns, and that themselves become packed with meaning. . . . For Americans, one magic number is, of course, 1492, the year marking the discovery of America, or 1776, the American Declaration of Independence. But April 1865 is another such pivotal date.[5]

If the president had been in a scribbling frame of mind, he might have scratched a note next to those words on pages xiv and xv—"and now September 11 is such a date as well."

Like Lincoln, who occupied the White House in April 1865, in the face of the crisis of September 11, Bush pledged to proceed with God's help, to seek to do God's will, and to ask for strength and wisdom through prayer. As Lincoln approached that pivotal month, he called on God in his second inaugural address to help him "see the right." When he bowed his head to kiss the Bible, artillery salvos could be heard in the distance.[6] On September 11, when commercial airliners were turned into bombs, crashing into skyscrapers in New York, a five-sided building in Washington, and a farmer's field in western Pennsylvania—the last of which was reportedly en route to the former governor's new Washington home at 1600 Pennsylvania Avenue—Bush, like Lincoln years before, suddenly felt thrust into a line of fire.

The forty-third American president found comfort in the way Lincoln reacted to the turmoil. On May 1, 2003, Bush spoke to a pensive group of religious believers in the East Room of the White House. It was 7:47 A.M. They were there early to kick off the

National Day of Prayer—which, to Bush, was a holiday to be taken seriously. Engaging the crowd, Bush said that Lincoln "knew that his burdens were too great for any man, so he carried them to God in prayer."[7] The Civil War president said he had been driven many times to his knees by the conviction that he had nowhere else to go. Bush already prayed daily. Now, especially, after the grim events of September 11, he began each day on his knees, praying for forbearance and guidance.

ON SEPTEMBER 11, 2001, ISLAMIC FANATICS, FINANCED by the homicidal mastermind Osama bin Laden and his Al-Qaeda terrorist network, pulled off the most vicious attack ever perpetrated on American territory. Thousands of Americans were pulverized. Cable networks debated whether or not to air video of New Yorkers in business suits leaping hundreds of feet out of burning windows, bouncing off lampposts like rag dolls, crashing through car roofs, and splattering on the pavement. The instant analysis forecast as many as twenty-five thousand dead at the bottom of the Twin Towers rubble; the final figure, fortunately, would be far lower.[8]

The news of the strikes was whispered into President Bush's ear while he sat in a Sarasota, Florida, elementary school. He was there to stump for the No Child Left Behind Act, a comprehensive education bill under which federal funds would be denied to any local school district that obstructed the religious rights of students, including prayer.[9] Stunned by the news, the president made his way to the media room at the Emma Booker Elementary School.

It was 9:30 A.M., roughly twenty-five minutes after United Airlines Flight 175 crashed into the World Trade Center's south tower and forty-five minutes after American Airlines Flight 11 smashed into the north tower. The president began a terse statement: "Ladies and gentlemen, this is a difficult moment for America." He asked the public-school crowd to join him in a moment of silence. He closed, "May God bless the victims, their families, and America."[10] He was then whisked away. He later told Bob Woodward: "They had declared war on us, and I made up my mind at that moment that we were going to war."[11] For the first time since a 1973 standoff with the Soviets (during the Yom Kippur War), the U.S. military went to DefCon 3 alert status.[12]

Eleven hours later, after a frightening day spent jetting among undisclosed spots in the sky aboard Air Force One, Bush spoke to the nation from the Oval Office. CNN's Jeff Greenfield called it "probably as difficult a speech as any president has ever made." MSNBC's Brian Williams agreed, saying that Bush faced the greatest domestic crisis of any chief executive since FDR.[13] The president's location suggested that the nation's top house was safe, and that perhaps some normalcy might be salvageable. Unbeknownst to the public, however, Bush himself had suddenly become more fatalistic: when he returned to the White House, it was out of a firm conviction that God was in control of his life.[14] "Today our nation saw evil, the very worst of human nature," said the president. He asked his fellow Americans to pray to "a power greater than any of us," who had "spoken through the ages" in Psalm 23: "Even though I walk through the valley of the shadow of death, I fear no evil, for You are with me."[15]

Americans had walked through a valley of evil that day. Bush spent the rest of his presidency telling them not to fear evil, but to take the offensive against it.

The weapons of choice for the terrorists were American airplanes, built by Americans with American money, and filled with American passengers. While the World Trade Center buildings and the Pentagon were still smoldering, there were news reports that

Flight 93, which had nose-dived into a western Pennsylvania field, was headed to Washington.[16] One can imagine the horror of the freshman president ordering U.S. fighter pilots to be ready to shoot it down, along with all its forty-four helpless civilians, if left no other option. It was a decision that reportedly made Bush the first president since Lincoln to instruct the military to fire on fellow Americans.[17]

Those watching on the cable networks, blow by blow, could contemplate how lucky their generation had been—a half century with no world wars, no sudden foreign attacks. That generation now had its Pearl Harbor. In terms of deliberate murder of innocents, it was the single worst such tragedy in American history.

The attack was also like Pearl Harbor in that it was a wake-up call. How often had terrorism come up in the presidential debates? September 11 awoke Americans to the threat abroad. It was fitting that the attack took place in the year 2001, for it signaled the threat of the twenty-first century: malicious, ruthless but elusive and unpredictable. In the twentieth century—the "American century," as Henry Luce called it—the United States had preserved its homeland from attack by the most formidable military powers in history. Neither Nazis nor Soviets could touch U.S. soil. Yet the damage on September 11 was caused not by a great power, but by a small band of terrorists.

The attack was, especially, a wake-up call to George W. Bush. He resolved never to forget the tragedy; as he said countless times thereafter, "everything changed" on that day. Like Pearl Harbor, September 11 meant American entry into a much larger war. It instantly galvanized American resolve. Japan's Admiral Yamamoto, after the attack on the Hawaiian base, had observed: "I fear that all we have done is awakened a sleeping giant and filled him with a dangerous wrath." September 11 filled Americans with a very similar wrath.

A New Yorker staring at the rubble the next day told television cameras: "I'm a bleeding-heart liberal, but right now I just wanted to bomb the hell out of something and ask questions later." Veteran *Time* reporter Lance Morrow fulminated about "retribution": "Healing is inappropriate now, and dangerous. There will be time later for the tears of sorrow. . . . Let's have rage. What's needed is a unified, unifying, Pearl Harbor sort of purple American fury—a ruthless indignation that doesn't leak away in a week or two."[18]

In the original translation, Japan's Yamamoto was said to have used the words *dangerous resolve* rather than *dangerous wrath*. Bush later said simply, "The evil ones awakened a mighty giant."[19] From the outset, the president spoke of resolve. "This is a day when all Americans from every walk of life unite in our resolve for justice and peace," he told the nation from the White House on September 11. "America has stood down enemies before, and we will do so this time. None of us will ever forget this day."[20]

The next day, September 12, started a sharp escalation in rhetoric—the kind of fighting words Americans have seldom heard from their own leaders. After a meeting with his national security team, Bush called the events of the previous day "more than acts of terror. They were acts of war." He would never back off. America was now engaged in a "war on terror." At 10:53 A.M., he spoke from the Cabinet Room:

> The American people need to know we're facing a different enemy than we have ever faced. This enemy hides in shadows and has no regard for human life. This is an enemy who preys on innocent and unsuspecting people. . . . But it won't be able to run for cover forever. This is an enemy that tries to hide, but it won't be able to hide forever. . . . [It] won't be safe forever.

This battle will take time and resolve. But make no mistake
about it: We will win. . . . This will be a monumental struggle of
good versus evil, but good will prevail.[21]

For Bush a line was drawn in the sand. The Texan was vigilant,
and ready to fight.

On September 14, he flew to New York to meet with grieving
families and with those who had stepped up to dig through the immense pile of concrete, steel, ash, and flesh at Ground Zero. A firefighter shook Bush's hand and graciously asked how he and the first
family were doing. "Freaked out, the girls are," said Bush. "My wife's
okay. She understands we're at war and she's got a war mentality. So
do I. Thanks for asking."[22]

He toured the site of the impact. At 4:40 P.M., at the corner of
Murray and West streets, he paused to say a few words. He stood atop
the rubble, wrapped his left arm around a hard-hatted firefighter,
grabbed a bullhorn, and began shouting. A rescue worker heckled
good-naturedly, "Can't hear you." Bush yelled back, to laughter, "I
can't go any louder." The wise-guy New Yorker pushed again, "I can't
hear you." To thunderous applause, Bush replied: "I can hear you. I
can hear you. The rest of the world hears you. And the people who
knocked down these buildings will hear all of us soon." The rescue
workers responded by chanting, "U.S.A.! U.S.A.! U.S.A.!"[23]

It was a powerful, patriotic, and spontaneous moment. Those on
the scene loved it, as did those watching on television across the country. Bush's staff later called it the defining moment of his presidency.

America had been hit with a "mighty sucker-punch," in the
words of a popular country singer, but Bush's statement helped pick
up the nation from its knees. That day, an ABC News poll registered

Bush with an 86 percent approval rating. A week later, a *Newsweek* poll found that 89 percent of the public approved of his handling of the crisis, and a *Newsweek* article comparing him to FDR said Bush had found his "true voice."[24] He would retain that level of popular approval until he pushed for war in Iraq fifteen months later.

Meanwhile, an unprecedented outpouring of international sympathy flooded into the United States, even from rogue regimes and dictators. Libya's Moammar Kaddafi sent his condolences; so did Cuba's Fidel Castro. Terrorist nations, and even some terrorist groups, expressed sorrow. There was only one exception: Saddam Hussein. The butcher of Baghdad stood conspicuously alone in not condemning the attack.[25]

EVIL, FAITH, AND SEPTEMBER 11

In Bush's eyes, the sheer iniquity of September 11 showed that in the new war on terror Americans should never be tempted by notions of moral equivalency. During the Cold War, advocates of moral relativism had held that the United States and the Soviet Union were equally culpable, that neither country could claim the moral high ground. In the war against terror, Bush wanted no such talk. He "wanted to cut that off right away," as speech writer David Frum recalled.[26] Bush dubbed the deed an "act of evil" by "evildoers," and in so doing ingrained those words in the public lexicon.

The events of that day had, in Bush's description, driven him to "bended knee." He maintained that the prayers that had rung out across the nation since that day were a part of "the good that has come from the evil of September 11." He often said that something good would come from the wreckage of those attacks, given his belief that God works all things for eventual good.[27] He also leaned on the words of German theologian Dietrich Bonhoeffer, who during the darkest days of Nazi rule had said, "I believe that God can and wants to create good out of everything, even evil."[28] George W. Bush turned to prayer for, in his words, "wisdom and resolve, for compassion and courage, and for grace and mercy."[29]

He had trouble talking about the tragedy without mentioning prayer. In describing what happened on Flight 93, he more than once noted that the passengers prayed. "They told their loved ones goodbye," said Bush of their final phone conversations. "They said a prayer—history will show they said a prayer. A guy said, 'Let's roll.' They took the plane to the ground."[30]

The religious community noticed his spiritual acuity during the crisis. "President Bush, from the day of the attacks on the World Trade Center, has led the nation with a deft spiritual presence that radiates solidarity with people of all faiths," began a cover feature in *Christianity Today*. "After the September 11 attack, Bush displayed great skill at expressing his spiritual and moral convictions." H. B. London of Focus on the Family asserted, "I think we're better able to face the tragedy and attack . . . because we see a president who's calm because of his dependence on God."[31] Brian Berry, who has known the Texan for over ten years, sensed that September 11 was an "almost supercharging moment for him. He has always said that he felt a purpose, but now it seemed to me like he really felt it." He sensed "a different look" about Bush, "almost an aura."[32] Presidential aide Tim Goeglein called the events "absolutely a spiritually defining moment" for Bush.[33]

Aides and observers spoke of Bush's post-9/11 sense of purpose. He seemed to carry a confidence, a feeling of destiny, a call, and a corresponding contentedness, that he had been placed in office at that grave moment in history.

On September 14, the president organized a service at the majestic National Cathedral to memorialize the dead. He picked the music, selected speakers, and carefully chose his words. The roster of speakers was an exercise in multiculturalism. The first six speakers included a woman bishop, two black ministers, a rabbi, a Catholic bishop, and a Muslim imam. This inclusiveness was deliberate—particularly the inclusion of Imam Muzammil Siddiqi of the Islamic Center of North America. For American Muslims, Bush did not want a repeat of the way Japanese Americans were treated after Pearl Harbor.[34]

The seventh and final religious figure to speak, before Bush rose, was Billy Graham. At eighty-two years of age, Graham was frail. In deference to Graham's condition, church organizers had directed all speakers, including the president, to use the lower stone pulpit, which was less ornate but closer to the audience than the magnificent upper pulpit.[35]

Bush had declared the day a National Day of Prayer and Remembrance. In preparing for his speech, he prayed that he could rise to the occasion and deliver his talk meaningfully in keeping with the somberness of the occasion. "I prayed a lot before the speech," he told reporter Bill Sammon, "because I felt like it was a moment where I needed, well, frankly, for the good Lord to shine through."[36]

Everyone in elite Washington was there: Former presidents Jimmy Carter and Gerald Ford sat in the third pew, as did Al Gore. The Clinton family sat in the front pew. Throughout the service, Bill Clinton wore his heart on his sleeve. Breaking protocol, he jumped up and led a standing ovation when Graham finished. Bush approached the platform at 1:00 P.M. He began:

We are here in the middle hour of our grief. So many have suffered so great a loss, and today we express our Nation's sorrow. We come before God to pray for the missing and the dead and for those who love them.

On Tuesday our country was attacked with deliberate and massive cruelty. We have seen the images of fire and ashes and bent steel. Now come the names, the list of casualties we are only beginning to read. . . .

Just three days removed from these events, Americans do not yet have the distance of history. But our responsibility to history is already clear: To answer these attacks and rid the world of evil.

War has been waged against us by stealth and deceit and murder. This Nation is peaceful, but fierce when stirred to anger. This conflict was begun on the timing and terms of others. It will end in a way, and at an hour, of our choosing.[37]

While he spoke, Bush looked for a figure to focus on. Every face was weeping. He did not make the mistake of looking at his parents up front. "If I looked down at my mother and dad," he said, "and they'd be weeping, then I'd weep."[38] He plowed on:

Our purpose as a nation is firm. Yet our wounds as a people are recent and unhealed and lead us to pray. In many of our prayers this week, there is a searching and an honesty. At St. Patrick's Cathedral in New York on Tuesday, a woman said, "I prayed to God to give us a sign that He is still here." . . .

God's signs are not always the ones we look for. We learn in tragedy that His purposes are not always our own. Yet the prayers of private suffering, whether in our homes or in this great cathedral, are known and heard and understood.

There are prayers that help us last through the day or endure the night. There are prayers of friends and strangers that give us strength for the journey. And there are prayers that yield our will to a will greater than our own.

This world He created is of moral design. Grief and tragedy and hatred are only for a time. Goodness, remembrance, and love have no end. And the Lord of life holds all who die and all who mourn. . . .

On this national day of prayer and remembrance, we ask almighty God to watch over our Nation and grant us patience and resolve in all that is to come. We pray that He will comfort and console those who now walk in sorrow. We thank Him for each life we now must mourn and the promise of a life to come.

As we have been assured, neither death nor life, nor angels nor principalities nor powers, nor things present nor things to come, nor height nor depth, can separate us from God's love. May He bless the souls of the departed. May He comfort our own, and may He always guide our country. God bless America.

With that, Bush closed his leather folder and walked away from the podium. Clinton, according to Bill Sammon, sat gnawing on his lower lip, his wet eyes pinned on Bush. When the president sat down, Bush's father reached across Laura and patted the president on the arm. At risk of losing his composure, the son dared not look back.[39]

Bush later said he viewed the speech not as an opportunity to rally the nation to war, but rather as a means of religious expression to help his country mourn. "I really looked at it from a spiritual perspective," he told Bob Woodward, "that it was important for the nation to pray. To me, the moment was more, it really was a prayer."[40]

The service concluded with an inspired rendition of "The Battle Hymn of the Republic," chosen by Bush. The congregation stood and belted out the war anthem in a loud and determined voice. "Glory! Glory! Hallelujah! His truth is marching on!" Tears streamed from the visages of grown men, all evidently prepared to loose the fateful lighting of a terrible, swift sword. As Woodward reported, when the presidential party left the cathedral, the rain and grayness of the morning had lifted, and now sunshine beamed through the blue skies above.[41]

An even larger public performance lay ahead for Bush a week later, on September 20, when the president addressed a Joint Session of Congress. In preparation a couple of hours earlier, he had met with a group of twenty-seven religious leaders from around the country, whom he summoned at the last minute. Prominent evangelicals like Franklin Graham, T. D. Jakes, and Max Lucado were flown in. To Bush, it was a bouquet of faiths: Hindu, Sikh, Buddhist, Mormon. New York's Edward Cardinal Egan was there. In the gathering, Bush connected his own suffering a decade-plus earlier with that of his fellow Americans now. "I was a sinner in need of redemption and found it," he told those assembled. Now, he said, the staggering nation—which, unlike him years earlier, had been sinned against—needed to be helped back on its feet.[42]

One of those who attended was Gerald Kieschnick, president of the Lutheran Church–Missouri Synod. He told Bush that he had just returned from the same spot where the president stood in Manhattan six days earlier, that he had seen what Bush saw and smelled what he smelled. "You not only have a civil calling, but a divine calling," Kieschnick instructed the president. "You are not just a civil servant; you are a servant of God called for such a time like this."[43]

A few minutes later, Bush addressed the world from the House Chamber of the embattled Capitol, as American fighter jets patrolled the surrounding skies. In a sign of the times, Vice President Dick

Cheney was absent, secured away at an undisclosed location. So intense was the interest in the speech that fans at the New York Rangers–Philadelphia Flyers hockey game demanded that authorities stop the game at 9:00 P.M. to show the speech on the giant-screen Jumbotron, a request that was granted.[44]

That night, George W. Bush spoke slowly, smoothly, and deliberately, with a measured resolve, a solemnity that bespoke controlled anger. He concluded this most-watched speech of his lifetime with these words: "Freedom and fear, justice and cruelty have always been at war, and we know that God is not neutral between them. Fellow citizens, we'll meet violence with patient justice, assured of the rightness of our cause and confident of the victories to come." They were words that spoke more for himself than for the millions of Americans and others around the world he hoped to lead in the two tumultuous years ahead. Likewise, the final words that followed were more a personal prayer: "In all that lies before us, may God grant us wisdom, and may He watch over the United States of America. Thank you."[45]

As he left, he literally reached out to Democrats. He shook the hand of the man seated behind him in Cheney's vacated spot, Senator Robert Byrd (D-WV), and then hugged Senator Tom Daschle (D-SD). He firmly grabbed the shoulder of Representative Dick Gephardt (D-MO) and gently patted the face of Representative Charles Schumer (D-NY).

In his message and tone, Bush showed his ability to rise to the occasion. The consensus was that it was difficult to imagine any president delivering a better speech at that moment; indeed, Bush seemed born for the address. *Washington Post* media analyst Howard Kurtz reported: "No pundit on the major networks uttered a negative comment. They were, in a word, wowed." NBC's Tom Brokaw called it "an eloquent speech." CBS's Bob Schieffer called it "especially powerful." MSNBC's Howard Fineman marveled: "At every step of the way, he rises to the occasion. . . . My breath was taken away."[46] *Washington Post* columnist David Broder, in an op-ed titled "Echoes of Lincoln," said that this "most unrhetorical of politicians" had achieved "what words alone can do," and that overnight polls showed the American people rallying "almost unanimously to his call for action."[47] Broder's colleague at the *Post* Jim Hoagland said Bush had "lifted the moment toward greatness."[48] Another veteran presidential watcher, *Time's* Hugh Sidey, said that America saw the "steel" in Bush's performance. "He was tough tonight," said Sidey. "That was West Texas."[49] Commentator David Gergen called the speech "extremely tough" but "eloquent"—"poetry in power."[50] The liberal commentator Gerald Posner, who said that ten months earlier he had personally done everything humanly possible to help the recount movement in Florida—so fearful was he of a Bush presidency—wrote an op-ed article titled "I Was Wrong About Bush," in which he lamented: "I must sadly admit that Bill Clinton, for whom I voted twice, could not have delivered that same clear speech."[51]

Democrats registered not a single complaint. Senator Joe Lieberman (D-CN) stated: "The president really rose to the occasion." His colleague Senator Dianne Feinstein (D-CA) called the speech "a ten"; Bush, she said, "inspired Americans, he brought us all together."[52] Senator Robert Torricelli (D-NJ) called it "George Bush's finest hour."[53] Senator Ted Kennedy (D-MA), who two years later would excoriate Bush's Iraq policy, said: "The president's speech was exactly what the nation needed: a message of determination and hope, of strength and compassion."[54] Senator Evan Bayh (D-IN) said that on his side of the aisle he heard "nothing but praise" for Bush: "For anyone who doubted if he had the gravitas, they can't doubt it any longer."[55]

Republicans were thrilled with their president's performance. Congressman Tom Delay (R-TX) cited Scripture in asserting that Bush seemed born for the moment.[56] Embattled New York mayor Rudolph Giuliani, not exactly a religious-right Republican, summarized the moment: "I thank God that George W. Bush is our president."[57]

TOLERANCE OF ISLAM

To the general public and the world, the aftermath of September 11 revealed something especially significant about Bush's faith-based thinking: his longtime tolerance of other religious faiths. That was never on greater display than when it came to his words about Islam. Despite the perception of many Americans, who perceived Islam as inherently hostile, Bush has consistently preached that Islam is a "religion of peace"—and that Muslim terrorists subscribe to a "faith of hate" completely disconnected from "real" Islam.[58]

At the time, this sentiment was not merely rejected but ridiculed by many of Bush's own supporters. Some conservative radio talk-show hosts began snidely referring to the "religion of peace" when they gave updates on the latest Muslim suicide bombing. Conservative columnists wrote op-ed pieces assailing Bush's insistence that Islam is inherently peaceful.[59] Billy Graham's son Franklin described Islam as "a very evil and wicked religion."[60] Agreeing in full, a number of conservative Christians rushed to Graham's defense.[61] Another voice, Jerry Vines, former president of the Southern Baptist Convention, reportedly labeled Islam's founder, Muhammad, a "demon-possessed pedophile."[62]

Particularly critical was Pat Robertson, who referred to Muhammad as "an absolutely wild-eyed fanatic" and "a robber and a brigand." To reach this conclusion, said Robertson, "all you have to do is read the writings of [Muhammad] in the Koran. He urges people to attack the infidels. He urges his followers to kill Christians and Jews. He talks about eradicating all of the Jews." "You read the Koran," Robertson continued, "it says wage war against your enemies. Kill them if you possibly can. And destroy anybody who doesn't agree with you. I mean, it's all laid out in the Koran."[63]

Robertson claimed that Muslim terrorists were not at all distorting Islam—rather, "they're carrying out Islam." He said that peaceful Muslims who argue to the contrary "don't really understand what their religion believes," just as, he said, there are many Catholics and Protestants who do not understand their own religion. The Taliban in Afghanistan, said Robertson, was simply carrying out fundamental Muslim teaching. Such violent behavior, he stated, was completely contrary to the teachings of Jesus Christ, who, talked of peace and loving one's enemies.

Robertson's views were not isolated. He spoke for not just many Christians or many conservatives but for many people generally, regardless of faith. He did not, however, speak for George W. Bush, who has repeatedly said precisely the opposite. It's fair to ask whether Bush has spoken so warmly of Islam for political reasons—to heal divisions after September 11—or because he truly believes Islam is a religion of peace. Judging from the extensive volume of remarks he has repeatedly offered on the subject, the latter seems more likely.

Beyond mere words, Bush has hosted Ramadan dinners. He visited a mosque. He calls the Koran a "holy" work that "teaches the value and the importance of charity, mercy, and peace."[64] He regularly meets with Muslim leaders. And he has sought to work with Muslim heads of state in rather extraordinary ways.

One example involved the new prime minister of Turkey, Recep Tayyip Erdogan. At the age of forty-nine, Erdogan walked into an extremely difficult job. He was facing a divided country and legislature over Turkey's position on the looming war in Iraq. Erdogan is a committed Muslim: "Before anything else, I'm a Muslim. I try to comply with the requirements of my religion." It was a conviction to which his U.S. counterpart could relate. In December 2002, when Bush met with Erdogan in the White House, what Bush said raised eyebrows: "You believe in the Almighty, and I believe in the Almighty," he reportedly told Erdogan. "That's why we'll be great partners."[65]

To Bush, in other words, what mattered most was the two leaders' shared belief in God. Some Christian theologians, of course, might have countered that Christians and Muslims do not believe in the same God, because of the Christian belief in the Trinity and the divinity of Christ, which Muslims reject. That did not matter to Bush: As committed believers, the American Christian and Turkish Muslim were kindred spirits.

Bush has been given due credit for working with and reaching out to Muslims. "Bush has gone to great lengths to reassure them [Muslims] that he admires their religion," reported Howard Fineman.[66] The *New York Times*'s Nicholas D. Kristof and Bill Keller admired Bush's efforts to distance himself from the unflattering assessments of Islam by Graham and Robertson. Kristof went further: "Mr. Bush displayed real moral leadership after 9/11 when he praised Islam as a 'religion of peace' and made it clear that his administration would not demonize it."[67] The *Washington Post*'s Jim Hoagland said Bush had ensured no "McCarthyite persecution" of Arab Americans.[68]

There is something quite interesting at work here. Many secular liberals treat tolerance and diversity in an almost sacred manner; they afford a reverence to tolerance. Many conservative Christians do not hold tolerance as reverentially. Yet a reverence for both the religion of Jesus Christ and tolerance generally seems to come naturally to

George W. Bush. His Christian faith, it seems, has led him to embrace the practice of Islam as a part of the American mosaic.

Just six days after September 11, Bush averred: "The face of terror is not the true faith of Islam. That's not what Islam is all about. Islam is peace. These terrorists don't represent peace. They represent evil and war."[69] Eight days after the dread event, Bush, while meeting with congressional leaders, told a group of reporters: "We don't view this as a war of religion, in any way, shape or form." He continued: "As a matter of fact, Islam preaches peace. The Muslim faith is a peaceful faith." And he promised: "for those who try to pit religion against religion, our great Nation will stand up and reject that kind of thought. We won't allow that to creep into the consciousness of the world." He took it upon himself to assure that "Muslim and Jew and Christian" would stand side by side.[70]

In the speech to a Joint Session of Congress the next day, Bush picked up that theme, asserting that throughout America prayers were being recited in "English, Hebrew, and Arabic." Charging that "the terrorists are traitors to their own faith, trying, in effect, to hijack Islam itself," he said that they practice "a fringe form of Islamic extremism . . . that perverts the peaceful teachings of Islam," and follow a "directive [that] commands them to kill Christians and Jews." Presumably, according to Bush, the Koran itself contains no such directive. He maintained that the "teachings" of Islam "are good and peaceful, and those who commit evil in the name of Allah blaspheme the name of Allah." These words were directed to Congress, America, and the world.[71]

A few weeks later, on November 19, the Christian president of the United States celebrated the Muslim holy month of Ramadan by hosting an Iftaar dinner at the State Dining Room in the White

House. "The terrorists have no home in any faith," he told his Muslim guests. "Evil has no holy days." He closed by wishing all a "blessed Ramadan."[72] A week and a half later, Deputy Secretary of Defense Paul Wolfowitz and Secretary of State Colin Powell also gave speeches at Iftaar dinners.[73]

On October 4, Bush talked to employees at the State Department, assuring them: "This is not a war between Christianity or Judaism and Islam."[74] Continuing with his message, in April 2002 he affirmed: "America rejects bigotry. We reject every act of hatred against people of Arab background or Muslim faith. America values and welcomes peaceful people of all faiths—Christian, Jewish, Muslim, Sikh, Hindu and many others. Every faith is practiced and protected here."[75]

Two months later, he commended Muslim countries for their "commitments to morality, and learning, and tolerance." He claimed that "those values are alive in the Islamic world today."[76] Such a statement about tolerance in Muslim countries was an extraordinary thing to hear from a Christian: indeed, it is widely accepted that nowhere in the world are Christians so routinely and mercilessly persecuted for their faith as they are in the Muslim nations of the Middle East.

As the first anniversary of September 11 approached, Bush sought to head off any anti-Muslim sentiment. On September 10, 2002, he held a roundtable discussion with Muslim American leaders at the Afghanistan embassy in Washington, where he told them: "All Americans must recognize that the face of terror is not the . . . face of Islam. Islam is a faith that brings comfort to a billion people around the world. It's a faith that has made brothers and sisters of every race. It's a faith based upon love, not hate."[77] A month later he spoke of

Islam as "a vibrant faith," and insisted that Muslim suicide bombers do not "follow the great traditions of Islam. They've hijacked a great religion."[78] Shortly thereafter, he hosted his second Iftaar dinner at the White House, where he said candidly that the dinner was intended to send a message: "Our nation is waging a war on a radical network of terrorists, not on a religion and not on a civilization."[79]

He then took this homily to world leaders. During a meeting with UN Secretary General Kofi Annan on November 13, 2002, Bush told reporters: "Some of the comments that have been uttered about Islam do not reflect the sentiments of my government or the sentiments of most Americans." He didn't stop there. "Islam," he declared, "as practiced by the vast majority of people, is a peaceful religion, a religion that respects others. Ours is a country based upon tolerance and we welcome people of all faiths in America."[80] The next week, during a press conference with Vaclav Havel in the Czech Republic, he reiterated: "Ours is a war not against a religion, not against the Muslim faith. But ours is a war against individuals who absolutely hate what America stands for."[81]

In his most sweeping gesture of all, in December 2002 Bush made an extraordinary overture to the Muslim community. He visited the Islamic Center in Washington, D.C., where he celebrated Eid al-Fitr—festivities that mark the culmination of Ramadan. The Islamic Center is the oldest mosque in the nation's capital, with a congregation representing Muslims from seventy-five countries. This was the first time an American president had ever visited a mosque to mark the end of Ramadan. Before he entered the mosque, the Texan removed his shoes as a sign of respect. Inside, he met Muslim schoolchildren who told him stories, recited poems about their special day, and showed him artwork.[82]

When it came time for Bush to approach the podium to deliver his

Eid al-Fitr message, the center's director, Dr. Abdullah Muhammad Khouja, told the president "Your visit today is greatly appreciated." Bush then took a moment to explain Ramadan to non-Muslims before openly hailing American Muslims for their "many contributions" in business, science and law, medicine and education, and other fields. He saluted Muslim members of the U.S. armed forces and his own administration, who "are serving their fellow Americans with distinction, upholding our nation's ideals of liberty and justice in a world at peace."[83] Speaking of Ramadan specifically, he added the following:

Over the past month, Muslims have fasted, taking no food or water during daylight hours, in order to refocus their minds on faith and redirect their hearts to charity. Muslims worldwide have stretched out a hand of mercy to those in need. Charity tables at which the poor can break their fast line the streets of cities and towns. And gifts of food and clothing and money are distributed to ensure that all share in God's abundance. Muslims often invite members of other families to their evening iftar meals, demonstrating a spirit of tolerance.

America treasures the relationship we have with our many Muslim friends, and we respect the vibrant faith of Islam which inspires countless individuals to lead lives of honesty, integrity, and morality. . . . Islam brings hope and comfort to millions of people in my country, and to more than a billion people worldwide. Ramadan is also an occasion to remember that Islam gave birth to a rich civilization of learning that has benefited mankind.[84]

The president stood with six local imams under a large bronze chandelier donated by the Egyptian government. The mosque was

a testimony to its Middle East heritage. Its high ceilings were deco-
rated with colorful painted verses from the Koran, drawn by Egyptian
artists. The carpets came from Iran. The tiles were donated by
Turkey.[85]

Bush later told reporters that the one thing he did after September 11 that was "most important" was visit the Islamic Center. He did
so to "send a signal" that the "evil people who hijacked a great religion" should not be used to condemn that religion. "Americans
shouldn't hold Islam accountable for the deaths."[86]

George W. Bush's countless presidential statements in support of
Islam demonstrate this devoutly Christian president's exception tolerance toward other faiths.[87] Indeed, it is difficult to find an American *Muslim* leader who has spoken so glowingly of Islam, and it is
impossible to identify another such president or politician in all of
U.S. history. Indeed, when a defensive Bush said at the White House
in June 2002 that an American president "should never promote a
particular religion," he was clearly referring only to his own Christian
faith, since his cheerleading for Islam was so ebullient that it arguably
bordered on promotion.[88] It was charged after September 11 that
mainstream Muslims had not done enough to purge the radicals from
their faith and to show the world that Islam was in fact a religion of
peace hijacked by extremists. George W. Bush, it could be argued, did
the job for them.

Christians who support Bush, when interviewed about the president's effusive statements on Islam—particularly the claim that Muslim extremists are practicing a perverted form of a peaceful
religion—simply smiled, shrugged, and dismissed the question: "Well,
he *has* to say that." As president of a diverse country, their logic goes,
Bush has made such statements for purposes of harmony, not because

he believes them. Yet, the president's glowing statements on Islam are so voluminous that it seems quite plausible that he is sincere.

Bush's kindness toward Islam and trumpeting of its peaceful nature may have gone a long way toward preventing a backlash of violence against Muslim Americans after September 11. Attacks took place, but they were surprisingly scarce. The Bush government did not respond in any way similar to the administration of Franklin Delano Roosevelt's mistreatment of Japanese Americans after Pearl Harbor. This was the polar opposite of Japanese internment—a profoundly important historical fact.

And yet what is perhaps most remarkable (and unrecognized) about George W. Bush is that his inclusive attitude toward Islam *predates* September 11. Indeed, Bush was the first president ever to mention mosques in his inaugural address. "I was floored by that," says professor of religion Paul C. Kemeny, an expert on civil religion. "The fact that he included 'mosque' before 9/11 is profound."[89]

Prior to September 11, the *Presidential Documents* archive lists six Bush references to mosques, five to Islam, and three to Muslims. Those fourteen references came in the eight months between Inaugural Day and September 11. Nearly every mention of mosques he made came alongside references to churches and synagogues and the positive role all three can play in American life. One such statement came during Bush's April 2001 proclamation for National Volunteer Week: "Church and charity, synagogue, and mosque form an essential part of our communities and their indispensable work must have an honored place in our plans and in our laws."[90]

While that statement was typical, it was not the only way Bush referred to Islam before September 11. He had even commemorated a Muslim holy day: on March 6, 2001, the Texas Christian extended "warm greetings" to those marking Eid al-Adha, when American Muslims "joined in spirit" their millions of brothers and sisters gathering in Mecca for the annual hajj, which Bush explained was the fifth pillar of Islam. "By educating others about your religious traditions," said the president to American Muslims, "you enrich the lives of others in your local communities."[91]

Bush spoke this way not just before the collapse of the Twin Towers, but prior to his presidency. In his Republican convention address in August 2000, he mentioned mosques and their role not just as places of worship but as places where Muslims came "to serve."[92] In a March 1999 speech to a Baptist church in Houston, the Methodist governor heralded the work of "churches and synagogues and mosques." "We must teach our children bedrock values," said Bush, "not the values of one denomination over another. . . . We're all God's children, and faith supplies what we need to treat each other in a decent and civilized way."[93]

GEORGE W. BUSH HAS FACED THE TYPICAL CRITICISM of modern Christians (usually uttered by non-Christians): that his faith makes him intolerant. That charge has been raised throughout the war on terror. And therein is a supreme irony: Bush's main targets in the war on terror would be Osama bin Laden, the Taliban, and Saddam Hussein—few were ever as intolerant. The true exclusivist, the real religious imperialist, was bin Laden, who began the battle by unleashing a "holy war" against Christians, Jews, and infidels. He and his minions targeted anyone who was not a Muslim, who was not a member of *their* faith.

Though careful to avoid such statements, Bush seemed to believe that reacting with force to September 11 was justified in God's eyes. "We believe," he affirmed, "as Franklin Roosevelt said, that

men and women born to freedom in the image of God will not forever suffer the oppressor's sword."[94] Bush believes that God wants all
humans to be free. There is, he assured, no godly reason why a free
people should be passively subjected to the sword of those of the terrorist stripe.

8.

Targeting Evil

"States like these and their terrorist allies constitute an axis of evil."

—*President George W. Bush,*
State of the Union address, January 2002[1]

"I think it will take years before we can repair the
damage done by that statement."

—*Former President Jimmy Carter on Bush's*
"axis of evil" remark[2]

President George W. Bush wanted Osama bin Laden's head, even
if on a platter. Speaking with a group of reporters, the Texan
evoked images of the Old West: "I want justice. There's an old poster
out West that I recall. It said: 'Wanted: Dead or Alive.'"[3]

Bush sought justice in Afghanistan, the nation that harbored
Osama and had sponsored the Al-Qaeda killers of September 11.
Brazenly and stupidly, Afghanistan's Taliban leadership not only

refused to hand over bin Laden, but refused to cooperate at all, despite repeated requests and dire warnings from a mighty, angry America. The Taliban needed to "cough up" bin Laden and his minions, said Bush: "In order to avoid punishment, they should turn over the parasites that hide in their country."[4] He demanded they do so unconditionally. The Taliban responded by offering to negotiate terms of release. Bush adamantly rejected the offer: "Turn him over. There is no negotiation. Period."[5]

If the Taliban did not turn over bin Laden, the president warned, it would face the "full wrath" of the United States. Bush was in no mood for leniency after visiting the families of the victims of September 11. "Time is running out for Afghanistan's Taliban militia to avoid being targeted for war," he said on September 17.[6] Such bellicose language from Bush would have been unthinkable just eight days earlier, when the only war on his mind was against illiteracy. By October, U.S. laser-guided missiles rained over Afghanistan. "The Taliban made a choice to continue hiding terrorists, and now they are paying a price," explained Bush. "We are deliberately and systematically hunting down these murderers."[7]

Since 1996, the Taliban had run Afghanistan as a theocracy—a state claiming full devotion to God. Yet it turned the nation into a sanctuary and training ground for terrorism, and was also the world's largest supplier of opium. As Bush himself had put it to the UN General Assembly, the Taliban leaders "call their cause holy, yet they fund it with drug dealing."[8] The Taliban perpetuated terrorism not just abroad, but against its own people. Bush called the Taliban "one of the most brutal and oppressive governments in modern times," accusing it of a "reign of terror" on the Afghan people.[9]

The president was particularly appalled by the Taliban's lack of religious tolerance, by the way its leadership—employing religion as its justification—created Islamic laws that prohibited women from singing in public or getting an education or even leaving the house without a male escort. In the name of God, the Taliban permitted amputation of the fingers of girls who polished their nails, and punished homosexuals by pushing walls onto them. Transgressors were hunted down by the morality police, known as the Ministry for the Promotion of Virtue and the Prevention of Vice. In a country where women were prevented from becoming professionals, women were not allowed to see a male doctor or be operated upon by a surgical team containing a male, unless a male family member was present. The Taliban was violently misogynistic and antihomosexual. To the UN General Assembly, Bush spoke of how women in Afghanistan had been beaten for wearing socks that were too thin, and executed in Kabul's soccer stadium.[10]

Forced religious conversion to Islam was commonplace, and the country harbored a disturbing brand of prisoner—the religious detainee. As Bush said, the regime had tried to control "every mind and every soul" in the country.[11] This enemy, he averred, sought to dictate "how to think and how to worship, even to fellow Muslims."[12] Bush noted that for Afghans, "Religion can be practiced only as their leaders dictate. A man can be jailed in Afghanistan if his beard is not long enough."[13] He told the United Nations that male citizens were jailed for missing mandatory prayer meetings.[14] Indeed, men were instructed to attend five daily prayers and Friday noon prayers at mosques, and neighbors were ordered to turn in any violators. Women, banished from mosques, were expected to carry out the prayer decree in their homes. Those who disobeyed prayer requirements were subject to severe beatings.

The nation's minuscule portion of 2,500 Christians fled underground. Proselytizing by non-Muslims was prohibited and was punishable by death, or deportation in the case of foreigners. In January 2001, Taliban supreme leader Mullah Mohammed Omar announced that any Afghan citizen who converted from Islam to Christianity, Judaism, or any other religion would be punished by death. Moreover, the Sunni Muslim Taliban directed acute repression at Shiite Muslims, especially the predominantly Shiite Hazara ethnic group—targeted because of its religious affiliation.

Bush took pains to make clear, as he would do in the case of Iraq later, that his war in Afghanistan was aimed at terrorists and the regime, not the Afghan people. He stunned his cabinet when he asked during one of the first war sessions: "Can we have the first bombs we drop be food?" Bush explained to reporter Bob Woodward that his thinking stemmed from "a larger question" of one's view of God—namely, that "We're all God's children." He wanted any attack on Afghanistan to be grounded in moral as much as military considerations. Though acknowledging that the military might be bemused by the president's thought, Secretary of Defense Donald Rumsfeld said he understood Bush's reasoning, and followed through on the request.[15]

Food was dropped, and so were bombs, though civilian targets were assiduously avoided. Despite warnings of "another Vietnam" by some critics, and the presence of millions of buried land mines left from the war in the 1980s, the American invasion was a rout. The Taliban and its sympathizers were quickly destroyed.

On November 10, 2001, standing before the UN General Assembly, Bush made a "promise" that the Taliban's days were "drawing to a close" and the world would soon wave "good riddance."[16] Just two days later, on November 12, 2001, came death for the Taliban regime. The leadership abandoned Kabul; it had lost to American airpower and U.S. Special Forces on the ground, aided by helpful Afghan Northern Alliance rebel troops. The residents of Kabul responded with a giant party. Women threw off their burkas and veils as if they were shackles and danced in the streets, actions that earlier would have resulted in whipping and imprisonment. Barbershops were filled with men shaving off beards. Music played throughout the streets. A regime that tried to elevate a religious faith had ended by degrading it.

The ultimate sign of the betterment of life in Afghanistan came in the mass movement of Afghans back to the country—a total reversal of an exodus that had lasted more than twenty years. After the Soviets invaded in December 1979, a staggering five to six million Afghan citizens, out of a total of 15.5 million (possibly as high as 40 percent of the population), fled the country. They lived in abject squalor in refugee camps in neighboring Pakistan—escaping the ravages of war and the repressive Soviet-supported Communist government. When the Taliban took over in 1996, refugees found no good reason to return home. Only the removal of the Taliban by the Bush administration moved Afghan citizens to return. By the end of 2002, a massive number of Afghans—1.7 to 2.5 million—had returned to their native country from Pakistan, India, Iran, and other countries.[17] The trend continued throughout 2003 and into the present.

Terrorism aside, Bush's removal of the Taliban was a triumph for a principle that was long dear to his heart—religious freedom. A couple of months after the regime's death, the president declared a Religious Freedom Day on January 15, 2002. In his official proclamation, Bush declared, "Today, as America wages war against terror, our resolve to defend religious freedom remains as strong as ever." The only nation he cited by name was Afghanistan, where, he said in celebration, a regime responsible for "an era of . . . religious repression" had been terminated.[18] The State Department likewise took note: in its 2002 International Religious Freedom Report, the cautious analysts reported "a significant change" and "major improvement" in religious freedom in Afghanistan.[19]

Religious freedom had been spurned in the nation before the Taliban. The Communist regime propped up by the Soviets in the late 1970s and through the 1980s was made up of a trio of horrifically repressive Marxists who orchestrated a brutal, atheistic campaign against religion, even Islam. When religious freedom came at the end of 2001, it had been absent for more than three decades.

The end of the Taliban also meant the end of bin Laden's protective regime. He now began a difficult life on the run—a dismal existence of hiding in caves or anywhere he could sleep for a few nights while U.S. Special Forces combed the region in search of the terrorist mastermind. American resolve to locate him continues.

Bush later quipped that bin Laden and his followers must have expected the president and his fellow Americans to curl up in a fetal position after the September 11 attacks. The enemy must have assumed that Americans were so "materialistic," "self-absorbed," and "selfish" that after the attacks they would simply "file a lawsuit or two." They were wrong, said Bush.[20] With the liberation complete and humanitarian aid under way, he asked, "May God bless the people of Afghanistan and of America."[21]

The war went so smoothly in Afghanistan that history will note the lack of rancor and criticism of Bush's actions. Such complete unity behind a president had not been seen in a long time. Former vice president Al Gore commended his adversary: "I felt that he did a terrific job in the aftermath of September 11."[22] So did the public. An October 2001 Zogby poll asked Americans who they would prefer as commander in chief during the current crisis—Bush or Gore's former boss, Bill Clinton. Bush got the nod by a margin of 72 percent to 20 percent.[23]

It was difficult to find anyone who disagreed with Bush's war on terror in Afghanistan. But the protests were not far off, as George W. Bush prepared to toss aside his post–September 11 political good-will—the accolades from all corners—to pursue a war in Iraq.

Axis of Evil

While the dust was still settling in Afghanistan, in his January 29, 2002, State of the Union speech, President Bush identified Iraq, Iran, and North Korea as three legs of an "axis of evil." Bush personally "loathed" North Korean Communist despot Kim Jong Il, whose economic policies led to the starvation of 10 percent to 15 percent of his country's population (2 to 3 million out of 22 million people) from 1995 to 1999.[24] Kim's public schools teach North Korean children that their leader does not defecate, and that a new star appeared the day he was born. His regime reportedly removes triplets from the care of their parents out of an irrational fear that one of those triplets will one day remove Kim. The dictator directs the nation's scarce resources into a nuclear weapons program he promised not to develop, which is funded partly by opium grown on precious farm acreage, partly by counterfeit U.S. currency, and partly by missile sales to the world's worst regimes.

To Bush, Kim was evil. And with such a moral declaration, he began stoking the flames of opposition. As with Ronald Reagan nearly twenty years earlier, the mere fact that an American president was invoking the idea of evil, and challenging it on moral grounds, drew lightning. As Reagan had seen, the response to biblical language in American public life often involves a helping of fire and brimstone.

Ours is an age of moral ambiguity. Those who subscribe to the tenets of moral relativism do not greet the prospect warmly when a conservative president calls the leadership of a specific nation evil. Yet those offended do not always object to describing certain regimes as evil. They themselves asserted that South African apartheid rule, Augusto Pinochet's regime in Chile, and the Nazi government in Germany were evil.

Supporters of Bush's language saw it as a salutary revelation to those ignorant of Saddam's tyranny, or Iran's state-sponsored terrorism, or Kim's madness. They welcomed the candor. The *Washington Post* published an editorial noting that what Bush said about the three countries "has the advantage of being true."[25] In retrospect, Bush's remark seemed a tactical maneuver, putting the world on notice that these nations were future targets in the war against terror, particularly because each either possessed or intended to procure weapons of mass destruction. Bush's aim may have been to get the public thinking and to ready Americans for a new level of pressure against these enemies.

The president's declaration of the "axis of evil," a phrase inserted within the speech only after much deliberation, was greeted with fiercely mixed feelings. Some saw the remark as diplomatically foolish. Chris Patten, the European Union commissioner in charge of international relations, logically protested the use of the word *axis* for a trifecta that was not actually a collaborative axis, even if they were independently evil: These three nations were hardly prone to working together. Others saw it as simply too absolutist in a world of gray.

The French foreign minister dubbed the declaration *"simplisme,"* or an oversimplification—a repeat of the reception of Reagan's remark about the "evil empire."[26] Chris Patten also accused the Bush administration of a precarious "absolutist and simplistic" stance toward the world.[27] Former Democratic president Jimmy Carter agreed, publicly calling Bush's description "overly simplistic and counterproductive." "I think it will take years before we can repair the damage done by that statement," said Carter.[28] Critics bristled at the image of a religious president applying morally absolutist terms to foreign policy. They viewed it as a dangerous intrusion of a man's biblically based beliefs.

And yet George W. Bush was hardly a latter-day convert to the concept of evil. In fact, he had used the word many times before September 11, and rarely angered his detractors when he did so. He used the word to describe the Holocaust and racism. In a June 2001 speech, he referred to the Nazi monster resisted by Polish Jews as evil.[29] Almost two years before September 11, the governor identified "smut and pornography," hate crimes, and the crime of defacing synagogues as evil.[30] In an August 2000 interview, he said the Columbine students who killed their classmates had "hearts" that were "taken by evil."[31] No one complained of these applications of the word *evil*; all sides silently nodded in approval.

CHINA AND RUSSIA

A month after the axis-of-evil remark, Bush headed to China. His trip was an official state visit, but his faith came along for the ride. Bush had had a special interest in China since the days his father was ambassador in the 1970s, and he paid particular attention to religious persecution there. The year before, in two separate incidents in May and June 2001, he spoke at length about China's lack of religious liberty. That same year, during a meeting with Chinese President Jiang Zemin in Shanghai, he had done something extraordinary: He shared his faith with Zemin, the leader atop the atheist regime. "I talked to him on very personal terms about my Christian beliefs," said Bush. "I explained to him that faith had an incredibly important part in my life, and it has a very important part in the lives of all kinds of citizens and that I would hope that he, as a president of a great nation, would understand the importance of religion in an individual's life." Bush talked about the Catholic church in China, interned bishops, the status of the Dalai Lama, and the situation with other faiths in the Communist nation.[32]

Now, in February 2002, Bush raised these issues again in China. At Tsinghua University in Beijing on February 22, he spoke of religious freedom. He told the students that Americans often take responsibility for helping others without being ordered to do so, motivated by good hearts and often by faith. "America is a nation," continued Bush, "guided by faith. . . . This may interest you: 95 percent of Americans say they believe in God, and I'm one of them." Bush then told the university that faith points to a higher moral law beyond man's law, and calls human beings to duties greater than mere material gain. "Faith gives us a moral core," Bush explained. He said that freedom of religion should not be feared but welcomed. He informed his audience that he had shared these thoughts with President Jiang Zemin a few months earlier.[33] He went on:

> Tens of millions of Chinese today are relearning Buddhist, Taoist, and local religious traditions, or practicing Christianity, Islam, and other faiths. Regardless of where or how these believers worship, they're no threat to public order; in fact, they make good citizens. For centuries, this country has had a tradition of religious tolerance. My prayer is that all persecution will end, so that all in China are free to gather and worship as they wish.

The president's Chinese hosts could not have been pleased with Bush's lecture or his prayer—words spoken in China's communist political capital.

Bush's next big trip, in May, was to Russia, a country once equally hostile to faith. With the Cold War over, of course, the atheism of the Soviet state was a matter of history; now, of all things, Bush and Russia's new leader, Vladimir Putin, found common ground over a cross. Bush had heard that Putin owned a cross that his mother had given him, which Putin had had blessed in the Holy Land of Israel. He asked Putin about it. "It's true," Putin confirmed. Bush said he was amazed that a Soviet Communist and KGB operative like Putin had dared to wear a cross around his neck. "That speaks volumes to me, Mr. President," Bush told him. "May I call you Vladimir?" Yes, said the Russian leader. Putin then followed with a story: One night he removed the cross and hung it on the wall of a house, which then burned to the ground. "The only thing I wanted recovered was the cross," said Putin, who gave those orders to one of the firemen. Not long after, the fireman appeared before Putin and handed him the crucifix—"as if it was meant to be," said Putin. Bush, impressed still more, replied: "Well, that's the story of the cross as far as I'm concerned. Things are meant to be." A month later at a meeting in Genoa, Italy, Putin showed the cross to Bush. The two had bonded on a personal and spiritual level.[34]

On May 24, 2002, Bush met with Putin again in Moscow, where they signed a historic accord to reduce nuclear weapons. After that, he met with a group of community and religious leaders, to whom he spoke about the "Creator's" inalienable rights and about the importance of faith; he said he appreciated their recognition of a "universal and gracious God." He closed: "May God bless you all. May God bless Russia. And may God bless the United States."[35] Two days later, he visited a church and a synagogue in St. Petersburg. During the Communist period, the church had been converted into a museum of atheism, as was the case for many Russian churches. Now, Bush rejoiced, it was once again a place where people went to worship God freely. "Freedom of religion," he told Russian reporters, is "one of the nonnegotiable demands of individual dignity."[36] It was a message he took to the world.

9.

When Bush Prays

"The nation's executive mansion is currently honeycombed with prayer groups and Bible study cells, like a whited monastery."

—Garry Wills[1]

With his first year as president ending with victory in Afghanistan, and war with Iraq on the horizon, 2002 served as a transition year between the two most significant actions of George W. Bush's presidency. These were events that entailed both fierce opposition and the hardest of decisions: to dispatch young men to die in combat. It was fitting, then, that even prior to his trips to Russia and China in 2002 and his axis-of-evil remark, the year began with an exchange between Bush and a citizen over the importance of prayer.

The exchange took place on January 5, 2002, in Ontario, California, thirty-seven miles east of Los Angeles. The weather was typical southern California; the times were not. It had been only four months since thousands of Americans were murdered by bin Laden bombers. George W. Bush was there to remind fellow Americans of their shared duty to confront those responsible. "They were fixin' to hurt the American people," said Bush of the terrorists, interchangeably speaking English, Spanish, and Texan. He promised they would pay. A concerned citizen spoke up: Mr. President, he began earnestly, how could he and others help their commander in chief during this difficult new war on terror? Bush had a simple answer: prayer.[2] He said he knew the American people were praying for him: "I can just feel it. I can't describe it very well, but I feel comforted by the prayer." He asked that Americans pray for "God's protection," a "shield of protection"—a "spiritual shield that protects the country."

Bush believes in "the power of prayer" and its transforming force. He seeks it for himself and his country. "I want to tell you," he lectured a lively May 2002 audience at the National Hispanic Prayer Breakfast, where he again spoke English and Spanish, "the greatest gift that people can give to a president or people in positions of responsibility . . . is prayer. I work the rope lines a lot, and people say, 'Mr. President, I pray for you and your family.' I turn to them, I look them in the eye, and say, that's the greatest gift you can give. . . . I mean it with all sincerity. And so I want to thank you for your prayer."[3]

He delivers that message repeatedly, down to the image of working the rope lines. James Dobson recalls Bush's address at the first National Day of Prayer of his presidency. A happy Dobson watched while Bush's voice quivered when he acknowledged all the people who said they were praying for him.[4]

During a later stop in Nashville, where he spoke to a group of believers at Opryland, Bush met privately with members of the executive committee of the National Religious Broadcasters. He mentioned that he knew people were praying for him, and that the prayers were working. One skeptic asked how he knew they did. Bush shot back, "Brother, if you have to ask, you just don't get it."[5]

FROM HIS FIRST DAY AS PRESIDENT, BUSH HAS BEGUN each morning with prayer, and by reading his daily Bible devotional. He often turns to a cabinet member to request a prayer before opening a cabinet meeting. Prayer is part of his presidency, and increasingly so after the "evildoers" dramatically elevated the gravity of his daily duties.

Other subsequent events brought him to prayer. When the space shuttle *Columbia* exploded, the president directed the nation's gaze upward. Seven "brave souls," Bush called *Columbia*'s crew, had perished. He and the first lady flew to Mission Control in Houston, where they prayed with the families of the victims. Bush said that he felt the "presence of Almighty God" not only in the hearts of the mourners but in the room itself. "There was such incredible strength in the room of those who were grieving that it was overwhelming," said Bush. He attributed that presence "to the fact that they, themselves, are in prayer." He shared this sentiment at the Prayer Breakfast in Washington, requesting prayer yet again for those grieving families.[6]

Yet, while prayer sustains the president, it has tended to annoy his critics, who see it as a symbol of Bush's excessive piety. It reflects what they do not like about his faith—its openness. They prefer that he privatize his faith—a sentiment that became pronounced after September 11, when a particularly pensive Bush turned to prayer more than ever.

CONSERVATIVE AND MODERATE CHRISTIANS

Though Bush's detractors detest his piety, conservative to moderate Christians adore Bush and the openness of his faith. Many conservative Christians I spoke with in the course of writing this book gushed in praise of the man. One Protestant minister said: "This is the first time in my life that I have really loved a President. He is the best role model for serious Christians in a long time."[7] On the other hand, many secularists, agnostics, and liberal Christians seethe with anger when Bush speaks about God.

Bush's appeal to conservative Christians, especially Catholics, is unprecedented for a Republican president. Though Bush and Gore split the popular vote in 2000, Bush ran the table among churchgoers. Among those who attend religious services weekly, he beat Gore by 57 to 40 percent. For those who attend more than weekly, he won 63 to 36 percent. (Gore won by 61 to 32 percent among those who said they "never" attend church, suggesting that the former vice president easily swept the atheist vote.)[8] These numbers would be even starker if not for the fact that African-Americans, who have high church attendance rates, voted almost entirely for Gore.[9]

Among whites who identified themselves as belonging to the "religious right," Bush beat Gore by 80 to 18 percent. He handily won over white Protestants by 63 to 34 percent, and white Catholics by 52 to 45 percent.[10] Bush advisers believe that it was the "religiously active Catholic" vote that narrowly brought him victory in 2000. By one estimate, more than half of Bush's 2000 votes came from serious Catholics and Protestants.[11]

Jack Graham, pastor of the 22,000-member Prestonwood Baptist Church in Plano, Texas, and president of the nearly 20-million-member Southern Baptist Convention, says that he expects evangelicals to head to the polls to vote for Bush "in record numbers" in 2004. "Our people didn't quite know George Bush in the last election," said Graham, "but they do now." He points to character above all as the attraction to Bush.[12]

A key factor for this appeal to churchgoers is that they believe Bush "walks the walk"—that he truly integrates his faith into his life. "I'm mindful of walking the walk," he said before he stepped into the White House. "That's the best thing I can do as president. And when you walk the walk, people of faith will walk right with you."[13]

A good illustration of that is James Dobson's reaction to Bush's opposition to abortion. "He continues to speak very eloquently about the unborn child and about his commitment . . . to life at all ages, and I deeply appreciate that," Dobson told his millions of listeners. "President George W. Bush has done more to protect life at all ages than any president in history. . . . The man really is committed to life. . . . I am very relieved and pleased that there is something in this man's heart." While worried about some "very tough battles" ahead with Congress, Dobson took solace "that there is a man at the helm who believes in the sanctity of life."[14]

Another influential evangelical who believes that Bush walks the walk is Marvin Olasky, editor in chief of *World* magazine. "He's our first modern president who is born again not only in his heart and mind but in his actions," says Olasky, who knew and advised Bush in Texas. "He shows his belief that Christianity makes a difference."[15] He is joined by Tony Evans, the nationally known African-American preacher from Texas, of whom Bush is a big fan. Evans says that the president is "doing a very admirable, very clear and profound job of showing faith to be a part of his life."[16]

One person with her hand on the pulse of evangelicals is Janet Parshall, longtime host of a syndicated radio talk show carried on 130

Christian radio stations, daily reaching 3.5 million. Parshall, a religious broadcaster—a job that Bush dubs "a great commission"[17]—says that she has never witnessed such an outpouring of sustained support for a president among Christians. "They call me and say they're praying for him," she says. "My callers like him and are thankful. They actually tell me they *cried* when they watched the State of the Union address. Imagine that! They love this man." A popular speaker at Christian conferences, Parshall speaks of how people stand in line long after her presentation simply to express their pleasure with Bush and to say that they pray for him. "That's unsolicited," says Parshall. "They just come up and say it."[18]

Like Olasky, she agrees that the positive reaction stems from the fact that Christians see Bush as the real deal—a man privately and publicly guided by his faith. "He's so unhesitatingly unembarrassed by his faith," says Parshall. "He works it into his verbiage, his public policy, his comportment. He's so comfortable with his faith. And he's sincere about it. His faith so totally defines him." She also believes that the evangelical community has reacted to Bush's personal integrity with the first lady—an important contrast from his predecessor.

This embrace of Bush is evident at major gatherings of conservative Christians. It was not unusual when the *Washington Post*'s Dana Milbank reported that at the February 2003 National Religious Broadcasters' convention Bush was greeted with "rock star adulation." Attendees yelled out "amen" while he spoke. Milbank quoted Glenn Plummer, the chairman of the broadcasters, who introduced Bush: "The United States of America has been blessed by God Himself to have George W. Bush as president."[19]

These conservative Christians are eager to share their affection for Bush. In February 2003, when interviewed on a separate topic, Reverend Louis P. Sheldon, chair of the Traditional Values Coalition, could not stop raving about the current president. That morning, Bush had spoken at the National Prayer Breakfast. "You *must* get a copy of that speech," Sheldon urged. From memory, he quoted Bush's reading from Isaiah in his space-shuttle remarks the previous Saturday. After that, he pulled from his desk a transcript of the president's State of the Union address from the previous week and read the closing paragraphs. "That's wonderful," Sheldon declared.[20]

THE OTHER SIDE — THE LEFT

On the other hand, there are plenty of liberal Christians—as well as secularists, agnostics, and atheists—who do not like Bush, in large part because of his piety.

One factor in their discomfort is that they simply disagree with him politically. Any suggestion that Bush's conservatism and policies stem from his faith strikes many liberal Christians as a misrepresentation of the Bible and Gospel of Christ. Bush's self-righteousness is belied by his positions, they say. His policies would not have been those of Jesus.

The liberal Christians are joined by nonreligious liberals, who are generally bothered by Bush's moral absolutes. Many of these individuals are relativists. It galls them to see a president ground his positions in a biblically based absolutism they feel is not valid.

Another group of nonreligious liberals, including secularists, agnostics, and atheists, are disturbed by the fact that the highest person in the land draws upon religious faith to mold his political choices and "carry" him through the day. They see this as a violation of a necessary separation of church and state. They would not mind so much that Bush is religious, they say, if he kept his faith completely out of the public arena.

Constitutionally, the church-state issue is often misinterpreted. The words *separation of church and state* are not found in the U.S. Constitution. They come from a letter by Thomas Jefferson, who, though obviously a vital founder, was neither a signer of the Constitution nor present at the Constitutional Convention. What the Constitution does say about religion is contained primarily in the First Amendment, where it relays two things: that government has no right to (1) establish a religion or (2) prohibit the free exercise thereof.

The establishment clause is the most debated of the two clauses. What constitutes establishment? Undoubtedly, it means that the government should not recognize any particular national religion or favor a single faith. That is clearly what the founders had in mind. Since that time, though, courts have interpreted the clause much more liberally, and separation-of-church-and-state voices have seized on these changes.

Less heralded by these voices is the free-exercise clause. Bush has called freedom of religion "one of the central freedoms" in the Bill of Rights, "the first freedom of the human soul, the right to speak the words that God places in our mouths."[21] A fair-minded reading of the Constitution suggests that it is critical to respect both clauses—a balance not always achieved by separation-of-church-and-state enthusiasts. While George W. Bush is not permitted to make Christianity the nation's official religion—and has no apparent designs to ever do so—the Constitution protects his right to exercise his religious freedom. He can pray, talk to God, talk about God, lean on God, attend church, and integrate his faith into his life. What he cannot do, as president, is implement a theocracy. The founders never intended that a president leave his faith at the front desk before walking into the Oval Office each day.

The cloudier question is to what extent the president can integrate his faith into his public actions and political positions. That is where the splits begin, and the way they take root is usually based on the ideology and political party of the president.

Those critical of Bush's piety almost always give their own political figures a pass when they, too, mix faith and politics. Liberals approve when faith enters the battle for civil rights, to reform mental hospitals, or to create better child labor laws. They cheered when Martin Luther King Jr. brought the values and rhetoric of the church into the public square. When the Reverend Jesse Jackson proclaimed at the 1984 Democratic convention, "God is not finished with me yet," many on the convention floor wept with joy.[22]

Liberals agree with the policies that spring from their faith-filled politicians, but are troubled by those of conservatives who appeal to God; in particular, they worry about a conservative president's association with the Christian right, a group that terrifies the left. When Bill Keller characterized Bush's faith as a cross between pop and frat-boy theology in the New York Times, he had not been critical enough for many in the Times's readership. "Bill Keller lets President Bush off the hook too easily," complained one letter to the editor. Another writer, from Queens, New York, feared that Bush and his administration had been consumed by "the far religious right." A third fumed that Bush "scares many of us . . . whether he's simply pandering to ultraright fundamentalists, or on some kind of religious crusade that could turn into Armageddon."[23]

Should conservative public officials silence their piety while liberal believers are granted free rein? Some liberals concede that there is a double standard, yet choose to defend it. When Vice President Gore and Senator Joe Lieberman spoke openly of their faith during the 2000 campaign, David Harris, deputy executive director for the

National Jewish Democratic Council, defended it: "Bush's [religious] declarations have an air of exclusivity. But Gore and Lieberman appear all inclusive on faith; [they suggest] that all must be made to feel welcome."[24]

Some resistance to Bush's religious orientation stems simply from anti-Bush partisanship, which intensified during the Florida election fiasco and eventually boiled over with the war in Iraq. Jonathan Chait, senior editor at *The New Republic*, wrote an op-ed piece for the *Washington Post* titled "Blinded by Bush-Hatred." Chait alluded to those "who distrust Bush so much that they automatically assume everything he says must be false," and said that perhaps the "most disheartening" development of the later war in Iraq was "the number of liberals who have allowed Bush-hatred to take the place of thinking. Speaking with otherwise perceptive people, I have seen the same intellectual tics come up time and time again: If Bush is for it, I'm against it."[25] Though Chait did not address the religious aspect, it applies; there are many on the left who are angered by the president's belief in prayer merely because it is Bush who is praying.

WHEN BUSH'S STAFF PRAYS

Critics are bothered not just by the thought of Bush praying, but also by the fact of his staff praying—especially in circumstances when the president has called on staff members to pray before a meeting.

Yet there appears to be no evidence of any staffer who has complained about being asked to pray. According to his staff, the president asks for prayer from those who do not mind being asked. Most of his staff, whether Jewish, Catholic, or evangelical, seem to be believers. Condoleezza Rice, for example, has been quite open about her spirituality. "I have a very, very powerful faith in God," says the former

Stanford professor, whose father was a preacher. "I'm a really religious person."[26] Since September 11, Rice says, she has "turned to God and prayer more and more."[27]

She is hardly an unusual case in the Bush administration. Chief speechwriter Mike Gerson is devout. The wife of Chief of Staff Andrew Card is a Methodist minister. Donald Rumsfeld happily obliges when called on to say grace. Attorney General John Ashcroft, a favorite target of the left, is the son of a minister. (Arthur M. Schlesinger Jr. has called Ashcroft a "religious fanatic"—an appraisal he offered immediately after singing the praises of John Quincy Adams, who wore his piety far more openly than Ashcroft.[28]) The atmosphere in the White House, reports Howard Fineman, "is suffused with an aura of prayerfulness."[29]

When not praying, some members of the Bush White House worship and study the Bible together, at times including the president himself. On Palm Sunday 2002, the president—who hates to miss church on important occasions—was stuck aboard Air Force One. So, along with Condoleezza Rice and speechwriter Karen Hughes, he decided to hold an informal religious service on the plane. According to Kenneth T. Walsh, three dozen officials huddled in the Air Force One conference room. Rice led the group in hymns. Hughes gave a short sermon. They ended with Bush's favorite hymn, "Amazing Grace." Then they all hugged one another. "There were a lot of religious people on the plane," recalled Bush. "It was a packed house. . . . And to be able to worship with people with whom you work in a unique spot is a special moment." He added: "You know, I did feel the presence of God amongst my friends on Air Force One."[30]

On the ground, the Bush White House is filled with Bible studies. The concept of such studies in the nation's executive mansion is not a radical one. The Clinton White House had a Bible-study group. In the Bush White House, however, Bible-study groups are everywhere—and apparently they have proven an irritant to some outsiders.

One British observer said that when the mere existence of White House Bible studies was disclosed, it confirmed the view in western Europe that a "fundamentalist crazy" president was itching to turn the United States into the Republic of Gilead. "To listen to the European reaction," he wrote, "one might have thought they were bringing back witch trials in Massachusetts."[31]

Many Bush staff members participate in the studies. There is, however, concern that a kind of peer pressure exists in which staff members are expected to attend. David Frum contributed to this view in his memoir of the early Bush administration, writing that Bible study in the White House "was, if not compulsory, not quite *uncompulsory*, either." This was "disconcerting" to a non-Christian like himself, Frum added, noting that the first words he heard in the Bush White House were "Missed you at Bible study."[32]

Opponents have seized upon these two quotes, sometimes quite angrily. Writing in *The Atlantic*, Jack Beatty began his column with the "missed you at Bible study" remark[33]—and went on to offer an assessment of Bush that was nearly hysterical with rage.

Garry Wills is also troubled. "The nation's executive mansion is currently honeycombed with prayer groups and Bible study cells," worries Wills, "like a whited monastery."[34]

Wills, like Beatty, zeroed in on Frum's comment as evidence of an us-vs.-them mentality among observant Christians at the White House. Yet the "missed you at Bible study" anecdote was not directed at Frum. It was aimed at his boss, Michael Gerson, with whom Frum was meeting. Gerson is a committed evangelical, schooled at Wheaton College, the prestigious Christian college in Illinois. He attends Bible study regularly, as both a vigorous participant and a leader. In the situation that Frum referred to, Gerson had missed the last study. Someone asked him where he had been.

Yet the line made Frum feel uncomfortable. And those concerned about the "not quite *uncompulsory*" aspect of his charge have a point. They feel it is wrong to pressure White House staff to think they must be, or ought to be, attending Bible study with fellow staff. Surely, that can be done elsewhere on Sunday, or even not at all. Prayer and Bible study are not requirements for public service. Not all White House staff members are spiritually devout, and not all must be devout in order to work in the White House.

That said, despite what the letters to the editor insist in the *New York Times*, a single comment, even told as colorfully as Frum does, cannot possibly "qualify as coercive religious indoctrination." It does not violate the spirit of the final clause of Article VI of the Constitution: "No religious test shall ever be required as a qualification to any office or public trust under the United States."[35] The Bush White House has no such test.

Of Bush staff who partake in Bible studies, Frum is careful to note that while secular people imagine the devout to be "censorious personalities, keen to forbid and punish," the evangelicals in the Bush White House were "its gentlest souls, the most patient, the least argumentative. They were numerous enough to set the tone of the White House, and the result was an office in which I seldom heard a voice raised in anger—and never witnessed a single one of those finger-jabbing confrontations you see in movies about the White House." Frum said that the antic tone of the television show *The West Wing* was so alien to the Bush White House that it might as well have been filmed aboard a Klingon starship.[36]

Disclosures like Frum's became public in 2002, after September 11 and during the period when the Bush administration was preparing the military and the world for an invasion of Iraq. Such religious revelations contributed to the unease some felt over the level of devoutness in the Bush White House, especially that of the president himself. Critics expressed discomfort more and more in the days following September 11. Interestingly, while data showed that the post–September 11 public went to church, read the Bible, and prayed more than ever in recent times, the president's detractors also complained more than ever about his demonstrations of piety during the same period.

10.

God and Democrats

"Our ministry is to do the work of God here on Earth."

—*President Bill Clinton to a church in Temple Hills, Maryland, August 1994*[1]

"God's work must be our own. And there are many questions before us now in this last Presidential election of the twentieth century, and the first Presidential election of the twenty-first century. . . . Our obligation is to help each other live up to what God meant us to be."

—*President Bill Clinton to a church in Newark, New Jersey, October 1996*[2]

"He [Jesus] was a Democrat, I think."

—*Presidential candidate Dick Gephardt to Democratic voters in Iowa, December 2003*[3]

George W. Bush's intense piety is nothing new among America's presidents, its founders, and its politicians. And it is not foreign to leading Democrats, past and present.

The nation's first chief executive unabashedly integrated his faith into public life. In the snow of Valley Forge, George Washington prayed on his knees for God's intervention, and did again as president. In his first inaugural address, Washington said, "It would be particularly improper to omit, in this first official act, my fervent supplication to that Almighty Being, Who rules over the universe, Who presided in the councils of nations." In his farewell address, he declared: "Of all the dispositions and habits which lead to political prosperity, Religion and morality are indispensable supports."[4]

Such ideas saturated the thinking of America's founders—among them John Adams (and his wife Abigail), John Jay, Benjamin Franklin, Benjamin Rush, Samuel Adams, and Patrick Henry. Henry is credited with the ultimate politically incorrect statement: "It cannot be emphasized too strongly or too often that this great nation was founded not by religionists, but by Christians; not on religions, but on the Gospel of Jesus Christ." Compared to the language of those at the Continental Congress, George W. Bush's religious invocations seem modest, almost tame.[5]

This kind of rhetoric has persisted throughout U.S. history, even finding its way into the statements of some of the twentieth century's great progressives. When Teddy Roosevelt, who had an encyclopedic recollection of Bible verses, found himself frustrated by his inability to secure the Republican presidential nomination in 1912, he informed his faithful: "We stand at Armageddon and we battle for the Lord!"

Like George W. Bush, TR was a Republican. Yet some of the most openly devout presidents have been Democrats. Consider four—all icons—from the twentieth century: Woodrow Wilson, Franklin Delano Roosevelt, Harry Truman, and John F. Kennedy.

Wilson, a liberal's liberal, was a Presbyterian elder who read the Bible daily; he felt "sorry for the men who do not read the Bible every day." The Bible, he argued, was "the one supreme source of revelation of the meaning of life." Wilson was prone to make explicitly Christian claims about his nation, even excluding the word *Judeo* from his characterization of the nation's religious heritage. "America was born a Christian nation," claimed the great liberal in 1913. "America was born to exemplify that devotion to the elements of righteousness which derived from the revelations of Holy Scripture."[6]

Wilson routinely invoked God's work as his own. He was a preeminent moralizer who saw things in terms of good and evil.[7] Arthur S. Link, the director of the Wilson papers at Princeton, has said that Wilson had a superb command of Reformed theology, and "drew his greatest strength from the sources of Christian faith." "It was no accident," writes Link, that Wilson "never thought about public matters, as well as private ones, without first trying to decide what faith and Christian love commanded in the circumstances."[8] One cannot talk about Wilson or his programs without discussing his faith. Eager to leave his mark on history, in his Fourteen Points Wilson took the opportunity to propose his dream of a League of Nations, which he felt would advance God's will:

> The stage is set, the destiny is closed. It has come about by no plan of our conceiving, but by the hand of God who led us this way. We cannot turn back. We can only go forward, with lifted eyes and freshened spirit, to follow the vision. It was of this that we dreamed at our birth. America shall in truth show the way. The light streams upon the path ahead, and nowhere else.[9]

The twentieth century's longest-serving chief executive was Franklin Delano Roosevelt. In survey after survey, academic historians and political scientists rank him the greatest president of the century. In a 1935 radio broadcast FDR declared:

> We cannot read the history of our rise and development as a nation without reckoning with the place the Bible has occupied in shaping the advances of the Republic. . . . Where we have been the truest and most consistent in obeying its precepts, we have attained the greatest measure of contentment and prosperity.[10]

In his second inaugural address, FDR pledged to do his utmost by "seeking Divine guidance."[11] He took that self-appointed mandate further on January 25, 1941, when he wrote a personal prologue to a special edition of the New Testament, which was distributed to millions of U.S. soldiers. "As Commander-in-Chief," Roosevelt wrote, "I take pleasure in commending the reading of the Bible to all who serve in the armed forces of the United States."[12] He believed that all American soldiers should have the opportunity to read the words of Christ in preparing for battle. Once, when joining those soldiers aboard a warship with Winston Churchill, FDR asked the crew and prime minister to join him in singing the hymn "Onward Christian Soldiers."[13] In his final inaugural address, FDR affirmed: "So we pray to Him for the vision to see our way clearly . . . to achievement of His will."[14]

FDR's public faith in Providence was carried on by his successor. A striking example of a president's faith influencing a major historical decision was Harry S Truman's recognition of the nation of Israel in May 1948.

David Niles, Truman's pro-Zionist assistant, had "serious doubts" that Israel would have come into being if FDR had lived.[15] That is quite a testimony to Truman's involvement—and not unreasonable, especially since most of the U.S. delegation to the United Nations was opposed, as was Truman's secretary of state, George C. Marshall, his State Department, Secretary of Defense James Forrestal, and numerous White House staff. Yet none of these advisers could stop Truman. And a central factor in Truman's decision making was his faith. As one of the few aides who supported him, Clark Clifford, recalled, Truman's "own reading of ancient history and the Bible made him a supporter of the idea of a Jewish homeland in Palestine, even when others who were sympathetic to the plight of the Jews were talking of sending them to places like Brazil."[16]

Truman was influenced by the direct lobbying of several Jewish religious figures. His longtime friend and business partner from Missouri, a Jew named Eddie Jacobson, pressured him to meet with rabbis like Chaim Weizmann. Especially effective was Rabbi Isaac Halevi Herzog, who told Truman: "God put you in your mother's womb so you would be the instrument to bring the rebirth of Israel after 2,000 years." David Niles, who witnessed Truman's meeting with Herzog, thought to himself, "I thought he [Herzog] was overdoing things, but when I looked over at the president, tears were running down his cheeks."[17]

Truman apparently took the pleas to heart. His formal announcement of de facto U.S. recognition of Israel came into the United Nations eleven minutes after Israel became a state. The U.S. delegation broke into laughter, thinking the announcement a joke. Ambassador Austin, who knew it was true, was so upset that he left without telling the others.[18]

George Marshall was furious. He had spoken harshly to Truman and lectured him in what Clifford called "a righteous God-damned Baptist tone."[19] He had told the president he would personally not vote for him in 1948 if he recognized Israel.[20]

Truman's faith was not the only factor in his thinking. On the heels of the Holocaust, he felt that creating a nation for Jews was simply the right thing to do. Still, the biblical influence was undeniable, and liberal Democrats have never complained.

Much can be learned about John F. Kennedy through his first presidential words. When he gave his inaugural address from the east front of the Capitol during a cold January day in 1961, the new president began by mentioning God twice. One of these was a very George W. Bush–like pronouncement: "The rights of man come not from the generosity of the state but from the hand of God." Halfway through the brief speech, JFK quoted Isaiah. His closing is famous for his statement "ask not what . . ."; that line falls amid important remarks about the role of America in history and its role in relation to God. The Democratic president claimed that in the annals of world history, only a select few nations had been granted "the role of defending freedom in its hour of maximum danger"—a duty he said that he personally welcomed. America, Kennedy contended, could spark a fire that could "truly light the world." After asking Americans to consider what they could do for their country, Kennedy followed: "My fellow citizens of the world: ask not what America will do for you, but what together we can do for the freedom of man." And he concluded his historic address with a forthright religion's invocation: "[L]et us go forth to lead the land we love, asking His blessing and His help, but knowing that here on earth God's work must truly be our own."[21]

Were these merely the musings of presidents from a bygone Democratic Party—the one that Ronald Reagan once claimed had left him? To an extent, yes. Yet leading Democrats today—including the party's presidential nominees and contenders—have not shied away from religious rhetoric. Consider just four contemporary cases: Hillary Rodham Clinton, the party's favorite for a future presidential nomination; Al Gore, the party's 2000 presidential nominee; Joseph Lieberman, its 2000 vice-presidential nominee and an erstwhile candidate for the 2004 nomination; and Dick Gephardt, longtime Democratic Party leader and another 2004 candidate.

Hillary Rodham Clinton is a Methodist and a subscriber to many of the political beliefs advocated by the liberal Methodist leadership. Quite unappreciated by conservatives, but accepted by liberals, is the degree to which the former first lady relied on her faith in surviving her husband's infidelities prior to and during the presidential years. In both of her bestselling books, she writes frequently of how her faith "sustains" her and of the "power and importance of prayer" in her life. While in the White House, Mrs. Clinton says, she too had "prayer partners" and a "prayer group."[22]

In *It Takes a Village*, Mrs. Clinton includes a full chapter on faith. She also expresses her policy preferences on issues like religion in schools. On that, she agrees with both Bush and her husband in insisting that "nothing in the First Amendment converts our public schools into religion-free zones, or requires all religious expression to be left behind at the schoolhouse door." Those words are actually her husband's, as are these, which she also quotes approvingly: "Religion is too important in our history and our heritage for us to keep it out of our schools." She sounds much like Bush in her comments on God and love, and in her firmness in following the biblical admonition to forgive and love enemies—a duty she admits she finds difficult to keep.[23]

Likewise, Mrs. Clinton relates her faith to her public service, and talks of her "sense of social responsibility rooted in my faith." She points specifically to John Wesley's teaching that God's love be expressed through good works. "I took Wesley's admonition to heart," writes the former first lady. The Christian life, she says, is about "faith in action."[24]

Hillary Clinton's religious sentiments are fairly conventional. The same cannot be said for Al Gore, a man whose spiritual beliefs defy categorization. This is apparent in his acclaimed but controversial *Earth in the Balance*, which carried the often neglected but apt subtitle *Ecology and the Human Spirit*; this environmental manifesto was a kind of spiritual autobiography by the former vice president.

In *Earth in the Balance*, Gore speaks of the environment in a religious way—with a kind of New-Age spiritual tone. This is especially evident in the chapter "Environmentalism of the Spirit," in which Gore declares that the "environmental crisis" demands "a new faith in the future of life on earth." In one heated section, Gore commends ecological activists as "resistance fighters" and "people of conscience" engaging in a just war akin to the World War II resistance of the Nazis. He foresees "a kind of global civil war between those who refuse to consider the consequences of civilization's relentless advance and those who refuse to be silent partners in the destruction." The rescue of the environment, Gore urges, must become the "central organizing principle" of all societies and modern civilization; this will require not just sacrifice and struggle but "a wrenching transformation of society." Predicting nothing short of environmental Armageddon, Gore takes the occasion to issue a call for a crusade.[25]

In light of this written record—Gore's own published words (he had no ghostwriter) in a bestselling book—it is astonishing that it was George W. Bush's faith, not Al Gore's, that became an issue in the 2000 presidential campaign. Bush merely acknowledged that Christ was his favorite philosopher. Somehow, Gore's spiritual declarations did not even register on the media's radar—quite a contrast to Bush's isolated remark.

The faith of another contemporary Democrat might be underscored: Gore's 2000 running mate, Joseph Lieberman. In his book *In Praise of Public Life*, Lieberman, an observant Jew, points to lessons from the Bible as practical instruction for public leadership. While on the job in the Senate, he says, he pauses three times a day to pray—honoring Jewish tradition and providing him "perspective and calm." The Democratic senator issues a plea for greater acceptance of religion in the public square.

By the mid-1980s, Lieberman charges, the Democratic Party had "moved too far to the left," particularly in its treatment of faith: "We cast out religion and faith as having no presence or value whatsoever in politics and public life." Instead, he said, America needs moral regeneration and a "spiritual awakening." He urges that religious principles and faith be reintroduced into Democratic politics. Lieberman states that America is, after all, "one nation, under God." Like the Clintons and Bush, he laments the way the courts and various public officials are "mistaking the Constitution's promise of freedom of religion for a policy of freedom from religion," and decries the fact that politicians today are being pushed to "hide their faith behind closed doors"—declaring, simply, "that's wrong."[26]

Another Democrat who has not pushed his faith behind a closed door is Missouri congressman Dick Gephardt. A Baptist who once considered becoming a minister, during the 2004 campaign Gephardt promised that if elected president he would help Americans fulfill their "God-given potential." While campaigning, he regularly quoted passages and language from the New Testament. George W. Bush has called terrorists evildoers; Gephardt has so referred to former Enron executives. He points to Jesus Christ helping the poor as a model for his fellow Democrats. "He [Jesus] was a Democrat, I think," Gephardt told a group of Democratic voters in Marshalltown, Iowa. He has not shied from judging the morality of the Bush administration, criticizing its trade policies as "immoral."[27]

THE "J-WORD" — BUSH AND CLINTON

Those most bothered by Bush's religious statements are a statistical minority on the ideological left. A June/July 2003 survey by the Pew Research Center found: "The public at large is quite comfortable with President Bush's evocation of faith and what many perceive as his reliance on religious beliefs in making policy decisions." A 62 percent majority believed that Bush had struck the right balance in how often he mentions his faith, and 58 percent deemed his reliance on his faith in policy making appropriate. Some 41 percent said that their political leaders' expressions of faith and prayer occur "too little," whereas only half that amount (21 percent) believed such expressions take place "too much."[28] As Carl Cannon notes in the *National Journal*, Molly Ivins may be struck by an "odd, personal religiosity about Bush," but the public is not.[29]

The record suggests that Bush's inaugural address was no more religious than the fifty-three previous ones, and during his presidency he has not been prone to "excessive" Jesus talk.[30] Ronald Reagan was fearless in his open talk of the literal Christ. Jimmy Carter frequently expressed his feelings about the Nazarene carpenter.

A comparison of the mentions of Christ by Bush and Clinton shows that through 2003, Bush mentioned Jesus, or Jesus Christ, or Christ—hereafter referred to as "Christ"—in fourteen separate statements, compared to forty-one by Clinton.[31] The references usually came in speeches. On average, Clinton mentioned Christ in 5.1 statements per year, which exceeded Bush's average of 4.7.

Bush's biggest year was 2001, when he mentioned Christ in seven statements. This was the year of September 11; he was especially introspective, and looked upward for strength. In 2002, he cited Christ in five statements. Most interesting, in all of 2003, the *Presidential Documents* display only two statements in which Bush mentioned his philosopher: the Easter and Christmas messages. It may be reasonable to conclude that hostile press reaction to Bush's Jesus talk has pressured him into circumspection.

Such pressure had never been placed on Bush's Democratic predecessor. President Bill Clinton's most frequent references to Christ came in 1996—the year of his reelection campaign—when he spoke of Christ in nine separate statements. Within a single year, Bush has never outdone Clinton in references to Christ. This goes against the assertion of Barry Lynn, executive director of Americans United for Separation of Church and State, who contends that Republicans like Bush "have tended to do more God-talking."[32]

Clinton's references to Jesus Christ were always most frequent during election years: nine separate statements in 1996, seven in 1998, six in 2000, and five in 1994. In total, Clinton mentioned Christ twenty-seven times in the four election years, compared to only fourteen times in the four non-election years.[33] He mentioned Christ almost twice as much in election years.

Among these Clinton references, the Democrat deemed it critical that a president like himself do "what you believe is right and you believe is consistent with the will of God."[34] In one case, Clinton spoke at the Museum of Women in the Arts, where he was stumping for Terry L. Lierman, a Democratic congressional candidate for Maryland's Eighth Congressional District. Speaking in support of hate crimes legislation, Clinton pointed to, in his words, "the parable of what Jesus said to the woman who was caught in sin and brought to him for stoning. And [Jesus] said to let he who is among you without sin cast the first stone." Clinton noted that this analogy had been made previously by a U.S. senator (whom he didn't name) on the Senate floor, and said he was touched by the analogy and "proud" of the senator: "The whole Senate was practically weeping when this guy spoke. It was so moving."[35] Clinton was citing the teachings of Christ in support of federal legislation—an audience of Democratic partisans applauded.

POLITICKING IN CHURCHES

Indeed, it is astonishing to note just how thoroughly President Clinton was given a pass by those who normally cry foul on separation of church and state. Clinton frequently gave campaign speeches in churches, particularly African-American churches; as late as October 31, 2000, Clinton spoke in a black church in New York City, the Kelly Temple Church of God in Christ in Harlem. As in most such talks, Clinton was joined by a contingent of fellow Democratic politicians. He began by reminding congregants why they were there:

> Now, we all know why we're here, and we can shout amen and have a great time, and we're all preaching to the saved. . . . But I want to talk to you about the people that aren't in this church tonight, the people who have never come to an event like this and never heard a president speak or even a mayor or a comptroller or a senator or anybody. But they could vote. And they need to vote, and they need to know why they're voting. And that's really why you're here, because of all the people who aren't here. Isn't that right? . . .

So what you have to think about tonight is, what is it you intend to do between now and Tuesday, and on Tuesday, to get as many people there as possible and to make sure when they get to the polls, they know why they're there, what the stakes are, and what the consequences are. . . . But I want to tell you tonight in public what I would tell you if I were sitting alone in a room with any of you, and you asked me, what's this election about, anyway?

I think there are three great questions that I want you to tell everybody you can reach in Harlem, everybody in New York State. If you've got any friends across the river in New Jersey or anyplace else, I want you to reach them between now and Tuesday, because this is a razor-thin election.[36]

President Clinton was speaking in a church in order to rally New York City voters for the November 2000 election, just days away. He then gave a lengthy campaign speech, doing precisely what a preacher cannot do in a church in America without jeopardizing the church's tax-exempt status.

Two days earlier, on October 29, the president campaigned for Vice President Gore in two churches at two different Sunday services. Speaking to the congregation of Alfred Baptist Church in Alexandria, Virginia, Clinton employed a Bible verse as justification to head to the polls:

The Scripture says, "While we have time, let us do good unto all men." And a week from Tuesday, it will be time for us to vote. . . . But I'm telling you, there are huge differences on economic policy, on health care policy, on education policy, on crime policy, on environmental policy, on foreign policy, and how we deal with arms control and how we relate to Africa and other emerging areas of the world. . . . When I hear people say, "This is not really a very signifi-cant election," it makes me want to go head first into an empty swimming pool. I mean, this is—we really do have a good choice here; I mean, a big, clear, unambiguous, stark choice. We don't have to get upset; we don't have to get mad, but we need to be smart. . . . On November 7th, you're just as important as the president. . . .

But the only thing I'm concerned about is people believing that it doesn't much matter whether they vote, that the conse-quences are not great, that there aren't any significant differences. Those things are not true.

It matters whether you vote. It's the most important election inarguably that you've ever had to vote in. . . . So I implore you, show up. Call every friend, family member, co-worker, and halfway interesting-looking stranger you see on the street between now and November 7th. It's a great chance for these kids here in this church to avoid some of the mistakes and trouble and heartbreak all of us had to live through—to keep making America the beacon of hope in the world.[37]

Clinton was joined by a collection of Democratic politicians, including U.S. Representative. Jim Moran (D-VA), who was up for reelection.

That talk came at 12:40 P.M. Earlier, at 9:40 A.M., Clinton squeezed in another campaign talk to the congregation of the Shiloh Baptist Church in Washington, D.C., bringing along "so many mem-bers of the White House staff." Also present was the D.C. delegate to Congress, Eleanor Holmes Norton. In his speech, Clinton gave a pitch for various types of federal legislation, including the D.C. College Access Act, bill H.R. 2879, and full voting rights for the

District of Columbia. He railed against tax cuts proposed by Republicans, and closed by urging the worshipers to get out the vote on Election Day:

> But I am pleading with you. . . . I have done everything I know to do. . . . But . . . you have to show. So talk to your friends, talk to your neighbors, talk to your family members, talk to your co-workers, and make sure nobody takes a pass on November 7th. Thank you, and God bless you all.[38]

None of these church talks in an election week had anything to do with religion. When Scripture was mentioned, it was tied to politics. In two of the three talks, there are literally no religious statements.

Moving back through the years, we see that some of Clinton's church talks were not as blatantly political. Speaking to the Metropolitan Baptist Church in Washington, D.C., in December 1997, he hewed to more religious themes, quoting New Testament books including Ephesians. Evoking Ronald Reagan, he spoke of the capital as a shining city on a hill.[39]

In other church speeches, however, Clinton was more overtly political. Speaking at the Metropolitan Baptist Church in Newark, New Jersey, in October 1997, the president gave a major campaign speech. A number of New Jersey politicians were there—a state senator, a mayor, a U.S. representative. He gave a pitch for State Senator Jim McGreevey, who was running for higher office. He also used Scripture to speak of a political vision. "The Scripture says," said Clinton, "'Where there is no vision, the people perish.'"[40]

A year earlier, during the campaign season, he had given a speech at another Baptist church in Newark, where he was joined by two congressmen, including senatorial candidate Robert Torricelli and two mayors—all Democrats. Clinton claimed:

> God's work must be our own. And there are many questions before us now in this last presidential election of the 20th century, and the first presidential election of the 21st century. You know them all: Will we have more jobs; will we have better education; will we continue to expand health care; will we give the little children that came to the airport to visit me today a cleaner environment to grow up in? . . . Our obligation is to help each other live up to what God meant us to be.[41]

The election, said the Democratic president, was about "God's work."

Other Clinton church speeches came during the 1996 election year.[42] In one address given at St. Monica's Episcopal Church in Washington, D.C., he warned that Republicans were seeking to take food from elderly people:

> Across this great country of ours, there are seniors like you and others who depend upon meals like this that are federally funded. In one year alone, more than 230 million of these meals are served to seniors all across America. And for a lot of seniors, this is the only really good, warm, nutritious meal they get every day. Now, these meals are one of the things that are threatened by the shutdown that was forced by the Republicans in the House of Representatives.[43]

President Clinton often advocated federal policy in churches. During the 1994 midterm election year, he made the following remarks at the Full Gospel A.M.E. (African Methodist Episcopal) Zion Church in Temple Hills, Maryland:

> I came here because your church stands for what our country ought to be and where it ought to go. I came here because the Bible says that good Christians are also supposed to be good citizens. And I ask you this whole week to pray for me and pray for the members of Congress, ask us not to turn away from our ministry. Our ministry is to do the work of God here on Earth. . . . And I ask you to pray and to speak to your friends and neighbors and to hope somehow we will all find the wisdom and the judgment to come back and do the will of God in our ministries, which is to make you as safe as we possibly can.[44]

This was a pitch for the Crime Bill, which, Clinton told fellow Methodists, Republicans had walked away from. God, in Clinton's judgments, wanted the Crime Bill. It was His will and the "ministry" of Clinton and the Democrats, whom "good Christians" ought to support.

Another such address occurred on September 25, 1994, at the Bethel A.M.E. Church in New York City. Aside from White House staff, it featured eight Democratic politicians, including Governor Mario Cuomo and New York City Public Advocate Mark Green. Cuomo and Green are nationally known liberals adamant about separating church and state. Cuomo, in particular, has taken great pains to describe how he, as a Catholic, can be pro-choice on abortion because as a politician he must separate his faith from his politics.

Clinton began his remarks with a tribute to Cuomo: "How many times in the Bible—I think two or three times—does our Savior say, 'A prophet is not without honor except in his own land'? Most places would give anything to have a leader like Governor Cuomo." He then compared his administration to that of Reagan and the earlier Bush:

> How long did we hear from our Government that the real answer to all of our problems was, bad-mouth the Federal Government, lower taxes on the wealthiest of Americans, burden the middle class, reduce investment in our future, and explode the debt? And all the time, the people that were in cussed the Government as they were doing their best to stay in the Government and keep drawing those checks. That happened for twelve years, right?

Earlier in the service, the pastor had quoted Isaiah: "They that wait upon the Lord shall renew their strength. They will mount up with wings as eagles." Clinton read the rest of that verse to the congregation: "They shall run and not grow weary. They shall walk and not faint." He used the verse to motivate the worshipers to vote. On Election Day, he did not want them to "be weary and stay home and not mount up with wings as eagles, not run or walk without growing weary or fainting." He read a New Testament verse from Paul's letter to the Galatians, which he again employed to exhort the faithful to vote for the New York Democrats gathered around the pulpit. He urged:

> Show up. Talk to the people in your neighborhoods; tell them to show up. Scripture says we're supposed to be good citizens, too. Mario Cuomo is the heart that you must not lose. . . . These people [Democrat politicians] are the heart that you must not lose. . . . Stay strong, mount up, go forward. God bless you.[45]

Yet another notable Clinton church address came in November 1993 at the Church of God in Christ in Memphis, Tennessee. Congregants included a governor, a mayor, and six members of Congress. Clinton told the congregation:

> By the grace of God and your help, last year I was elected President of this great country. . . . We want to pass a health care bill that will make drug treatment available for everyone. . . . We need this crime bill now. . . . Scripture says, you are the salt of the Earth and the light of the world. That if your light shines before men they will give glory to the Father in heaven. That is what we must do. . . .
>
> So in this pulpit, on this day, let me ask all of you in your heart to say we will . . . somehow by God's grace, we will turn this around. We will give these children a future. We will take away their guns and give them books. We will take away their despair and give them hope. We will rebuild the families and the neighborhoods and the communities. We won't make all the work that has gone on here benefit just a few. We will do it together by the grace of God.[46]

Such church talks occurred throughout Clinton's presidency—and scores of Democratic politicians, public officials, and White House staff accompanied the president. None included Republican candidates; these were purely partisan talks that endorsed one party.

Not every Clinton speech in a church was political, and some of those that avoided partisanship were quite moving—particularly remarks at two memorial services in 1995 and 1996.[47] Yet no politician in modern times melded politics and religion as freewheelingly as Bill Clinton did.[48] Bush supporters might best pray for the same tolerance. Thus far, however, they need not worry: The *Presidential Documents* list only three incidences of Bush speaking in a church through his first three years in office[49]—and none of these appearances involved vote pushing or campaign rallying.[50]

By contrast, Clinton spoke in churches twenty-one times. Of these, more than half (twelve) came in election years.[51] In a separate category, Clinton spoke an added eight times at the National Cathedral. All were memorial services that presidents routinely attend. He kept politics out. Bush, for his part, has spoken at the National Cathedral once, for a September 11 memorial service.

Clinton's campaigning in churches did not end with his presidency. On September 14, 2003, he appeared at the First A.M.E. Church in South Central Los Angeles with California Governor Gray Davis, who was facing a possible recall. The Democratic governor had been appearing in churches for at least a year. His campaign candidly explained the reason for the appearances: "The Governor was at the First AME Church in Los Angeles to urge increased voter participation," said a press release by the Governor Gray Davis Committee. "This coming Sunday," it added, "the Governor will address the congregation at the West Angeles Church of God in Christ to encourage them to vote."[52]

Though Davis was no rookie at this kind of thing, he knew where to find the help of a veteran. He appeared with former President Clinton at the South Central Los Angeles Church of Pastor Cecil Murray, described by CNN as "a prominent recall opponent" who "urged his parishioners to vote to keep Davis in office." "We are his [Davis's] posse," the reverend told his flock. Clinton eagerly campaigned for Governor Davis at the church.[53]

HILLARY RODHAM CLINTON AND AL GORE IN CHURCHES

Bill Clinton was hardly alone in trying to rally votes in churches. So did Vice President Al Gore and First Lady Hillary Rodham Clinton. On the eve of the 2000 election, all three of these top Democrats barnstormed churches seeking votes.

While George W. Bush made routine campaign stops in Florida on November 5, senatorial candidate Hillary Rodham Clinton appeared at as many New York churches as she could. "In a day of gospel and politics," began an article in the *New York Times*, "Hillary Rodham Clinton preached and prayed her way through seven churches in seven hours yesterday, moving to close out her campaign by urging black parishioners in New York City to turn out to support her tomorrow." From the Bronx to Queens to Brooklyn, said the *Times*, at churches large and small, the first lady "pleaded and cajoled churchgoers to vote the Democratic line. . . . The same striking scene was repeated again and again throughout the day." "It would be a shame if we stayed at home this Tuesday," Mrs. Clinton shouted into a microphone at the center of the massive Allen A.M.E. Church in Queens. Then, after putting down the microphone, she said, "One more church, one more rally." The Reverend Charles E. Betts Sr. proclaimed, "God is raising up another woman of God."[54]

Usually sensitive to church-state separation, the *New York Times* seemed unbothered by this blurring of the lines. Reporter Adam Nagourney wrote enthusiastically of the "rustle of excitement and raised hands and swell of organ music and gospel song" that accompanied the first lady. His article ran beside a picture of an African-American woman from a Bronx church holding a sign that read ALL SOULS TO THE POLLS.

Similarly, Vice President Gore campaigned in a number of churches in the closing days of the 2000 campaign—mostly African-American churches in Detroit, Memphis, Pittsburgh, and Philadelphia, where his message was clear: A victory by George W. Bush would be a calamity for black Americans. In a Detroit Baptist church on October 29, he was introduced by the Reverend Charles Adams as a defender of civil rights—in contrast to Bush, whom Adams described as a protector of the wealthy. With an uncanny accuracy that no one else foresaw, Gore correctly informed African-American worshipers that they possessed "the ability to decide this close election."[55]

From there, the vice president traveled south to his home state of Tennessee, where he addressed a congregation in Memphis. There, he boiled down the choice between him and Bush as one between good and evil. "Deep within us," said Gore, "we each have the capacity for good and evil. I am taught that good overcomes evil if we choose that outcome. I feel it coming. I feel a message from this gathering that on Tuesday we're going to carry Tennessee and Memphis is going to lead the way." It was up to the worshipers to ensure that evil—which, Gore hinted, would involve a Bush victory—would not prevail.[56]

Moving on to Pittsburgh, on Saturday, November 4, Gore held a rally at the Wesley A.M.E. Zion Church. He was introduced by Pastor Glenn Grayson, who told his congregants: "It's Saturday night, but I've got a Sunday feeling! And I'm here to agitate and encourage African-Americans to vote." He prophesied that the African-American vote could sway the election on Tuesday. Gore then ascended the pulpit. "Then they rose up like a mighty army and they went to the polls!" he yelled to a crowd of over one thousand. "Let us vote together on Tuesday." As he had before other African-American audiences, Gore pointed to the murder of James Byrd Jr., a black

Texan dragged to his death by three white men in 1998.[57] Gore then warned the congregation about the kind of law and justice he believed they could expect under a Bush presidency—suggesting that more James Byrds would be killed if the Texas governor became president. He also warned of the strict constructionist judges Bush might appoint—harking back to an earlier era, when strict constructionists insisted that black Americans be considered three-fifths of a person.[58]

Gore's dire admonition frightened the worshipers. "I'm concerned now about the future of my kids," said Raushana Ellison, twenty-three, of Pittsburgh's Hill District. Though she had been registered to vote for five years, Ellison had never voted before. Now, however, she would run to the voting booth. Also attending Gore's church talk was sixty-seven-year-old Willa Mae Tot of the Overbrook section of Pittsburgh, who was now worried about Bush and the Republicans: "Their decisions will affect our children and grandchildren. That's who we have to look out for now."[59]

The next day, just two days before the election, Gore was in Philadelphia; there he appeared with James Byrd's sister, who described in vivid detail her brother's mutilation. The graphic moment was described by the *New York Times* as "the emotional high point" of Gore's day; the Texas murder during Bush's governorship, the *Times* reported, was how Gore "rallied his base." Gore also politicked in two black churches in Philadelphia. At the Mount Carmel Baptist Church he told his audience that their votes would decide whether America would move "toward inclusion" and "toward justice."[60] Then he headed to the Morris Brown A.M.E. Church, where he told churchgoers: "There is an old African proverb—when you pray, move your feet. Tuesday is the day to move your feet."[61]

These three leading Democrats—the sitting president, sitting vice president, and sitting first lady—made more church appearances in one campaign week than George W. Bush did in his entire presidency. Furthermore, Al Gore and Bill and Hillary Clinton spoke exclusively to *Christian* congregations, not reaching out to mosques and synagogues.

Conceding that liberals apply "a bit of a double standard" to Republicans like Bush, Barry Lynn explains, "Republicans have a long history of seeking votes on a religious basis." Mark Pelavin, associate director for the Religious Action Center of Reformed Judaism, agrees; he says that liberals become upset by Republicans' talk of faith because Republicans have a history of using religion for politically partisan purposes.[62]

Yet Democrats have a history every bit as rich. They have long brought their faith into their politics—a line runs from Wilson and FDR to Clinton and current Democratic presidential candidates. The better question is why there is zero tolerance for similar thinking or remarks when they leave the lips of George W. Bush.

11.

Saddam

"Three whom God should not have created: Persians, Jews, and flies."

—*Saddam Hussein family proverb*

If George W. Bush's opponents were uncomfortable with presidential prayer and Bible studies, they were about to become apoplectic over his next stop in the War on Terror: as 2002 drew to a close, the president was preparing to send his troops to Baghdad.

Under the surface, in this period, a tempest was brewing in the policy rooms of the White House. The Bush administration concluded that in the long war ahead the surest way to prevent future September 11 tragedies was to act preemptively. Such a course was chosen because the Bush team assessed the new enemy as one that could not be deterred. Unlike America's Cold War foe, this one embraced death as service to Allah and a ticket to paradise, and pointed to the Koran itself as the source for such a view.

It can be argued that preemptive action against terrorists and the nations that harbor them is not really preemption, but rather the only response to a war begun by terrorists against the United States long ago—certainly since at least the attack on the U.S. military barracks in Beirut, Lebanon, on October 23, 1983, which killed 241 Marines. Nonetheless, with preemptive thinking in mind, on September 17, 2002, the Bush administration publicly released "The National Security Strategy of the United States of America" (the "NSS"). The report came one year to the week after the attacks on the World Trade Center and Pentagon—that inspired it. Assessing the bold new doctrine, Yale professor and Cold War historian John Lewis Gaddis claimed that the strategy represented the "most sweeping shift in grand U.S. strategy" since the *beginning* of the Cold War. In scale and significance, he called it a "truly *grand* strategy."[1]

The NSS laid out a legal basis for preemption, stating that international law recognizes "that nations need not suffer an attack before they can lawfully take action to defend themselves against forces that present an imminent danger of attack."[2] The NSS states that the Bush administration would always seek to act multilaterally—"to enlist the support of the international community." Yet, said the NSS, the United States "will not hesitate to act alone, if necessary, to exercise our right of self-defense by acting preemptively against such terrorists, to prevent them from doing harm against our people and our country."

This drama would be played out in Iraq in 2003, as George W. Bush sought out the most ruthless terrorist of them all—Saddam Hussein. Here, too, some argued that Iraq had long ago targeted and killed Americans, and thus a U.S. invasion should not be considered preemptive. Yet the primary intent of a war in Iraq would be to head off a perceived possible disaster down the road, making it preemptive in the broadest sense. Moreover, the NSS included a less noticed but

equally ambitious—indeed, monumental—long-term goal: the ultimate means of removing Middle Eastern tyrants and the terrorism
they support, it argued, was to spread democracy. "Freedom," the report opened, repeating Bush's constant refrain, is "the birthright of
every person."

The United States had imposed democracy at the tip of a bayo-
net in Japan after World War II; from there it eventually spread to
other parts of Asia. The Bush team hoped the same might occur in
Iraq, perhaps replicating the pattern elsewhere in the Middle East.

The degree to which Bush's actions in Iraq (and earlier in
Afghanistan) were cemented in the NSS has been widely overlooked.
And most unappreciated is the extent to which the strategy—though
carefully crafted by a team and infused with the thinking of advisers
like Condoleezza Rice—is a direct by-product of Bush's own worldview.

And it should be understood in particular that the National Security Strategy carries Bush's imprint with regard to religion: Quite
unusually for a security document, from its first paragraph the NSS
speaks repeatedly of freedom of worship. Building on earlier Bush
pronouncements in May and June 2001, it advocates "religious tolerance" and declares that America will "take special efforts to promote
freedom of religion and conscience and defend it from encroachment
by repressive governments." The invocation of religious freedom as
an explicit goal in such a formal policy document is unprecedented.
And it would become reality in Iraq in 2003.

GEORGE W. BUSH'S EXPERIENCES WITH SADDAM HUS-
sein have long been deeply personal, predating his presidency by a decade. On April 14, 1993, a group of Iraqi terrorists put the final
touches on a 170-pound bomb, equipped with a radio-controlled

firing system, built into the body panels of a Toyota Landcruiser and smuggled the vehicle into Kuwait in the dark of night. The vehicle was positioned at Kuwait University, where it was poised to take the life of ex-President George H. W. Bush during a three-day visit honoring him for liberating Kuwait two years earlier.

The plot failed. The Kuwaiti government arrested sixteen people, including eleven Iraqi nationals. The Kuwaitis eventually identified two vehicles loaded with remote-controlled bombs. Altogether, several hundred pounds of explosives were seized. The explosives held enough firepower to kill not just the former president but also his entourage.[3]

"I was forced into this operation," later confessed one Iraqi saboteur, Raad al-Assadi. "Our regime does not permit us to object." His partner in crime was fellow Iraqi Wali Abdelhadi al-Ghazali, a male nurse by profession, who, in attempting to kill the former president, forsook any Hippocratic oath. He was the driver of a van packed with explosives. He was also instructed in how to detonate the Toyota. To ensure success, Ghazali was fitted with a belt packed with explosives—a suicide vest—if the vehicle bombs failed.[4]

There were two American responses to the incident.

When news of the botched assassination reached the new Clinton administration, one of those who was especially alarmed was Vice President Gore. Though he'd been on the job for only a few months, he was not naive to the implications of the plot. Though Iraq was suspected, its exact role was not immediately known. Yet even before the FBI and CIA reports were completed, Gore smelled a rat. He knew the foiled assassination attempt had Saddam's bloody fingerprints all over it, and he undertook his own personal inquiry into the plot.[5]

Saddam was behind this, Gore told Clinton. Doing nothing would make the freshman president appear weak and rekindle concerns that Democrats were too wishy-washy about employing force. He firmly steered the president, who had at the time no foreign-policy experience, toward retaliation, insisting that Iraq be punished. As *U.S. News & World Report* reported, Gore "concluded that retaliation was not only appropriate but required."[6]

On the weekend of June 25–27, 1993, the Clinton administration struck hard with a volley of missiles on Baghdad. The strike killed a number of Iraqis, but left Saddam in power and unscathed.

The Clinton administration did not seek UN approval for the strike—a fact that annoyed some UN Security Council members, including France's representative, Jean-Bernard Mérimée. They were bothered that the Clinton team proceeded on its own evidence, prior to the end of the trial of the saboteurs. Yet Madeleine Albright, U.S. ambassador to the United Nations, insisted that classified American intelligence confirmed that Saddam's regime was behind the plot. According to Albright, U.S. evidence alone was sufficient for U.S. unilateral action; UN approval was not necessary, and neither was any type of UN investigation. Albright, Clinton, and Gore were adamant: the United States did not need UN approval to use force against Iraq.[7]

The second American response to the assassination attempt sat two thousand miles away, out west. George W. Bush was seething. The Butcher of Baghdad had attempted to take the life of the man he idolized. "The SOB tried to kill my dad," he said later.[8]

Saddam would later target George W. as well, at least in an oblique way. In October 2002 he dispatched his vice president, Taha Yassin Ramadan, with this offer to the world: a duel between George W. Bush and Saddam Hussein, to be held at a neutral site with UN Secretary-General Kofi Annan as the referee.[9] Despite the antiquated gesture, there's every evidence that Saddam was deadly serious.

By the time Saddam made his visible overture, a line had been drawn in the sand. A real death struggle between the two gunslingers was about to ensue; only one man would win.

Two Lives

After September 11, President George W. Bush kept a personal list of most-wanted Al-Qaeda operatives in the top drawer of his Oval Office desk. When one of these evildoers was killed or captured, Bush, like a Dodge City sheriff, pulled out the list and, with quiet satisfaction, crossed out another name or face with a big X.[10] Late in 2002 he had added another name to the list: Saddam Hussein.

The lives of these two men were a study in contrasts. George W. was raised by loving parents and neighbors. He had a wonderful home with all the conveniences. Saddam Hussein, on the other hand, grew up barefoot in a mud hut. His parents—a woman named Subha Tulfah and father called Hussein al-Majid—were landless peasants who struggled through an impoverished life in the town of Tikrīt, some ninety miles north of Baghdad on the Tigris River.

George W. lionized his father; Saddam never met his. His father vanished a few months before Saddam was born, for reasons that remain mysterious. Some believe he was murdered by bandits. Others say he simply abandoned the family. Still others say he never really existed, that Saddam's mother was a village whore impregnated by an unknown sperm donor.[11] Saddam's mother was reportedly depressed by her husband's disappearance.

Things only got worse for Subha Tulfah. Saddam's thirteen-year-old brother died of a brain tumor in a Baghdad hospital only weeks before Saddam's birth. His mother became despondent to the point of suicide, and she tried to abort him. She made numerous attempts, some brazenly in the open, leaving bystanders aghast and in doubt about her sanity. In one instance, she jumped under a bus. A passerby quickly yanked her out of harm's way. One account claimed that on-lookers heard the deranged woman screaming: "I am giving birth to the devil!"[12] Some witnesses recall the horrible sight of the pregnant woman banging a door against her distended belly.

Against all odds, Saddam survived his mother's prenatal on-slaughts. When he was born, she gave him the name Saddam—meaning "the one who confronts." This sick, unloving woman produced a sick, unloving child.

At around the age of nine or ten, Saddam was orphaned. He did find a home, with a racist, politically radical, and highly disturbed un-cle. This substitute father helped forge the Saddam of history, becom-ing Saddam's role model.

Where George W. Bush's parents and faith taught him respect and tolerance of other creeds, Saddam learned just the opposite. When Saddam was an adolescent, his uncle published a pamphlet entitled "Three Whom God Should Not Have Created: Persians, Jews, and Flies." Saddam lived that credo. As a dictator in the late 1990s, he reissued his uncle's pamphlet. It was circulated throughout the nation.

Racism is one unappreciated component of Saddam's madness. It was a turn of mind he learned at home, where he was taught that God detested certain races. For generations, racists have cited God and the Bible to try to lend credibility to their bigotry. Saddam was one such figure.

Saddam Hussein grew to be an adolescent thug and teen gangster on his way to the job of young professional assassin. Early in life, he be-gan murdering his political opponents—the first victim a low-level lo-cal politician running for office against his uncle. He would ultimately set his sights much higher, organizing a group that overthrew Iraq's leader, paving the way for his own ascendancy to the top spot.

THE REPUBLIC OF FEAR

Saddam came to power in 1968; in an arrangement that must have tried his patience sorely, he shared the throne off and on for the next eleven years. Though technically second in the hierarchy, Saddam was often assumed to be in command. Absolute power came in July 1979, and so did megalomania. Saddam instantly transformed Iraq into a monument to himself. The dictator's visage was omnipresent—a giant banner here, a painted side of a building there. The Iraqi landscape was graced by giant gold-plated and bronze statues of the man from Tikrīt.

Saddam saw himself as a kind of biblical figure. From the outset, he pursued the grandiose goal of rebuilding the ancient biblical city of Babylon. This fit with his thinking of being the modern incarnation of Nebuchadnezzar, the most important of the Chaldean or neo-Babylonian kings, who ruled from 605 to 562 B.C. In 597 and 586, Jerusalem was besieged and captured by Nebuchadnezzar; the second time, the king destroyed the city and carried the Jews off into their Babylonian captivity. In Babylonia, and most conspicuously in Babylon itself, Nebuchadnezzar engaged in numerous extravagant building projects. Picking up the mantle some 2,500 years later, Saddam embarked on a $200 million remake of the ancient city of Babylon, in addition to the construction of his untold number (perhaps as many as sixty) of ornate personal palaces.

In this recreated Babylon, every tenth brick (among the 60 million) was inscribed "Babylon was rebuilt in the reign of Saddam Hussein," as they had once borne Nebuchadnezzar's name. This was

Saddam's most precious project—his apotheosis, his crowning touch—though it alone would not suffice to satiate his starved ego. It was also a futile attempt by the dictator to try to salvage some semblance of national pride for the Iraqi people, out of the refuse of the national degradation he had wrought.

Saddam invited the world to his spectacle. In the late 1980s, he began hosting an International Babylon Festival. Charles H. Dyer, professor of biblical exposition at Dallas Theological Seminary, attended the second festival in September 1988. The Bible, notes Dyer, forecasts Babylon's rebuilding, but also forecast that the rebuilt city would be quickly devastated in such magnitude that no single stone will ever be stacked there again. Both the Old and New Testaments prophesy Babylon's destruction.[13]

In seeking to reconstruct Nebuchadnezzar's vaunted city, Saddam had objectives of literal biblical proportions. The only man who stood to foil them was George W. Bush, a pious Texan who regularly asked God to use him as an instrument of His will.

With megalomania, Saddam's ascendancy to absolute power brought a river of blood. His inaugural came with a July 1979 address to the Iraqi parliament in which he called out the names of twenty-one alleged "plotters" against his government, all of whom were then summarily executed.[14] The nation's legislature watched in terror as the unfortunate were lifted one by one from their chairs and escorted to their graves. It was the start of the Republic of Fear.

For the next twenty-four years, nothing changed. From 1980 to 1988, a devastating war with Iran left over a million men dead. Chemical weapons were employed by Saddam on a scale not seen since World War I. He used them not just against Iranians but also on the defenseless Kurdish minority (including thousands of children) in his own nation. A couple of years after that campaign, in August 1990,

Saddam invaded Kuwait for its oil. His troops proceeded to rape Kuwait's natural resources and women and torture its men. In the process, he moved his troops to the border of Saudi Arabia, suggesting that he was going there next. Had he been successful in the enterprise, he would have single-handedly controlled the majority of the world's oil supplies—his grand objective.

The reaction of George H. W. Bush and the world community he rallied became known as Operation Desert Storm. In only six weeks—and despite predictions of mass U.S. casualties and "another Vietnam" from Democrats and war opponents—Iraqi troops were driven from Kuwait in a rout. Americans killed in the war numbered a little over one hundred; so many thousands of Iraqis were killed or wounded that to this day most figures are unreliable. George H. W. had denied Saddam his dream.

The night the war began, Billy Graham was at the White House. Graham spoke to the senior Bush and his staff about the importance of "a people of faith" turning to God for hope.[15] Speaking of wartime generally, and a war against Saddam specifically, George H. W. spoke words that must have rung indelibly in his son's ear: "One cannot be president of our country without faith in God. God is our rock and salvation, and we must trust him and keep faith in him."[16] Though he'd always been reticent and uncomfortable in discussing his faith, this was a sentiment the senior Bush shared more than once, claiming in November 1989: "Without God's help we can do nothing."[17]

During literally every year of Saddam's first decade in power, his nation had been at war, his own people brutalized at home. His regime's methods of torture were imaginative in their barbarity. Men were slowly fed, feet first, into giant industrial shredders (human meat grinders); women were hung upside down for hours in front of their families while they menstruated.[18] Iraq's women had a unique taste of hell: Hundreds of thousands were widowed by husbands who died in wars they were forced to join; some were beheaded in front of their children in one especially horrific Baathist campaign; others saw their children imprisoned in small cages; many were raped in front of their daughters and sons until their husbands talked. Videos of the grisly acts were taped for posterity and mailed to relatives.[19]

Torture was so pervasive during the regime of Saddam Hussein that it was imposed not just by men with guns but also by men with scalpels. In Iraq, doctors were forced to become torturers and executioners. Saddam's government mandated that all surgeons brand the heads and cut off the ears of army deserters. That was the price for any young soldier who refused to fight the Iranians, Kuwaitis, or Americans. In one hospital, every type of surgeon, from general to neurosurgeons, cardiac surgeons, and others, was required by a 1994 decree to perform this unique practice of mutilation. Surgeons who refused to brand skulls or amputate ears would themselves face branding and amputation.[20]

Some of the murders were performed by Saddam himself, as a routine part of his ongoing life of criminality. There were occasions over the decades in which he casually pulled his gun out of the holster and executed a cabinet member foolish enough to disagree with him.

With the help of his two unbelievably vicious sons, Uday and Qusay, Saddam imposed a vast reign of terror. When the Hussein regime was eventually toppled, Secretary of Defense Donald Rumsfeld said that Saddam now occupied his rightful place on the ash heap of history, alongside names like Hitler, Stalin, Pol Pot, and Ceauşescu.[21] George W. Bush correctly identified Saddam as a "student of Stalin."

Throughout this time, Saddam was also involved in pursuing and procuring weapons of mass destruction.[22] He acquired gallons of chemical and biological weapons. He used chemical arms and probably employed bioweapons in some form, possibly on groups like the Marsh Arabs, and almost certainly on human subjects. His arsenal of bioweapons was staggering, from anthrax to botulinum toxin to a dozen other agents. His country remains the only one in history to weaponize aflatoxin, a substance that slowly causes liver cancer and has no battlefield utility whatsoever; its "best" use is to give cancer to entire ethnic groups.

Much more elusive were nuclear weapons. Yet Saddam undertook herculean efforts to make Iraq a nuclear nation. In the mid-1990s, the United Nations Special Commission on Iraq (UNSCOM) learned that Saddam had an enormous nuclear weapons program that dated back to the 1970s. Spread among twenty-five facilities, it employed fifteen thousand technical people. Basing their research on a Manhattan Project bomb design, Iraqi scientists actually pursued five different methods for separating uranium. Saddam pumped $10 billion into the program.[23]

It was this relentless pursuit of weapons of mass destruction that forced the international community, through the United Nations, to apply sanctions on Iraq throughout the 1990s and beyond—from 1991 to 2003. These sanctions required Saddam to accept UN inspections of any and all suspect weapons facilities. As part of the 1991 Gulf War cease-fire, Saddam agreed to the inspections. But he quickly reneged on his promise, and inspectors endured endless cat-and-mouse games in trying to do their job. The inspectors eventually achieved notable success: By the mid-1990s they had found and destroyed an enormous amount of weapons. By the late 1990s, however, Saddam's regime was again obstructing inspectors at every turn; they had become too successful.

By December 1998, the Clinton administration had had enough, and once again unleashed a flurry of cruise missiles aimed at Iraqi military targets.

These strikes, which Clinton ordered repeatedly throughout the 1990s, were ineffective in stopping Iraq's pursuit of weapons of mass destruction. The strikes may have destroyed buildings and killed Iraqis but they failed to uproot Saddam and his regime.

The sanctions were equally ineffective. They did prevent a large amount of money from flowing into Saddam's hands—funds he would have funneled into his arms. But they also killed thousands of innocent Iraqi civilians. They did not, and could not, end the nightmare: Saddam and his rule. That was never their intention.

Throughout this time, Saddam continued to support terrorism. In April 2002—almost exactly one year before he would flee from American tanks—he publicly upped the payment from $10,000 to $25,000 for the families of Palestinian suicide bombers who blew themselves up in the service of killing Israel's Jews. Abu Abbas and Abu Nidal, probably the two most wanted terrorist ringleaders of the last twenty years, were both living with safe haven in Baghdad. Hundreds of bin Laden's Al-Qaeda members were operating throughout Iraq. Saddam operated his own terror camps. One of the most chilling was a clandestine facility south of Baghdad called Salman Pak, which drew attention after September 11 when it was reported that terrorists there (prior to September 11) had conducted training missions on an actual 707 fuselage, where they practiced the art of hijacking an aircraft without guns, using only knives and utensils. Just like the September 11 hijackers (possibly coincidentally), these terrorists were allegedly of Egyptian and, predominantly, Saudi origin. Satellite photos of Salman Pak were published and circulated widely.[24]

These reports led to speculation that Saddam might have

collaborated with the masterminds of September 11, and at the very least that he had a pre-9/11 relationship with bin Laden and Al-Qaeda. Articles on a potential nexus appeared in publications that traverse the ideological spectrum, including serious sources like *The New Yorker* and *The New York Times*.[25] To this day, reports of alleged links continue to surface, especially as information flows from Iraqi officials interrogated since the U.S. invasion of Iraq.[26] The Bush administration, however, has been extremely cautious in openly asserting that Saddam was in any way behind September 11.[27] Rather, the president's team has preferred to argue that Saddam was *capable* of sponsoring a 9/11-style attack, and that such a possibility was an unacceptable danger that further merited his removal.

BUSH RATIONALE FOR OPERATION IRAQI FREEDOM

After 9/11, George W. Bush memorably said that the attacks had "changed everything," including how the United States should view Saddam.[28] It brought home the sobering reality of American vulnerability. It demonstrated that America's enemies hate it enough to do more than just burn the stars and stripes in a Middle East capital. It showed that terrorists with financial backing, whether from a wealthy transnational criminal or a regime in a nation like Iraq or Iran, could wreak havoc on the American way of life. Worse, it kindled thoughts of the devastation possible not only by terrorists using commercial airplanes but by men equipped with real bombs and, one day, with weapons of mass destruction (WMD).

Saddam's pursuit of such weapons and sponsorship of terrorism—and, most crucial, the inability of the world to stop him—were the two primary reasons George W. Bush decided to invade Iraq in 2003.

There were four publicly articulated reasons: (1) the suspected *presence* of WMD; (2) Saddam's past and potential use of WMD; (3) his support of terrorism; and (4) the liberation of Iraqis from the atrocities they endured for decades. The Bush administration stuck to this script in explaining its war rationale.

A fifth reason that was equally significant—and more prominent in the president's statements after the war—was the notion that removing Saddam might enable the development of democracy in Iraq, sowing the seed for further democratization in the Middle East. Was this a utopian goal for a nation like Iraq? Not necessarily: Iraq, prior to Saddam's rampage, was one of the most liberal, cosmopolitan nations in the Middle East. If any culture in the region had the slightest chance of building a democracy, and a corresponding chance at freedom, it was Iraq. This fifth reason was seen in the Bush administration's National Security Strategy.

Among the main reasons, the fourth—liberating Iraqis from human rights atrocities—was not necessarily as instrumental as the others, since human rights alone are rarely considered a sufficient justification for an invasion. Still, the human rights factor should hardly be discounted. To the 24 million Iraqi people who withstood decades of mass degradation and mass graves, this was the one reason that mattered most.

An illustration was the experience of the human shields. These were war protesters who traveled to Iraq from the West, particularly from the United States and Britain, in late 2002 to try to block the Bush and Blair governments from pursuing war. One of them was Reverend Kenneth Joseph, a young American pastor with the Assyrian Church of the East. When he arrived, Joseph was sickened as Iraqis quietly told him about the human shredders—"people put in a huge shredder for plastic products," Joseph later described, "feet first so they could hear their screams as bodies got chewed up from foot to head."[29]

Joseph said his visit shocked him back to reality. Angry Iraqis slipped him aside and read him the riot act: "They told me they would commit suicide if American bombing didn't start. They were willing to see their homes demolished to gain their freedom from Saddam's bloody tyranny. They convinced me that Saddam was a monster the likes of which the world had not seen since Stalin and Hitler." Iraqis told him: "Only war will get us out of our present condition. . . . Everything will be all right when the war is over. No matter how bad it is, we will not all die." They went on: "We cannot wait anymore. We want the war, and we want it now. . . . Please bring on the war. We may lose our lives, but for our children's sake, please, please end our misery."[30] (A Gallup poll after the war confirmed this assessment: by a margin of 62 to 30 percent, residents of Baghdad said the ousting of Saddam was worth the wartime hardships; in Sadr City, the margin was 78 to 16 percent.[31]) Tears streamed down the startled pastor's face as guilt overwhelmed him. "How dare I claim to speak for [these] people?" he bitterly reproached himself.

The same was experienced by Daniel Pepper, a twenty-three-year-old American photographer living in London. He and a friend headed to Iraq to serve as shields. When they got there, Iraqis reprimanded them: "Of course the Americans don't want to bomb civilians. They want to bomb the government and Saddam's palaces. We want America to bomb Saddam." As Pepper was lectured by a taxi driver who described Saddam's horrors, his friend shook his head and repeatedly muttered, "Oh, my God." Pepper said "it hadn't occurred" to him and his friend that Iraqis might actually be pro-war. He said the taxi driver's most emphatic statement was: "All Iraqi people want this war."[32]

The total number of Saddam's victims is unclear. Once he was gone, Gallup tried to get an idea through polling. Baghdad residents were asked a bizarre survey question: whether a member of their *household* had been executed by Saddam's regime. A ghastly 6.6 percent said yes. Based on that percentage, Gallup estimated that 61,000 individuals *in Baghdad alone* had been killed under Saddam. Execution, Gallup aptly noted, was Saddam's chief weapon of mass destruction.[33] For the record, various authorities, from the U.S. administrative authority in Iraq to human rights groups like Amnesty International to the exiled Iraqi National Congress, estimate that anywhere from 300,000 to 1 million Iraqis were shot and shoveled into mass graves.

RELIGIOUS REPRESSION IN IRAQ

Also of keen interest to George W. Bush was religious repression under Saddam. Saddam was literally responsible for the deaths of more Muslims—from his own people to Kurds to Marsh Arabs to Iranians to Kuwaitis—than any other man walking the face of the earth. Still, by resisting the United States and launching Scud missiles at Jews in Israel, he had endeared himself to much of the Arab world, despite his treatment of Iraq's Muslim women, its Muslim minorities, and its Muslim neighbors.

One of Saddam's methods of ingratiating himself to Arabs was his Faith Campaign. Begun in 1996, this was Saddam's attempt to wrap himself publicly in the green-and-white Muslim flag, exploiting Islam for political purposes. (During the Gulf War, Saddam had inscribed the words *Allah Akbar*, or "God is great," on the Iraqi flag.) He could be seen on television daily kneeling in prayer facing Mecca. He constructed an elaborate $7.5 million "Mother of All Battles" mosque in Baghdad, surrounded by minarets shaped like Scud missiles, and sought to make Saddam University an educational mecca for advanced Islamic studies. The state increased religious instruction and provided religious scholarships. Koranic studies became mandatory in high schools. Saddam was even said to have donated twelve quarts of his own blood as "ink" for a large-type, 605-page copy of the Koran.[34]

This abuse of Islam for political purposes was not new. Saddam's regime hid weapons in mosques, and during Operation Iraqi Freedom, his military fired upon U.S. troops from inside mosques. Non-Muslim/non-Arabic American and British soldiers honored the mosques by refusing to return fire.

The reality is that certain ethnic and religious groups were targeted not merely for persecution but extermination, in many cases because of their faith. Iraq's more than 14 million Shiite Muslims faced severe restrictions. Saddam enacted a ban on communal Friday prayer for Shiites, whose numbers make them Iraq's majority faith.[35] He also halted circulation of books from Shiite mosque libraries. Even Shiite funeral processions—not to mention media activities and other religious rites, pilgrimages, and observances, including the holy month of Muharram—were restricted or banned by Saddam's regime. Countless Shiite clerics and leaders were arrested, imprisoned, tortured, and executed; their mosques were desecrated, their property confiscated, their families ripped apart. Following the 1991 insurrection in southern Iraq, as many as sixty thousand Shiites were killed. Freedom House reported: "Iraq's policy of eliminating senior Shi'a clerics threatened the very future of Shi'ism in Iraq."

Christians also faced persecution. Importation of Christian literature was limited or halted altogether, as was evangelization, and Christian schools were closed down by the state. Christians who married Muslims were required to convert to Islam. Unofficial discrimination existed in employment practices, and Christians in Basra complained of threats they would be raped, kidnapped, or killed for their faith. Some Christian minorities faced forced relocation. As recently as 2002, the Iraqi government issued a law that placed all Christian clergy and churches under the control of the Ministry of Islamic Property.[36]

SANCTIONS, JUST WAR, AND NONWAR

America's final step toward war with Iraq came when the Bush administration concluded that the United States had exhausted all peaceful alternatives. The word *peaceful* should be used guardedly. The world had spent twelve years pursuing alternatives to war, including the implementation of history's most rigorous sanctions regimen. No country had ever been subjected to so many different forms of sanctions so comprehensively by so many nations. Walter Russell Mead of the Council on Foreign Relations, citing well-known figures from the United Nations (namely UNICEF), noted that sanctions against Iraq—which supporters viewed as a policy of containment that was preferable to war—were responsible for the deaths of five thousand Iraqi children under the age of five each month, mostly through the deprivation of vital food and medicine. This alleged death toll of sixty thousand children per year continued throughout the sanctions period.[37] If those UN numbers are accurate, containing Saddam for another ten years would kill hundreds of thousands of additional Iraqi children. In all, the sanctions could have taken the lives of over one million Iraqi youth, without ever threatening Saddam's regime. (By comparison, says Mead, the Gulf War killed twenty-one thousand to thirty-five thousand Iraqis.) In short, the sanctions route was not peaceful; such containment enabled slaughter of the innocent.[38]

In addition, by not employing force to remove Saddam—the only option that would actually expel him from power—thousands more Iraqis would be maimed and killed. Saddam in power was also not a peaceful prospect to the neighbors he had invaded and fired upon over the years. The White House feared a still worse nonpeaceful scenario: Saddam with WMD.

Most important, the peace option never meant an absence of military action: for eight years, the Clinton administration had punished Saddam's noncompliance with air strikes against suspect WMD facilities and governmental buildings. Each time, the international community became more fractured and, worse, more Iraqi innocents were killed. These strikes could not and did not remove Saddam himself; they never had that intent. As long as Saddam remained in power, these bombings would continue. While this, too, was an alternative to a U.S. invasion, it was hardly peaceful.

Exhausting all peaceful alternatives is a fundamental condition of just-war doctrine, which comes from Augustine, a fourth- to fifth-century church father canonized by the Catholic church, and one of history's most prominent Christian theologians. His ruminations on everything from salvation to the Trinity to free will remain required reading for the serious seminarian. His just-war doctrine was an influential interpretation of the conditions under which war could be said to be biblically, morally, and ethically just.

Some Christians, particularly liberal ones, insisted that a war in Iraq did not meet just-war standards. Yet for each such claim, there was a counterassertion. The debate was complicated by the preemptive aspect of U.S. action. Among those interviewed for this book, for every Christian (usually a liberal) who maintained that preemptive war did not meet just-war standards, there was another Christian (usually a conservative) who retorted just as strongly that Augustine's just-war doctrine does *not* preclude preemptive action.

Conservative Christians were exasperated with this criticism. "The doves have hijacked just-war theory to justify their pacifism," said one professor who teaches the doctrine. "They are ramming it down our throats to protest what they believe is a preemptive war. However, just-war doctrine does not preclude preemption. No way. They are butchering the theory for their own purposes."[39]

Within that quote is a provocative thought—"what they *believe* is a preemptive war." Many war supporters believed that an invasion of Iraq, pursued to remove Saddam, did not constitute preemption, since Saddam had attacked and killed Americans before, and had tried to assassinate a former president. He had shot and gassed people of many nationalities, inside and outside his country, and was a sponsor of terrorism. The Bush team had declared a war on terrorism, and in a war against terror, Saddam had long ago become an active enemy.

One such thinker was Richard Land, president of the Southern Baptist Convention's Ethics and Religious Liberty Commission. Land spearheaded a letter of support for Bush policy, which was endorsed by a number of high-profile conservative Christians, including D. James Kennedy, president of Coral Ridge Ministry; Prison Fellowship's Chuck Colson; and Bill Bright of Campus Crusade for Christ. Land argued that military force against Saddam was defensive in light of Saddam's previous actions. Thus, it would be a "just cause."

David Earle Anderson, the liberal editor of Religion News Service, dubbed Land's reasoning "his spin on just-war theory."[40] Anderson was not alone in that view, as we will see. Moreover, this theological disagreement was mild compared to the rancor ahead.

12.

God and War in Iraq

"President Bush: Your war would violate the
teachings of Jesus Christ."

—New York Times *ad by Religious Leaders
for Sensible Priorities, December 2002[1]*

"I cannot profess Christ as my Savior and simultaneously support preemptive war. I can deny Jesus and support war but I will not."

—Jim Winkler, United Methodist Church, on
the war in Iraq, February 26, 2003[2]

As war swirled amid the desert sands of Iraq in early 2003, each
side dug in—and not just the military divisions. The debate
over war was intense. Also under fire during this time—a war target
itself—was George W. Bush's religious faith.

Bush's faith took heat in a number of ways during this period.
One came in the six weeks preceding the mid-March invasion:

Reporters raised questions of wartime political motivations in Bush's invocations of God. Several such articles appeared in influential publications like the New York Times, Washington Post, and Newsweek.

In the February 9, 2003, New York Times, Laurie Goodstein reported: "The president continues to talk and lead like a preacher. In recent weeks, there has been growing debate over whether the president's use of faith has gone too far." As she observed, "Over the last two weeks, President George W. Bush has delivered several speeches laced with references to his religious beliefs."[3]

Bush had indeed recently delivered several such speeches; it was the time of year when the National Religious Broadcasters held its annual convention and when the National Prayer Breakfast convened. Each year at that time, presidents speak at these religious venues and make religious references. In addition, the Columbia space shuttle tragedy had recently occasioned a statement of remembrance for the Columbia victims—one in which Bush mentioned God, as most presidents would.

Bush's references to God in this period were no more frequent than usual. According to the Presidential Documents, in January and February 2003, Bush made twenty-eight speeches or statements in which he mentioned God. In January/February 2001, he made twenty-nine such mentions; notably, that period began after Bush's January 20 inauguration. In that short January, Bush had mentioned God twenty-two times. By comparison, in all of January 2003, the period covered by Goodstein's article, there were only eleven statements—half his 2001 total. If anything, the president was cutting back on his references to God.

It was also suggested that Bush's alleged increased religious talk was politically motivated because of the war. "With war in Iraq looming, and much of the world opposed to his position," reported the

Washington Post's Dana Milbank on February 10, "the president in re-cent weeks has adopted a strongly devotional tone. In a series of speeches . . . Bush has far more openly embraced Christian theology."[4]

On the contrary, the tone Bush had adopted was strikingly non-denominational. The *Columbia* statement contained one religious reference, from the Old Testament. Milbank focused on the presi-dent's February 10 address to the National Religious Broadcasters' (NRB) Convention in Nashville. As to Christ-specific comments, Milbank cited none from Bush. Instead, he quoted Christians who in-troduced Bush at the NRB in a Christian way. "President Bush has addressed countless audiences as a commander in chief," began Mil-bank. "Today, he was introduced as 'our friend and brother in Christ.'" Milbank's next line noted that Bush spoke before a back-drop that read "Advancing Christian Communications." Bush's Christian hosts made their Christianity clear.

What was notable is that Bush did not. Milbank's article was no-tably devoid of any Bush references to Jesus Christ at the convention—because the president managed to speak to the NRB without once mentioning Christ. Perhaps mindful that he wanted to avoid the kind of article that Milbank had written, Bush left out his philosopher-king. Christians might have wondered why a committed brother like George W. did not utter their Lord's name. Ironically, Bush's clearly conscious effort not to mention his Savior was the only thing unusual about his appearance at the convention. Otherwise, he spoke of faith-based programs and made the usual points he makes at religious gatherings. Despite Milbank's assertion, it was not at all a "strikingly religious address" by Bush.[5]

Other articles at the time implied that Bush's religious outspo-kenness, and perhaps even the origins of his faith itself, had political roots.

In a March 10 cover story for *Newsweek*, Howard Fineman reported: "Bush turned to the Bible to save his marriage and his family. But was he also thinking of smoothing his path to elective office? We'll never know for sure."[6] Fineman, a fair and talented Bush observer, devoted a full section suggesting Bush may have done just that.

Newsweek doubled the political-motivation point: alongside Fineman's feature was a piece by theologian Martin E. Marty. In the second paragraph, Marty wrote of Bush: "On the path to the presidency he saw that his newfound faith appealed to a core constituency of religious conservatives and they appealed to him. His religious rhetoric became more public and more political."[7]

With such suspicions now part of mainstream reporting, others followed suit. "George W. Bush and Jesus are pals," began Michelle Cottle in *The New Republic*. The president was suddenly "employing 'God talk' more and more often in the run-up to war." She said that people were "uneasy by Bush's conviction that God is on our side" and, generally, "Bush's wartime God-talk."[8]

Such skeptical articles in major secular publications did not grace the cover of religious publications like *Christianity Today* or *World* magazine; nor was there such speculation on the nation's hundreds of Christian radio stations.

The effect of these explosive claims was grave. The *New York Times*'s dispatches become headlines for the rest of the media. The full impact of these articles was reflected by left-wing Web sites. Many Bush-bashing sites spewed vitriol over "the fact" that Bush was marshaling religion solely for political purposes, shamelessly employing his faith to kindle the flames of war. The seething hatred of Bush that now exists in liberal circles solidified in this period.

Bush bristles at the suggestion that his faith is politically motivated. "I don't bring God into my life to be a political person," he insists.[9] Those who know him resent the charge. "He is actually very sensitive about wearing his faith on his sleeve," says Brian Berry. "He knows that you shouldn't do that." Berry claims that Bush's frequent invocation of God and prayer stems from the fact that it is so much a part of him—and is highlighted, perhaps unfairly, because others—especially secular reporters—constantly ask about it.[10]

Others have come to Bush's defense. David Gergen, who served both Republican and Democratic administrations, including the Clinton White House, assured *The New York Times*: "I've seen presidents in the past who wear their religion on their sleeve as a political gesture, but that's not what we're seeing here."[11]

The Religious War

There were numerous protests against George W. Bush's war policy in Iraq, including a heated debate among spiritual believers. Here are both sides:

Supportive Christians, usually conservatives, spoke of Bush's being chosen for the moment. Asked in February 2003 if she felt that Bush seemed chosen by God for "this moment in history," Janet Parshall replied, "As a Christian, I think that. It sounds political to say that, but it does seem true to me. I think that God picked the right man at the right time for the right purpose." She continued: "In God's sovereignty and goodwill, I think He has allowed George Bush to be president at this time."[12]

Jim Cody, a Christian broadcaster from Tennessee who listened to Bush speak at the February 2003 NRB convention, furthered the idea: "It seems as if he is on an agenda from God. The Scriptures say God is the one who appoints leaders. If he truly knows God, that would give him a special anointing." A fellow Tennessean, Steve

Clark of the Faith Baptist Tabernacle in Jamestown, agreed on the role that "Divine Providence" seemed to be playing in Bush's actions: "At certain times, at certain hours in our country, God has had a certain man to hear His Testimony."[13]

Lieutenant General William "Jerry" Boykin, one of the top military officials leading the hunt for Osama bin Laden, was denounced far and wide when reporters got hold of a private videotape of him telling a church gathering: "Why is this man [Bush] in the White House? The majority of Americans did not vote for him. He's in the White House because God put him there for a time such as this." There were swift calls on Bush to fire Boykin for these and other religious comments.[14]

Among Operation Iraqi Freedom's detractors, the objections were many. Some envisioned a bloodbath. The Battle of Baghdad, they predicted, would be a dark day in U.S. military history, as coalition soldiers became mired in house-to-house shooting with Saddam's Republican Guard and Fedayeen. The war would hopelessly rage on, soon becoming another Vietnam. Others predicted a rash of domestic terror in retaliation. Some projected that Saddam would fire Scuds at Israel and draw Prime Minister Ariel Sharon into the conflict, further escalating the fighting in the Middle East. Protesters shouted that Iraq was just the start: the Bush team would next invade Iran and North Korea.

One common criticism was that the Bush administration should not expect the Iraqi people to welcome U.S. troops. Eric Alterman asked if Bush officials were "really so ignorant of history as to believe that Iraqis would welcome us as 'their hoped-for-liberators'?" Professor Edward Said likewise warned that the Iraqis would not cheer Americans. "The idea that Iraq's population would have welcomed American forces entering the country," he wrote in the *London*

Review of Books, was "utterly implausible."[15] In the *New York Times*, Nicholas Kristof opined: "If President Bush thinks our invasion and occupation will go smoothly because Iraqis will welcome us, then [he] is deluding himself."[16] This particular concern had itched at pundit Chris Matthews for some time. Writing in the *San Francisco Chronicle* in August 2002, Matthews ominously foretold: "This invasion of Iraq, if it goes off, will join the Bay of Pigs, Vietnam, Desert One, Beirut and Somalia in the history of military catastrophe."[17]

These, of course, were nonreligious criticisms. Among the most caustic complaints, however, were those of liberal theologians who concluded that the president was not pursuing a just war, and was not following the teachings of Christ.

One early religion-based demonstration against Bush policy in Iraq came on October 7, 2002, in Detroit. It was composed of a few hundred protesters, including a number of Methodists. The same Michigan area housed the strongest group of supporters of Bush policy, Iraqi exiles, who would be celebrating in Detroit six months later.

The October demonstration was held just hours before Bush's nationally televised speech in Cincinnati, which began laying out the case for action against Saddam.[18] "We can't sleep through this rush to war," said Reverend Ed Rowe of Detroit Central United Methodist Church. "Killing innocent victims makes us the terrorists we hate."

The protest did not attract a lot of national media attention. David Earle Anderson, in a cover story for *Sojourners* magazine, described the demonstration as "a drop in what has become an ocean of faith-based opposition to the Bush-Cheney-Rumsfeld plans for war on Iraq." Anderson claimed that "most of the religious response" came down against the president's unfolding Iraq policy.[19]

Jim Wallis, editor in chief of *Sojourners*, was also quite vocal. "Saddam Hussein is an evil ruler, no doubt about it," began Wallis in a November/December piece. "But that is not enough for war." Echoing the consensus on Saddam's WMD, Wallis added: "Iraq has weapons of mass destruction. But that is not enough for war either."[20] The issue was a matter of choosing the best response: "Christian peacemaking calls us to seek alternatives to war in resolving conflicts." Wallis insisted there were alternatives for dealing with Iraq's WMD, and the Bush team had not sought them. Wallis had no doubt whether or not the Bush policy was a Christian one: he said the policy forced American Christians to choose between their faith and their government. Unfortunately, he said, American Christians would now be forced to "learn to be Christians first and Americans second."[21]

Wallis zeroed in on just-war standards: "Neither international law nor Christian 'just-war' doctrine allow pre-emptive military action by one state against another."[22] Writing in the Boston Globe, Wallis contended that "the strong majority" of Christian leaders had "concluded that a doctrine of preemptive war to change a regime, however evil or threatening that regime may be, is not acceptable."[23]

Among Bush's most active antagonists was the National Council of Churches (NCC). On November 16, 2002, the council adopted a resolution against war, and urged the White House to "do all possible, without going to war, to ensure Iraqi compliance" with UN resolutions. The group complained that the president "rhetorically divide[s] nations and people into camps of 'good and evil.' Demonizing adversaries or enemies denies their basic humanity and contradicts Christians' beliefs in the dignity and worth of each person as a child of God."[24]

Reverend Bob Edgar is general secretary of NCC. A Methodist and former Democratic congressman from Philadelphia, he was especially strident in his opposition to war, signing multiple full-page protest ads in newspapers. One petition he spearheaded ran with 125 signatures from bishops, clergy, nuns, and parishioners in the *New York Times* in December 2002. It instructed: "President Bush: Jesus changed your heart. Now let Him change your mind. Your war would violate the teachings of Jesus Christ. It is inconceivable that Jesus Christ, our Lord and Savior and the Prince of Peace, would support this proposed attack."[25]

Frank T. Griswold, presiding bishop of the Episcopal church, said he was embarrassed by the Bush administration. He complained that he would like to be able to travel "somewhere in the world" without needing to apologize for being an American. "Quite apart from the bombs we drop," said Griswold on January 10, "words are weapons and we have used our language so unwisely, so intemperately, so thoughtlessly . . . that I'm not surprised we are hated and loathed everywhere I go."[26]

Like the NCC, Griswold was particularly angered at Bush's application of the word *evil*. Like other liberal Christians, however, he had no problem personally leveling the charge. Charging that the United States would spend more on the war in Iraq than on AIDS, he called that policy "a manifestation of evil" and a "form of sin from which we as a nation are called to repent." He did not acknowledge that Bush had recently shocked the world by announcing the largest AIDS package ever offered by a nation.[27]

On the Catholic side, opposition was led by Bishop Thomas Gumbleton of Detroit, who visited Iraq in January 2003. "The Bush administration's war on Iraq violates every value we hold as people of faith and conscience," he said on March 24, as the Third Infantry Division streaked across the desert. "Faith and conscience compel us to actively oppose this war in word and deed, to do what we can to halt the killing." Gumbleton helped coordinate a March 26 antiwar rally in Washington, which labeled the Bush action a "Crime Against Peace." The rally was sponsored by Pax Christi USA, the Fellowship of Reconciliation, Sojourners, and the Maryknoll Office for Global Concerns.[28] Among them, Dave Robinson of Pax Christi USA emphasized the need "to draw the world's attention to the immorality of this war. We can't stand by as men, women, and children die because of the callousness and greed of this administration."[29]

These assessments of Bush were actually tame compared to others. Writing in the *Catholic New Times* in March 2003, Gary Kohls stated:

On February 10, George W. Bush was introduced as "our friend and brother in Christ" [at] the National Religious Broadcasters convention. . . . The president was hailed as a man who "unapologetically proclaims his faith in the Lord Jesus Christ." The kind of Christian, the kind of Christianity broadcasters are gleefully supporting is a president who is unapologetically planning the un-Christ-like mass slaughter of innocent Iraqi children? Isn't the slaughter of innocents the job of people like Herod? What kind of god do these "pious" people think they are praising and worshiping? What kind of scripture passages are they reading that justify their participation in an evil so monstrous that only the forces of the satanic could easily approve? It certainly isn't Jesus' Good News manifesto—the Sermon on the Mount.

Certainly that type of Christian, that type of Christianity, that type of Christian radio broadcasting and that type of god are not of the same divine spirit of the nonviolent Jesus, who would have nobody radiated by uranium shells, nobody suffering when the cruise missiles explode and nobody thrown into the flames.

Certainly their type of god is not the true God as revealed by Jesus. . . .

It's no wonder that the right-wing, theologically punitive Christianity of George W. Bush is so despised by the rational world. . . . Jesus might say to George W. Bush and others who claim to be followers of Jesus: "And right now, your final judgment test is going to be how you treat my beloved Iraqi children."[30]

Such questioning of Bush's faith was popular among antiwar Christians. Therein lay an irony: liberal Christians chastised Bush for allegedly believing that he knew God's will, and being convinced that God was on his side. And yet they themselves claimed that Bush was not following Christ's teachings. In so doing, of course, *they* too were presuming to know God's will—and that God was on *their* side.[31]

Some saw Bush as diabolical; others assumed he simply did not understand things. Norman Mailer wrote in the *London Times*: "George W. may not know as much as he believes he knows about the dispositions of God's blessing." Mailer claimed that the real reason Bush went to war was "to boost the white male ego," which he said had suffered irreparable damage to its machismo by the success of the black athlete.[32]

Special outrage was aimed at the doctrine of preemption codified in the administration's National Security Strategy. Writing in the *Christian Century*, Robert N. Bellah, the academician credited with founding the notion of civil religion as a field of study, called the NSS "the most explicit blueprint in history for American world domination." The document, claimed the professor emeritus at the University of California at Berkeley, "is nothing if not a description of empire."[33]

REBUKES FROM METHODISTS

Much of the dissent was pitched at Bush personally. This was particularly true for some top officials in the Methodist church, the faith of both Bush and Vice President Dick Cheney. In one case, Methodist Bishop William Dew penned a Christmas 2002 message to his flock that appeared to draw a moral equivalence between Bush, Saddam, and Osama: "In the days of Bush, Saddam Hussein, Osama bin Laden, in the days of violence to children, lack of trust in financial institutions, incurable disease and threat of terrorism, Christmas comes to give us songs of hope to sing."[34]

Another major Methodist action at the time was a pastoral letter sent to the denomination's 8.4 million members by Bishop Sharon Brown, president of the United Methodist Church's Council of Bishops. She wrote in the letter that preemptive action against Iraq would go "against the very grain of our understanding of the gospel . . . To be silent in the face of such a prospect is not an option for the followers of Christ."[35]

Another vocal antiwar Methodist was Jim Winkler, general secretary of the United Methodist General Board of Church & Society. On February 26, he offered a blistering indictment of Bush policy.[36] Winkler attacked the prevailing assumption that war was inevitable, and listed his personal activities in support of finding a peaceful solution. Among these, two weeks earlier he met with Gerhard Schroeder—the first German leader to refuse to swear on the Bible during his oath to office—to support the chancellor's antiwar stance. Winkler stated:

> Nothing I understand about Jesus Christ leads me to believe that
> support of war and violence are necessary or tolerable actions for

Christian people. Someday, Christians will have to face up to the choice between their faith in God and the Prince of Peace and their willingness to participate in war. Why not today? War is an immoral choice.

Winkler, too, was especially alarmed at preemption, and called the Bush NSS "a dark vision of eternal war." He said it was both immoral and a violation of international law. "We who follow Jesus simply cannot support this," said Winkler.

He was also troubled by the ignorance that he felt had pervaded the thinking of war supporters: "I am concerned how few Americans have a sense of Middle East and Islamic history and culture." More so, he worried:

> I am deeply concerned about the impact of an invasion on the people of Iraq. Half the Iraqi population is children. Think about that. The United Nations has determined that 1.26 million Iraqi children are at risk in the event of war. . . . We are intending to unleash hell on Iraq. I have worshiped with Iraqi Christians and walked the streets of Baghdad. The people of Iraq are not our enemies.

Winkler then declared, "The people who carried out the horrible attacks of September 11 were seriously misguided." Warning that fundamentalism in all religions, Christianity included, is a dangerous force, he concluded:

> My opposition to war is deeply rooted in my faith. I cannot profess Christ as my Savior and simultaneously support preemptive war. I can deny Jesus and support war but I will not. . . . My opposition to war is . . . a faithful response. Jesus has shown us a better way.

Winkler's remarks were made at the Dirksen Senate Office Building at the Capitol. No one objected that he was improperly infusing church thinking into state business.

THE RELIGIOUS LEFT

These thoughts represented an influential segment of American church opinion leading up to and during the war. They were not the ramblings of the radical Riverside Church in New York City, the source tapped by the *New York Times* for a quote on Bush's faith. (Riverside Senior Pastor James A. Forbes Jr. told the *Times*: "He [Bush] has brought God in in handcuffs. This war is not coming from the council of heaven, it is coming from a council on earth that has not checked with God about their deeper motivations."[37]) These were the voices of top officials from the mainline denominations.

Representative of mainstream church leadership, these criticisms also embodied the prevailing opinion among the religious left, which routinely engages in protests and a myriad of political demonstrations; its list of crusading causes is at least as lengthy as that of the religious right. Its influence and very existence go unacknowledged by the major press.[38]

Recognition of the religious left has not been lost upon the two George Bushes. In a private July 1982 letter to Yale University President A. Bartlett Giamatti, who had apparently written to Vice President Bush expressing concern about the religious right, George H. W. fired back: "Why do you feel a threat from the Religious Right but not the [Religious] Left?" Pointing to Yale's own Reverend William Sloane Coffin, Bush asked rhetorically, "Why is it all right for Coffin to urge defiance on Viet Nam, tolerance on Khomeini, or advocate 'gay marriages' but it's not okay for the [Religious] Right to get to-gether and work against abortion or for prayer in school[?]" Bush re-minded his friend that they considered it "okay" when the religious left got involved in politics, and they ought not apply a double stan-dard to the religious right.[39]

His son observed the religious left at the Methodist church he visited in Washington in the late 1980s, as he had in the 1960s at Yale with Coffin; in both cases, leftist ministers preaching politics in-sulted his father. George W. was now seeing the religious left during his own presidency—and this time its sights were set on him.

Whether or not these antiwar messages from the pulpit had much impact on the pews is another matter. A February 2003 Gallup poll showed that two of every three Americans who attend church at least once a week supported war. A March survey by the Pew Research Center revealed that 62 percent of Catholics, and the same percent-age of mainline Protestants, supported war. Pew found 77 percent support among evangelicals.[40]

These figures did not affect the thinking of the NCC. Respond-ing to the poll numbers, Bob Edgar noted that none of the Old Testa-ment prophets had a majority. "My position is that prophetic voices are always way out ahead of the congregation," he said, presumably speaking of himself. "They should understand pretty clearly that the rank and file take a little longer to focus and to follow."[41] That view of the rank and file was shared by former NCC President Reverend M. William Howard Jr., who explained that church leaders have "an informed" and "critical assessment" of the Bush administration and the war. The church laity, he said, lacked this informed view because it relied on the popular media for information.[42]

THE CARTER CRITIQUE

Joining these critical church officials was President Jimmy Carter. Though Carter's language was not marked with fire and brimstone, his standing as an ex-president and well-known outspoken Christian made his an objection that would be taken seriously.

Carter's statements on Iraq represented a notable break with presidential protocol. Among former presidents, there is an understanding—a time-honored tradition—that they refrain from public criticism of sitting presidents, especially in wartime. Harsh or excessive criticism is considered off-limits. Eisenhower muted his outrage over Kennedy's handling of the Bay of Pigs until the two men met in person—a story relayed only years later by historians.[43] The tradition stems from the fact that ex-presidents, better than anyone, understand the rigors of the White House—or, as Harry Truman called it, the Great White Jail. They know that the last thing a sitting president needs is public protest by a former commander in chief.

Carter, in contrast, evaluated Bush's Iraq policy out in the open. In "The Troubling New Face of America," a September 2002 op-ed article for the *Washington Post*, he bemoaned the "belligerent and divisive voices" in the Bush administration and its "struggle" to define a "comprehensible" Middle East policy.[44] Though critical, the *Post* piece did not take an explicitly religious stand. For that, Carter saved his guns for the *New York Times* op-ed page. On March 9—exactly one month before ecstatic Iraqis would pounce on a fallen statue of Saddam—Carter launched a cruise missile at Bush's Iraq efforts. His *Times* piece was titled, "Just War—or a Just War?"[45]

Carter began with nonreligious criticisms, asserting that the Bush administration's policy changes had been so detrimental that they had reversed two centuries of "consistent bipartisan commitments" in U.S. foreign policy.[46] He also charged that the president's war policy lacked international support.[47]

Then, however, Carter turned theological. He stated that these two centuries of purported bipartisanship had been predicated on three factors: (1) foreign alliances; (2) respect for international law; and (3) basic religious principles. Bush's decision to launch war against Iraq, Carter maintained, was "a violation of these premises." Chief among them, he focused on the religious principles.

"As a Christian," Carter stated, he was "thoroughly familiar with the principles of a just war." A "substantially unilateral attack" on Iraq, he warned, "does not meet" just-war standards—and pointed to what he called "an almost universal conviction of religious leaders" that an attack would be unjust. In his exegesis, Carter then laid out the various ways he believed that Bush's plan violated just-war standards. Among these, he asserted that U.S. bombs and missiles would be launched at the "defenseless Iraqi population" and nonmilitary targets. The Pentagon was furious over that charge, insisting that it was planning on avoiding such targets at great financial cost and at the risk of lives of U.S. soldiers.

Carter's critique was remarkable not merely because it breached presidential protocol to give such an open, comprehensive criticism of a sitting president, but because it invoked religious grounds in doing so. Whether intentionally or not, Carter had questioned George W. Bush's understanding of Christian moral-ethical principles, if not Bush's understanding of the Christian faith.

It is important to stress the fact that just-war theory is an explicitly Christian doctrine, based on Saint Augustine's reading of the New Testament teachings of Christ and the Apostles. It was through that theological lens that Carter filtered Bush's policy prescription, offering it as an acid test to judge whether the current president's policy option in Iraq met the standards of political legitimacy. The *New York Times* supplied the venue.

The *New York Times* editorial board is very wary anytime a president interjects theology into policy. But rather than denounce Carter's use of his faith to question another man's understanding of a Christian doctrine, which would usually infuriate the *Times*'s editors and readership, in this case the paper provided him a platform. Carter used his Christianity—which, in past editorials, the *Times* has insisted that presidents keep private[48]—to criticize another president's public policies openly. The thirty-ninth president was not separating church and state. He was intertwining church teachings and state policy.

THANK GOD HE THANKS GOD

On the supportive side, one of the more unique faith-related analyses of the war was published by Michael Gove in the *London Times*.[49] Focusing on the faiths of Bush and British prime minister Tony Blair, another devout Christian, Gove noted that he had become accustomed to fellow Britons belittling their leader's faith. But he was particularly taken aback by recent incidents. When the prime minister was asked about his faith in an interview with *Vanity Fair*, one of his advisers cut in: "We don't do God." Blair's handlers persuaded him not to end his Iraq war address with the phrase "God bless you" because "people don't want chaplains pushing stuff down their throats." It was this "vampiric aversion" to faith by the prime minister's own advisers that compelled Gove to write about faith and the war in Iraq.

In a piece clearly directed at readers on both sides of the Atlantic, Gove acknowledged the prevailing secular belief that religion is the handmaiden of inflexibility and arrogance. According to Gove, such nonbelievers make a grave mistake. Rather, he argued, by adhering to Christian beliefs, Bush and Blair subject their actions to a higher authority; they make themselves answerable. This inclines them to humility, and places a deeper constraint on their decision making—a constraint beyond the judgment of parties or voters. Gove wrote:

> Christian faith . . . compels an examination of the conscience. As well as weighing the consequences of an action, the genuinely Christian politician will examine the sincerity of his intentions and be acutely aware of the fallibility of human reason. Far from encouraging rashness, Christian belief creates another hurdle a politician must clear before he acts. Subjecting decisions to extra moral tests that have nothing to do with strictly political calculation can only help to foster responsible leadership.

Bush himself alluded to this effect of faith in the March 1999 speech he made to Ed Young's Baptist church in Houston. "Faith gives us conscience to keep us honest," stressed the Texas governor, "even when nobody else is looking."[50] Many contemporary Christians operate under a slogan, "WWJD?"—a now-famous acronym for "What Would Jesus Do?" Christians exhort one another to consider that credo before they act, especially prior to major decisions. If Bush asks himself "WWJD?," he has added a layer of moral scrutiny that entails eternal consequences. He has appealed to a much higher moral plane.

In reference to the war in Iraq, Bush has emphasized how "prayer teaches humility," and has observed that sometimes a petition to a higher power may yield an answer that a mere mortal was not expecting. Through prayer, said Bush, "We find that the plan of the Creator is sometimes very different from our own."[51]

Even many non-Christians might appreciate the WWJD process. After all, many non-Christians have conceded that Christ was a great moral teacher, even if they do not accept him as divine. If so, then applying Christ's morality to decision making ought to be generally a salutary process.

What Gove speculates on from afar, David Frum has spoken to firsthand. Writing on how Bush's faith affects his decision making about war, Frum has addressed the fear that the president's faith "biases him toward aggression," making him "too quick to act, too eager to root out whatever he regards as evil." "Those fears are misplaced," states Frum. "If anything, Bush's religion biases him toward caution and restraint."[52]

In another point, Gove notes that secular critics find it hard to understand how Bush and Blair, who ground their respect for life in their faith, could prosecute a war that took life. "But it is precisely because both take religion seriously," Gove answers, "that they appreciate that inaction is itself a positive moral choice, with consequences one cannot escape." The president subscribes to the aphorism that all it takes for evil to prevail is for men to do nothing. He believes that if he and Blair did nothing to stop Saddam when they could, they would be poor leaders. Choosing not to act is itself a choice—and in this case, Bush felt, the wrong choice. Would Jesus be more disappointed if Bush did nothing, knowing he could stop a madman from more slaughter? Would there be a moral consequence for *inaction*? Gove continued:

Blair has previously talked of his fascination with [Pontius] Pilate, the quintessential politician who listened too much to his advisers, bowed before public opinion and acquiesced through inaction in the perpetration of evil. To have left Saddam Hussein in power, and let him pursue his ambitions unmolested, would have invited terrible consequences, not just for the Iraqi people but the concept of international order. Blair could not wash his hands of the problem, because inaction would have left them steeped in far more blood.

Gove's point is that a Christian politician who integrates his faith runs head-on into such considerations. To the contrary, a Christian politician like Ted Kennedy or Mario Cuomo, who insists on a full separation of one's religious beliefs from one's political actions, thereby forfeits this added layer of moral scrutiny, for better or worse. Kennedy and Cuomo acknowledge that this explains how they can support abortion rights while their Catholic church condemns abortion as immoral and unacceptable.

Faith and Going to War

In the run-up to war, Bush took special comfort in Scottish theologian Oswald Chambers. Each morning he read from Chambers's *My Utmost for His Highest*, which pledges: "My determined purpose is to be my utmost for His highest—my best for His glory." The book features a daily Bible excerpt and accompanying commentary.[53] Chambers, who died tragically at age forty-three in November 1917, after returning from preaching to soldiers fighting in the Arab world during World War I, remains one of the most widely read Christian thinkers, known for the depth of his work.[54] Chambers wrote frequently of war, and much of what he said resonated naturally with the situation in Iraq.[55]

To dodge the bullets and arrows, George W. Bush called upon

his faith-based confidence; it steeled him within the crucible of war and lent serenity to his decision making. Bush contends that a leader identifies what he perceives as a problem and pursues a solution despite doomsayers, and does not pass the buck to a successor; he leads.

Right or wrong, Bush did this throughout the Iraq crisis—in the face of tremendous opposition at home and abroad, including that of nations as powerful as Russia, China, France, and Germany. One member of the German government compared him to Hitler; the Canadian prime minister's director of communications called him a moron. The war protests on February 15, 2003, blindsided hawks; the mobilization was so vast that it appeared that dissent was not confined to the fringe left. The CBS Evening News reported 150 protests in American cities that day, including hundreds of thousands of marchers in New York City—a city Bush feared would be subject to more terrorist attacks. CBS reported that there had been roughly six hundred such protests around the world, with more than a million participants in the streets of London alone.[56]

The president faced an onslaught; he would call on his faith to weather it.

Time magazine dubbed it "Bush's Lonely March." Howard Kurtz of the Washington Post called it "Bush's Moment of Fate." NBC's Andrea Mitchell reflected, "I can't recall a time when we faced so many challenges in this country, both at home and abroad."[57] She was referring not just to Saddam and Iraq, but to the daily terrorist threats and the dangerous and seemingly unanswerable North Korean nuclear fiasco. That February the newly created Department of Homeland Security placed the nation on "high" terror alert, and gave directions, accessible through an 800 telephone number, on how to purchase and use a gas mask. The department advised that some home owners in high-risk areas buy plastic and duct tape for their windows in case of a chemical or bioweapons attack. One Connecticut man responded by covering his entire house.

Among war supporters, there was realistic concern that an invasion of Iraq could be a slaughter for U.S. troops if they were greeted with chemical and biological weapons. Soldiers trained in gas masks and heavy suits in extremely hot temperatures. If those weapons had been used, American boys would have faced a hell on earth. "This is the biggest gamble any president has taken in my lifetime," said a nervous Bush supporter and analyst at the Heritage Foundation.[58]

By March, however, polls were showing that the public, though initially lukewarm, strongly supported Bush, usually by margins of 70 to 20 percent.[59] Buoyed by a faith-based confidence and sense of reassurance, Bush tried to lead the country and a reluctant world. Remarkably, by March 18 Secretary of State Colin Powell announced a U.S.-led coalition of thirty to forty-five nations[60]—not only larger than the huge Gulf War coalition, but one of the biggest military coalitions in all history. The coalition included Afghanistan, Australia, Britain, the Czech Republic, Hungary, Italy, Japan, Lithuania, the Netherlands, Poland, South Korea, Spain, and dozens of others.[61] Such a multilateral stamp of approval was precisely what critics had clamored for. And the fact that it included a nation once run by the Taliban, and once Osama's home, was extraordinary.

And yet, rather than commend the Bush team's diplomatic ability, Democratic Congressman Lloyd Doggett ridiculed the coalition: "While the president's directive to Saddam . . . is tough," he mocked in an official statement, "the posse announced today is mighty weak." He sneered that the list included "such military powerhouses as Eritrea and Estonia," two nations which the administration considered a sign of the broad opposition to Saddam around the world.

The coalition, said Doggett, was "an embarrassing indication of the administration's foreign policy failure."[62]

The announcement of the coalition did not mute the complaint that the Bush administration was orchestrating a virtual "unilateral" effort against Saddam. The day after Powell announced the vast coalition of countries contributing troops to the effort, Thomas Friedman, using cowboy imagery, wrote in the New York Times: "We're riding into Baghdad pretty much alone and hoping to round up a posse after we get there."[63] The frustrated president pointed out repeatedly that the coalition was multinational, but to critics it didn't matter. At one point, an exasperated Bush told reporters that opposition from France and Germany did not make a multilateral effort unilateral.[64]

Another accusation that frustrated the White House came from Senator Ted Kennedy (D-MA), who claimed that Bush was pursuing war for political purposes: "This was made up in Texas," said Kennedy, "announced . . . to the Republican leadership that war was going to take place and was going to be good politically."[65] In fact, at the moment Bush decided to pursue a highly risky path to war, he was still surfing an unprecedented wave of popularity. Political scientists speak of the rally-the-round-the-flag phenomenon—a boost that presidents receive during national tragedy. Typically, this lift lasts a few weeks. Yet Bush's post–September 11 jump lasted more than a year—the longest rally-round-the-flag peak ever recorded. And he gave it up to go to war, sacrificing political fortune for what he thought was right. Bush never regained that post–September 11 upsurge; moreover, if the body bags piled up during the war, there was a chance that he could be a one-term president.

Oswald Chambers wrote that the "true test" of spiritual life comes in exhibiting the power to descend from the mountaintop. "If we have only the power to go up," wrote Chambers in My Utmost for His Highest, "something is wrong."[66] In pursuing war, Bush willingly chose to descend from the mountaintop of public opinion he reached after 9/11.

Everything came to a head on March 17–18. In Britain, former foreign secretary Robin Cook, now Blair's government leader in the House of Commons, gave an emotional speech announcing his resignation. Not incorrectly, he said that if not for a few hanging chads in Florida in 2000, Al Gore would be president and war against Saddam would not be looming. The next day, by a two-to-one margin, the British Parliament rejected a Labor Party amendment that claimed that all diplomatic means had not been exhausted. It then voted 412 to 149 to use "all means necessary" to disarm Iraq.[67]

In the United States on Monday, March 17 at 8:01 P.M. EST, President Bush addressed the nation from the White House. "All the decades of deceit and cruelty have now reached an end," he said of Saddam and his regime. "Saddam Hussein and his sons must leave Iraq within forty-eight hours. Their refusal to do so will result in military conflict, commenced at a time of our choosing."[68] There was no response from the Hussein boys. By midweek, U.S. fighter jets were bombing Baghdad.

The same night that Bush gave Saddam forty-eight hours, Senate Minority Leader Tom Daschle (D-SD) said that he was "saddened that this president failed so miserably at diplomacy that we're now forced to war." Speaking to a university audience in Madison, New Jersey, retired CBS News anchor Walter Cronkite decried the "arrogance" of Bush and forecast a "very, very dark" future for the country.[69] Congressman Pete Stark (D-CA) said bombing Iraq would be "an act of extreme terrorism" and "a terrorist act."[70]

Bush might have hoped that such dissent would quiet down once soldiers were on the ground fighting. That didn't happen. In a March 23 op-ed piece for the *Los Angeles Times*, Arthur M. Schlesinger Jr., noted Harvard historian and special assistant to John F. Kennedy, dubbed Bush's action in Iraq a "misadventure" that was "alarmingly similar to the policy that imperial Japan employed at Pearl Harbor." Because of Bush's decision, said Schlesinger, "today it is we Americans who live in infamy." The Bush doctrine of preemption assigned America the role of "the world's judge, jury and executioner. . . . The cause of our rush to war was so trivial as to seem idiotic. It was the weather."[71] At a peace rally at Columbia University on March 26, Professor Nicholas DeGenova wished for "a million Mogadishus" on U.S. soldiers in Iraq, a reference to the Somalia tragedy a few years earlier, when the corpses of American boys were spit upon and dragged through the streets—all filmed for the world (and families) to watch.[72]

In an April 2 speech in New Hampshire, Senator John F. Kerry (D-MA) wished for a regime change: "What we need now is not just a regime change in Saddam Hussein and Iraq, but we need a regime change in the United States."[73] That same day, Shiite leader Ayatollah Ali al-Sestani, who for over a decade had been under arrest in the Iraqi holy city of Najaf, was freed as American troops entered the city. The cleric issued a fatwa, a sacred edict, calling on all Iraqi Muslims not to resist the U.S. coalition.[74]

COURAGE AND WISDOM THROUGH PRAYER

Bush said he prayed for wisdom, guidance, strength, for the safety of the troops, and for the lives of innocent Iraqis.[75] In El Paso, Texas, just before the cruise missiles were launched, Bush's father said that every night he thanked God for Tony Blair—whose political and moral support for his son was crucial beyond description.[76] Web sites offered prayer for Bush. One of these, titled simply Pray for Our President, received about seventy thousand hits per day once war started.[77] A mid-March poll found that 61 percent of Americans had prayed for Bush.[78] Bush said that he knew the American people were praying for him because he could feel it.

Once the war began, the president thanked these prayer warriors. He also commended an online service that allowed Americans to adopt a soldier in prayer and the "prayer bracelets" used to intercede for military personnel. He spoke warmly about a Catholic church in Green, Ohio, that made two thousand rosaries for the troops, and about a woman in Fountain, Wisconsin, who collected over eighty Bibles to mail to those serving in Iraq.[79]

Bush especially needed the courage and wisdom he said he draws from prayer. Correctly or not, as he faced his inquisitors he might have recalled the moment in that Austin church in January 1999 when Pastor Mark Craig had spoken of how Moses was called to lead. "The people won't believe me," Moses protested, in Bush's words. "I'm not a very good speaker." Moses proceeded, as Bush said, "relying on God for strength and direction and inspiration."[80] Craig told Bush that people were "starved for leadership." It was not enough for a leader to have a moral compass; America needed leaders with "ethical and moral courage." "[Craig] was calling on us," inferred Bush, "to do good for the right reasons. And the sermon spoke directly to my heart and changed my life."

Bush interpreted Craig's words as a call to seek the presidency. They also spoke to how a leader acts once president. Bush may not have seen himself as a modern Moses rallying the country to war in Iraq, but he did feel he was doing the right thing—and that it was part of his duty as a man and leader of faith to do so.

Bush never claimed to his advisers that he was summoned by the Lord to defang the evil Saddam. Yet he says that he relies on his faith for wisdom. A fair question from the public is how that process works. How does a mortal tap into such a thing? Does the president flip through the Bible in search of a certain passage?

Bush does not make decisions that way. The pages of Scripture do, however, provide him with a moral framework, a certain understanding of good and bad, a moral compass. During the Iraq crisis, he tended toward faith-based generalities: "God intends people to be free," for example, or the contention that "freedom and liberty" are "the birthright of each individual." He publicly made this "freedom" declaration at least ten times between November 2002 and the first half of 2003.[81]

One might assume, then, that Bush viewed the human rights justification for war in Iraq as something God would welcome.[82] But he was rarely, if ever, more specific than that.[83] Garry Wills, in a lengthy piece in the New York Times, charged: "The conviction that we might benefit by removing Saddam is not the same as believing that God wills it—except in George Bush's mind."[84] Yet Bush has never said this. He never claimed God told him to invade Iraq, or that he was doing the Lord's work in seeking Saddam's removal. Even if he thought so, he knew better than to say so. Consider the rebukes he received without publicly saying such a thing.

I posed this question to several people who work with Bush in the White House: "Have you or anyone you know ever heard President Bush claim that God called on him to invade Iraq and remove Saddam Hussein?" Typical was a May 2004 response I received from a White House source: "That quote does not exist; he [Bush] has never said that."[85] Dan Bartlett, assistant to the President for communications and an old Bush friend, agreed. "The President actually said," Bartlett confirmed in a June 2004 written statement, "'Going into this period, I was praying for strength to do the Lord's will. . . . [But] I'm surely not going to justify war based on God.'"[86]

Bush's words to reporter Bob Woodward struck much the same tone: "I'm surely not going to justify war based on God. Understand that. . . . In my case I pray that I be as good a messenger of His will as possible. And then, of course, I pray for personal strength and forgiveness."[87] Similarly, he told NBC's Tom Brokaw: "I ask God to help me be a better person, but the decision about war and peace was a decision I made based upon what I thought were the best interests of the American people. I was able to step back from religion, because I have a job to do. And I, on bended knee to the good Lord, asked Him to help me to do my job in a way that's wise."[88]

While the remark to Brokaw conforms to the record, Bush did not step back from religion totally. He has said that he relied on God for wisdom and strength. His point to Brokaw was that he did not remove Saddam because the Bible instructed him, or because he felt God was prodding him.

In his State of the Union speech approaching war, the president laid out a lengthy case against Saddam. "We do not claim to know all the ways of Providence," he began. Yet we can trust in them, placing our confidence in the loving God behind all of life and all of history. May He guide us now."[89] Three critical points in those sentences reflect the spiritually driven Bush: (1) faith provides confidence; (2) faith offers guidance; and (3) faith does *not* mean that a leader can automatically think he knows all God's ways. There is also a fourth point: God is behind all of life and history. While human beings are instruments of His will, they cannot always know that will ahead of time. Bush has consistently expressed that very human inability. His theology does not count on God for a crystal ball.[90]

That same January, while he considered the decision to go to war, Bush read a selection in his book of daily devotionals by Oswald Chambers. Chambers affirmed that one of the most difficult questions for a Christian is to know what God expects him to do. "The only thing you know," answered Chambers, "is that God knows what He is doing."[91]

The closest reference from a credible source that reported explicitly that Bush felt called by God to lead generally was a *Time* piece by Michael Duffy.[92] "Privately," wrote Duffy, "Bush even talked of being chosen by the grace of God to lead at that moment, and perhaps he was." Duffy wrote this in September 2002, long before the drums of war in Iraq.[93] Perhaps closer to the truth was the *Post*'s Dana Milbank, who, in a report on the impending invasion of Iraq, speculated on Bush's general spiritual thinking: "Bush implies but does not directly assert that he is doing God's work."[94]

And yet, if Bush had directly claimed he was doing God's work, he would not be out of step with previous presidents, including Bill Clinton. Moreover, if he sensed that God chose him for this special moment in history—and, further, placed him in the Oval Office to remove Saddam—Americans should hardly be appalled. Like most of the billion-plus Christians, Bush believes God is in control of events—an idea taught by both the Old and New Testaments. During the Clinton years, it was not uncommon to encounter a conservative Calvinist who lamented, "Oh, well. God is in control. And he has Clinton in there for a reason." Bush, who subscribes to this thinking, surely assumes God has placed him in this spot for some reason. This is not unusual theology.

Though his remarks were less pointed, Prime Minister Tony Blair revealed similar thinking in his Churchillian July 2003 address to a Joint Session of Congress. Near the end of his talk, in which he laid out the global challenges he said America must assume, Blair posed the question "Why America?" His response: "The only answer is, Because destiny put you in this place in history, in this moment in time, and the task is yours to do."[95] If that is the case, then Blair must believe that destiny—and presumably the Controller of destiny—must have put George W. Bush in that place at that moment with that task. Being Christians, Blair and Bush also believe that God places people at certain points in history. The Bible is a rich record of such accounts.

"[Bush] really does believe," wrote David Frum, "that after he has done his best to make the right decision, the rest is up to God." This gives him an ability, says Frum, to take "terrible risks" while remaining "serene and confident."[96] Bush feels he is ultimately left to his own recognizance, while praying for strength and guidance. He never knows if the godly wisdom he calls for is exactly what he gets. His humble grasp of that ambiguity comforts, rather than frightens, his followers, especially in time of war.

13.

War and Freedom in Iraq

"I believe that Allah worked through Mr. Bush to make this happen. If I met Mr. Bush, I would say, 'thank you, thank you, you are a good human, you returned me from the dead.'"

—*Juad Amir Sayed, Iraqi Shiite Muslim, on April 2003 liberation of Iraq*[1]

A few weeks after the cessation of war in Iraq, *New York Times* columnist Nicholas Kristof visited the country. Like the *Times* itself, he had adamantly opposed the war. Now he had to come to grips with the undeniable freedom wrought by the liberation, and the gratitude that Iraqis felt for George W. Bush. One Iraqi told Kristof: "A thousand thanks to Bush! A thousand thanks to Bush's mother for giving birth to him!" Kristof admits he did not expect this reaction. He tracked down a man named Mathem Abid Ali. For deserting the army, Ali's ear had been amputated. "Children looked at me, and turned away in horror," he told Kristof, and added: "I'd like to make a statue in gold of President Bush."[2]

Kristof admitted that such facts "got in the way" of his plans for his column. He conceded that it was important that doves like himself encounter Saddam's victims and their joy at being freed. Doves "need to grapple with the giddy new freedom that—in spite of us— pullulates from Baghdad to Basra. I got a warm and fuzzy feeling each time I saw an Iraqi newsstand, overflowing with vibrant newspapers and magazines that did not exist six months ago."

The liberation of the Iraqi people, as we've seen, was only one of the reasons Bush went to war. What remains to be explored is what the liberation meant for Iraqi *spiritual* freedom.

From the moment pilgrims arrived at Plymouth Rock, through the signing of the Bill of Rights in Philadelphia to today, religious freedom has been one of America's most cherished liberties. Americans take it for granted; Iraqis, an intensely religious people deprived of such freedom, do not. To be sure, this new freedom could create long-term problems: fighting among differing sects, a repressive theocratic government in the Iranian mold, Shiite-funded terror; all exact opposites of the Bush administration's intent. The administration, aware of the dreadful possibilities, hopes to head them off. Still, as of April 9, 2003, Iraqis—like generations of Americans before them— are enjoying religious freedom at last.

THE PEOPLE OF IRAQ WILL NEVER FORGET THAT DATE. Neither will the president of the United States. On that day, one of Saddam's many monuments to himself crashed to the ground in Firdos Square in central Baghdad, where it was greeted by stomping Iraqi feet. In Arabic, *firdos* means "paradise" or "heaven." This was the closest to paradise the Iraqi people had come in thirty-five years.

For almost two hours, beginning a little before 9:00 A.M. EST, the world watched as American Marines made their way into central Baghdad. At first the situation was tense; soldiers ducked for cover. Soon they realized that all was clear. The Iraqi people slowly poured out to celebrate.

Within half an hour, the battle-weary soldiers were out of crouch position to pose for snapshots with smiling Iraqi families. One troop was tugged aside by an Iraqi mother and father who wanted a picture of him holding their two little daughters. Another was pulled away by an Iraqi man who insisted on frying him an egg. Women held up their babies for soldiers to kiss. Some adult men were so swept up by the emotion of the moment that they rushed into the streets wearing only their underwear, awkwardly embracing Marines in full combat gear. "We were nearly mobbed by people trying to shake our hands," said Major Andy Milburn of the Seventh Marines.[3]

Quickly, attention turned to malice against anything related to Saddam. There, begging for abuse in the town square, was a twenty-five-foot-high statue of Saddam—a statue notable for its resemblance to Joseph Stalin. It was erected the previous year in honor of the Iraqi ruler's sixty-fifth birthday.

As the international media fixed its cameras upon the statue,[4] a crowd of determined Iraqis encroached—initially a wary handful, then soon a hungry crowd of one thousand or more. They first feebly tossed their shoes at the statue, a major sign of disrespect in the Arab world. Then they tossed rocks. Someone brought a ladder. Men smacked the structure lamely with the ladder. A hefty Iraqi man in a muscle T-shirt began hitting the base of the statue with a sledgehammer, chipping off a few shards. Tired after a series of blows, he passed it on.

A helmeted Marine sat atop his tank with his arms crossed and feet up, enjoying the spectacle, watching as if he were home at a movie theater in Kansas. He and his comrades had all the firepower on hand to blow the obstacle to smithereens, but they didn't. They let nature take its course.

After considerable frustration, the Iraqis summoned the Marines. The tank crawled up the platform. As the vehicle positioned itself, Iraqi boys climbed on top to play a part. A winch was raised and a chain wrapped around the dictator's neck. Momentarily, Corporal Edward Chin draped Old Glory over Saddam's face before hoisting up an Iraqi flag. His family, who until then had no idea where he was, watched on television from New York. "Oh, my son, you are making history," exclaimed his mother, who dashed across the room to hug the TV set.[5]

Chin fitted Saddam with an iron necktie. George W. Bush's statement about the noose tightening around the neck of the Iraqi despot was being fulfilled before the world's eyes. In a scene reminiscent of the fall of the Berlin Wall over a decade earlier, the statue tumbled to the ground at 10:48 A.M. EST.

The crowd went wild, unleashing thirty-five years of repression on a hunk of metal. Saddam's onetime subjects rushed at the fallen sovereign and angrily stomped the statue.

The statue, of course, was a mere replica. But it was the closest thing to Saddam the Iraqis could get their hands on. It would do. And though no amount of punching could make up for the human meat grinders, rape rooms, and chemical baths, it still felt good to hit.

"They got it down," said a satisfied Bush as he watched from the White House. He had just emerged from a 9:45 briefing by Secretary of Defense Rumsfeld. He returned to the Oval Office for a meeting with the president of Slovakia.[6] He watched for only those precious few minutes; his response was generally subdued. "I don't have time to sit around watching TV all day long," said the president, explaining his exit.[7]

By 11:10 A.M., Iraqi citizens were dragging Saddam's head through the streets. Once the crowd cooled a bit, individuals got their own whacks well into the night. "I'm 49, but I never lived a single day," said Yussef Abed Kazim, a holy man from a local mosque, in between sledgehammer smashes. "Only now will I start living." His colleagues interrupted to prod the preacher, "Hit the eye! Hit the eye!"[8]

Soon, ten-year-old boys were riding the gigantic head of Saddam like a donkey through the streets of central Baghdad, slapping its ears with their shoes and kicking its chin with their heels.

As one CNN reporter observed, it was the first time in their lives that the Iraqi people could mock Saddam without fear of death.

Watching the statue go horizontal half a globe away in Dearborn, Michigan, Alan Owanainati, a Baghdad native, wept. "Oh, my God, it makes me cry. I never believed I would see this day." He was joined by a fellow Baghdad native, a Chaldean named Hany Choulagh, who raved: "President Bush has made our dreams come true."[9]

There was a sense of near disbelief. "I couldn't believe my eyes when I saw Saddam Hussein's statue toppled," wrote Awad Nasir, an Iraqi poet exiled in London. "For three decades . . . I dreamed of an end to the nightmare of the Baathist-fascist regime. But I had never dreamed that the end, that is to say Iraq's liberation, would come the way it did."[10] Nasir stared at the TV to make sure it was true. A call from his sister convinced him. Yes, she assured, "the Vampire" had fallen. "The nightmare is over," she shouted into the telephone. "We are free. Do you realize? We are free!"

In a piece entitled "Thank You," Nasir took to his pen to express gratitude. He noted that it was not the mullahs of Tehran and their Islamic Revolutionary Guards who liberated the Iraq Shiites, nor was it Turkey's army, the Arab League, or the European left. Nasir wrote:

> No, believe it or not, Iraqis of all faiths, ethnic backgrounds and political persuasions were liberated by young men and women who came from the other side of the world—from California and Wyoming, from New York, Glasgow, London, Sydney and Gdansk to risk their lives, and for some to die, so that my people can live in dignity. . . . They have gained an eternal place in our hearts.[11]

American GIs abroad had not seen such a reception since the crowds that greeted them on the streets of France in the summer of 1944. Iraqis shouted, "We love you!" to American troops, and cheered Bush's name. In shock, Mohammed Abdel-Amir, a thirty-four-year-old Shiite Muslim from Karbala, asked a reporter nervously: "Are you sure the regime is gone?"[12]

Majid Mohammed, a forty-seven-year-old electrical engineer, demonstrated that he was sure. "Saddam is a dog, a son of a dog," he coolly assessed, using one of the worst insults in the Arab world; it was a statement that would have gotten him impaled just a day earlier. His twelve-year-old daughter, Sara, lamented: "They stole our freedom. Until now, I haven't been able to speak my feelings about [Saddam]."[13] In broken English, an Iraqi boy who watched the tanks roll in told David Shater of ITN television that he finally felt safe—a feeling that came over him only with the presence of U.S. tanks.[14]

In the neighborhood known as Saddam City, a densely populated Shiite area, men jumped in jubilation, waving makeshift Iraqi and American flags. One middle-aged man held up a big portrait of Saddam and defaced it with his shoe. "This man has killed two million of us!" he yelled to passerby.[15]

In central Baghdad that day, grown men kissed pictures of George W. Bush. One smooched a placard he carried of Bush, with the words HERO OF THE PEACE.[16]

This Iraqi adulation for Bush was fleeting. A Gallup poll of Baghdad residents taken five months later, in mid-September, found that only 29 percent held a favorable view of Bush, compared to 50 percent who viewed him unfavorably. (Tony Blair polled even worse.) This was not a sign of general discontent with Americans or the American occupation; the U.S. chief administrator L. Paul Bremer III was viewed favorably by a two-to-one margin. Moreover, 70 percent of the same Iraqis said they expected their country to be a better place in five years—numbers almost identical to results found in a Zogby poll taken at the time.[17]

On April 9, however, Iraqis might have voted Bush king for life—so great was their joy over being freed. In the northern Iraq city of Maqloub, people chanted "George Bush! George Bush!" In the city of Arbīl, giant crowds partied all night.[18] The village of as-Sulaymānīyah was just as raucous. People waved anything red, white, and blue they could find. Women wore their best dresses. "There could be no better reason for dressing up," explained one. Another counted on her fingers the men missing from her family: "My brother . . . my husband's brother . . . They've all been killed. We've all been damaged by Saddam." Two men nearby agreed. "He's been a dictator for everybody," said a man named Star Arif, "even babies in the womb." Another hoped: "It's over for dictators. [Saddam] has sucked our blood mercilessly."[19]

Furious over what they saw as pro-Saddam, anti-American news coverage by Al-Jazeera, the CNN of the Arab world, a group of freed

Iraqis in southern Iraq chased an Al-Jazeera reporter and camera crew all the way across the Kuwaiti border.[20] There was little tolerance for those who opposed the Bush effort, particularly the human shields. Two Iraqi men strolled through Baghdad with a large sign that read GO HOME HUMAN SHIELDS: YOU U.S. WANKERS![21]

Thousands of miles away, in Dearborn, Michigan, there was also rejoicing. "If President Bush will allow, I would like to shake his hand," hoped one native Iraqi. Near him was Feisal Amin al-Istrabadi, a Chicago lawyer who went to work late because he couldn't pry himself away from his television as the statue wobbled. "This is a day we've been waiting for for 35 years," he shared. "I'm very, very proud to be an American today, as well as an Iraqi."[22] Gulala Abraham, a fifty-one-year old bilingual teacher at Dearborn's Fordson High and a native Iraqi of Kurdish descent, pointed to Bush personally. She stressed the role of his confidence and courage in the liberation: "I believe if it wasn't for his courage . . . this big project wouldn't have happened." Ali al-Ghazali, a forty-six-year-old native of southern Iraq, declared April 9 a new birthday for all Iraqis.[23]

On America's West Coast, a large crowd of ethnic Iraqis filled Colby Avenue in Seattle to dance in the streets, chanting, "Thank you, President Bush" and "Thank you, USA." Hasan al-Emeri was still seething at Saddam—"*he* did all this to Iraqi people, our people, to Muslim people." "This is the happiest day in our lives," said Ayad Jeraiw, a thirty-two-year-old taxi driver who lives in Everett, Washington.[24]

In New York, outside the United Nation headquarters, Iraq's ambassador suddenly said he no longer had any relationship with Saddam—a bold admission. The dictator had personally shot health ministers for less. "The game is over," the ambassador announced.[25]

A Day for Iraqis and a Day for Bush

The Bush team was careful not to be overly euphoric. The reaction of the president's political adviser, Karl Rove, was telling. In an unpublicized appearance, Rove visited Grove City College in western Pennsylvania on that April 9.[26] With such a huge win, the nation's chief political operative could have been expected to brag. His hosts were shocked when he chose not to bring up the events of that morning. When the issue was finally raised in the form of a question, Rove shook his finger and insisted, "No gloating." The temptation to milk the incident for poll points must have been enormous, considering all the criticism the administration had absorbed for its position. Nonetheless, Rove bit his tongue, echoing Bush's own "be-humble" attitude. His reaction also showed that the Bush team understood that difficulties, including sporadic combat, did not cease on April 9.[27]

Interestingly, much of the cheerleading over the fall of Saddam came from those whose job it was explicitly *not* to cheerlead for him. *Newsweek*'s Howard Fineman wrote that it was George W. Bush "who toppled that statue."[28] Fineman's point seems self-evident, but a quick review of the diplomatic landscape before the war reminds us of just how critical Bush's personal resolve was in topping the scales.

By mid-March 2003, there were basically two approaches for attempting to disarm Iraq. One favored negotiations and diplomacy and further UN weapons inspections. This approach aimed to "contain" Saddam by leaving sanctions in place.

The world argued over whether this approach would work. Bush and his administration believed it would not. This containment option was spearheaded by Jacques Chirac's French government and included the German government of Gerhard Schroeder, Vladimir Putin's Russia, UN Secretary General Kofi Annan, UN weapons chief Hans Blix, and China. Its advocates included the majority of the permanent members of the UN Security Council, not to mention much of the political left, untold grassroots war protesters, and many of the president's domestic political opponents, including some vocal Democratic presidential candidates.

In Bush's view, this French-led approach contained a fatal flaw: it permitted Saddam to remain in power. Thus, it precluded the liberation of Iraq. Bush was joined in this view by British Prime Minister Tony Blair.

The second option was Bush's own approach. The president maintained that the only way to truly disarm Saddam was to depose him and his regime. This approach sought removal, and with it liberation for the Iraqi people. Real disarmament, said Bush, would occur only with Saddam's elimination. It would transpire only through a U.S.-led invasion of Iraq. That, of course, was the option the administration pursued—and that is how liberation happened.

The invasion of Iraq had been under way for three weeks. On April 9, coalition troops liberated Baghdad, and thus the nation. Several days later, on April 14, the Pentagon announced that some aircraft carriers and Stealth bombers were already on their way home. This was exactly ten years to the day after George H. W. Bush arrived in Kuwait City, where Iraqi agents under orders from Saddam were poised to assassinate him. Rather than Saddam removing Bush, a Bush had removed Saddam. George W. had gotten "the SOB" who had tried to kill his father.

Wasting no time, on the following day, a Bush delegation hosted the first official meeting on replacing Saddam with a democratic government in Iraq. Symbolically, the meeting was held in the ancient Iraqi city of Ur, the biblical city of Genesis, believed by many Christians to be where life began.

On April 20, the *New York Times* ran a chart listing U.S. soldiers killed in battle: 85 for Operation Iraqi Freedom, compared to 148 for the 1991 Gulf War, 47,414 for Vietnam, 33,741 for the Korean War, and 291,557 for World War II.[29] The invasion of Iraq was not another Vietnam. A country the size of California with a military force of 400,000, plus another 600,000 reservists, was freed in less than a month, with very few civilian casualties. The extremely low number of Iraqi civilians killed was a stunning feat, and a testimony to the precision of modern American warfare.

The French-led approach could never have liberated the Iraqi people; that was not its goal. As Iraqi poet Awad Nasir has said, his country was "not liberated by Jacques Chirac, Vladimir Putin, [or] Kofi Annan."[30]

The apparent ease of the liberation had many detractors rethinking. "The Americans have won the war—in only three weeks," declared *Le Figaro*, the French daily that had excoriated Bush throughout the war. "It is a victory for George Bush." Former French Prime Minister Alain Juppé lamented: "Two weeks ago, everyone was taking their hats off to France. Today they're starting to say we were wrong."[31]

Thanking God and Bush

On April 9, the debate over the war's justness was joined by a new faction, suddenly free to speak for the first time in decades: newly freed Iraqis, predominantly Muslims, who not only advocated war but also professed a belief that George W. Bush had been the handmaiden of God in liberating them from the clutches of their slave master.

"I believe that Allah worked through Mr. Bush to make this

happen," said Iraqi citizen Juad Amir Sayed. "If I met Mr. Bush, I would say, 'thank you, thank you, you are a good human, you returned me from the dead.' "[32] Juad lives in the village of Karada, ninety miles southeast of Baghdad. At the age of twenty-four, he had buried all of his books in a flour sack, burned his identity card, and constructed a tunnel and three-by-five-foot concrete cell under the family kitchen. He entered on December 2, 1981, and lived there for the next twenty-two years.

Juad dug a tiny three-inch-diameter hole deep into the ground from which he sucked water. This was his well. A smaller peephole provided a ray of sunlight during the day. Juad deemed this his only chance of survival under Saddam. He had a plan to escape the country, but shelved it when his cousin, who tried first, was nabbed. His cousin was hanged for his religious views; the same happened to many of Juad's Muslim friends.

His crimes? The young man deserted the Iraqi army in the early stages of the Iran-Iraq War rather than murder Muslim brothers. He was also a scholar and a leading Shiite theologian. His violations were political and theological. Saddam's secret police were told that Juad must be apprehended at all costs. Juad knew what would happen if he was caught. Daily life in a concrete closet with little air and a tiny toilet was preferable.

Juad's only company was a Koran and a radio with headphones that he kept tuned to the Arabic Service of the BBC. His moment of greatest hope came near the twentieth anniversary of his confinement, when he heard a speech by President Bush on the September 11 attacks. "Mr. Bush gave a speech in which he said the terrorists of the world would be hunted down," recalled Juad. "The next time my mother brought me food I told her of my conviction that [Saddam] would not last." Juad assumed that any hunt for terrorists would naturally include Saddam Hussein.

As the events of April 9 became reality, Juad entered the light of freedom for the first time in over two decades. He now looks far older than his years. Still, frail and withered, he says he has the energy of a young man. His mother, now seventy-four, says she feels as though her son has been born again. "Now my job is done and I can die in peace," she says.

In his belief that God worked through Bush to secure his freedom, Juad was not alone. Other Iraqis saw a divine explanation; in some quarters, Bush and Allah were mentioned together. Throughout Baghdad, joyful Muslims could be heard following their holy credo, "There is no God but Allah," with: "Bush No. 1, Bush No. 1." "Thank God this has happened and the Americans have come," said Baghdad resident Maysoun Raheem.[33]

One witness, army journalist James Matise, was taken aback by an elderly-appearing Iraqi. An injured veteran from the Iran-Iraq War, the broken man had been beaten by Baathist thugs when he asked for compensation for his family. His disabilities left him unemployable. "It is the will of Allah," he explained of the U.S. invasion.[34]

Mustafa Ridha, a fellow Iraqi Muslim, safely ensconced in his home in Tampa, Florida, called the April 9 liberation a miracle. "[Saddam's] regime is over," cheered the forty-six-year-old owner of Submarine Gyros, a restaurant in Tampa's Orient Road section. "I can't believe it. I just can't believe it. This is wonderful. This is a miracle to [the Iraqi] people."[35]

Raised in Baghdad, Ridha had fled to the United States in 1979, the same time that Saddam solidified his grip by publicly arresting and executing the twenty-one "plotters" against his regime. To articulate his explanation for Saddam's fall, Ridha reached for the divine. It was an American effort ordered by President Bush, he agreed. It was also a "miracle."

Georgette Shaya went further. Born in Tel Kaif, a Chaldean community, she said in a celebration in Dearborn: "Even God couldn't help the Iraq people before, but George Bush did. God bless him."[36] In Paterson, New Jersey, residents Jabbar Alrouni and Jamael Murssidy both echoed the sentiment: "God bless America," Alrouni said, "and God bless Bush." Murssidy noted that for twelve years he had not seen his family nor Iraq. "I loved Iraq," he said. "I can't believe I will see Iraq again. And I can't believe I'll see my father and mother again."[37]

These Muslim voices were joined by those of other Iraqi Christians. Christians make up under 5 percent of Iraq's population—more than a million long-repressed Christians. On April 20, as Iraqi Muslims readied for a long-obstructed pilgrimage to Karbala, Iraqi Catholics celebrated Easter freely for the first time in a generation.

One such Christian was Selma Dawood, a seventy-five-year-old widow who lived in the small farming town of Qaraqosh in northern Iraq. Residents claim that the ancient town is 99 percent Assyrian Christian. Its landscape is marked by two towering Assyrian Christian churches, one for Catholics and the other for Orthodox believers. On April 20, 2003, there were finally more churches in Qaraqosh than murals of Saddam, though in their zeal to tear down anything Saddam, townspeople missed a giant painting of the god-man on horseback slaying a dragon with his spear.[38]

Dawood has a world-famous relative. She is the aunt of Iraqi Foreign Minister Tariq Aziz, the top Christian in Saddam's government. "Let them [American troops] arrest him," she said of her sister's son. "It's not important to me." Asked if her nephew had ever lifted a finger to help Iraq's Christians, she responded with a terse *no*: "Zero. Zero. He's very, very bad." Aziz had never acted to protect Christians, and she saw no need to try to protect him. Aziz's role in a "criminal regime," according to Dawood, had not made the family proud. She had this to say about the American-led action: "Saddam is finished and we are okay. We are very happy and merciful to God and the Americans, our uncles. God bless America. God protect America."[39]

Quotes like these from the Iraqi side abounded. Before U.S. Marines secured Baghdad, they took the town of Safwan. A man named Ajami Saadoun Khlis, whose son and brother were executed by the regime, grabbed the shoulder of a translator for Britain's *Guardian* newspaper and sobbed like a child: "What took you so long? God help you become victorious. I want to say hello to Bush, to shake his hand. We came out of the grave."[40] In Saddam's hometown of Tikrīt, a thirty-year-old carpenter named Munhal Taleb rejoiced: "[Saddam] destroyed us. We ask God that he never returns. . . . God willing, things will be better."[41]

In Dearborn on the day Baghdad was freed, a Shiite imam from the nearby Karbal Mosque took to the stage under a giant banner that read THANK YOU PRESIDENT BUSH FOR EVERYTHING! The holy man led the crowd in a chant of "Praise Allah!"[42]

While war protesters in the West reserved their opprobrium for George W. Bush, Iraqis lashed out in the other direction. In May, about a month after the liberation, a crowd of Iraqis mourned beside a grave of ten thousand lost corpses in the town of Mahaweel in central Iraq. It was one of hundreds of mass graves that had been newly located. There, onlookers cried for their deceased loved ones and chanted: "There is no God but God, and the Baath [Party] is the enemy of God." BABYLON WEEPS, read one headline in the *London Times*.[43]

KARBALA AND NAJAF

The liberation of Iraq, estimated *The New Republic's* Robert Lane Greene, "will allow Islam to flourish in the country much more than it ever did under Saddam Hussein."[44]

Changes were immediate. With the April 9 arrival of American troops, the slum known as Saddam City in eastern Baghdad was quickly renamed Sadr City in honor of a Shiite cleric assassinated by Saddam's regime in 1999. In the city's Jamila district sits the popular Mohsin Mosque, shut down by Saddam. The mosque opened its doors for the first time in four years the day U.S. troops arrived in central Baghdad.[45]

For Muslims, American tanks could not have liberated Iraq at a better time: two weeks after April 9, Shiites from Iraq and throughout the Middle East walked northward to the holy city of Karbala. In Karbala stands a shrine where Shiites pay homage to the son-in-law of Muhammad. This destination was a pilgrimage for Shiites everywhere, until the reign of Saddam. "In the days of Saddam, if anyone did this march, he was killed," claimed marcher Hussein Saman, forty-eight, imprisoned for eleven years by the Iraqi regime for practicing Shiite rituals. "The least penalty was prison, for life."[46]

On April 23, nearly 2 million Shiites from Iraq, Iran, and other countries took to the streets for a pilgrimage that culminated on April 24. The entire week, they said, had seemed blessed. The day before, one of Saddam's most vicious lieutenants, Muhammad Hamza al-Zubaydi, was arrested by U.S. forces. He was number eighteen— the queen of spades—in the U.S. military's "most wanted" deck of cards. Known as "Saddam's Shiite Thug" for his role in the bloody suppression of the 1991 uprising, in which tens of thousands were slaughtered, Al-Zubaydi was one of the most hated men in Iraq.[47] His arrest during that Karbala moment was viewed by Shiites as heaven-sent.

When the pilgrims arrived, Karbala was packed with people shoulder to shoulder under a blazing sun. The ninety-degree tempera-tures further taxed the many who walked barefoot for miles as a form of self-sacrifice. Roving watermen hosed down the masses.

Among the frenetic worshipers was a group of a hundred men in white robes who slashed their foreheads with swords in a self-mutilation ritual that sprayed blood on those nearby. This was done to show solidarity with the suffering of the martyred imam who was killed 1,300 years earlier at the Battle of Karbala. The martyr's head had been placed on a stake and taken to the caliph Yazid. "God curse Yazid and Saddam!" pilgrims shouted. Some who cut their heads had to be carried away by ambulance for medical treatment. This specta-cle was widely televised in the West, though only a tiny minority par-ticipated.[48]

Some in the throng denounced the U.S. presence. Many ex-pressed a "thank you, America, now please leave" attitude. Asked if he was concerned by the sight of emotional Shiites bloodying their skulls and chanting against America—a frightening show of chaos as U.S. soldiers tried to bring order to a postwar Iraq which was being looted daily—Bush stated: "I'm not worried. Freedom is beautiful, and when people are free, they express their opinions."[49] Bush's press secretary, Ari Fleischer, said that Bush had expressed "joy" over the Shiite observance.[50]

While many of the Shiites assailed the United States, others were aware of how they got that new liberty. "All this freedom is thanks to the Americans," said Abu Zahra, a hotel employee in Karbala. Yes, agreed Firas Abdulrazak, a merchant sitting in his stall in a market across from the mosque, "This is the first year of our freedom."[51]

Another Shiite named Abed Ali Ghilan saw God's hand: "This year we thank God for ridding us of the dictator Saddam Hussein and for letting us visit these shrines."[52]

Amid signs that read NO TO AMERICA, NO TO ISRAEL, YES TO ISLAM and BUSH EQUALS SADDAM, and DOWN U.S.A., there were others urging thanks. One Shiite stepped forward to tell an AP reporter that he wanted to thank President Bush personally for "breaking the prison" that was Saddam's Iraq. "God bless him," he added.[53]

Saddam was the prime target of anger that day. Men and women in the crowd shouted that the event was "the revenge of Karbala" against the despot. He had prevented them from coming by foot. Saddam's removal, read a number of green banners swirling among the throng, was THE REVENGE OF GOD.[54]

Karbala was not the only Muslim religious gathering. Next came Najaf, the other Shiite holy city in Iraq, home of a sacred burial shrine. On May 11 and 12, it was the destination of Shiite leader Ayatollah Mohammed Baqr al-Hakim. The sixty-four-year-old cleric, returning from a twenty-three-year exile in Iran, addressed a huge crowd in Najaf.

The ayatollah filled stadiums and rooftops on his way to the city. At one stop in Samāwah, sixty thousand people, came to hear him, some hanging on stadium lights. Some shouted, "Yes! Yes for Islam! No Americans! No Saddam." Al-Hakim's words were more akin to what President Bush hoped to hear: calls for a widespread embrace of Islam, democracy, freedom, unity, and tolerance of other faiths.[55] Tolerance is something the ayatollah could appreciate: when he fled Iraq in 1980 he was escaping the fate of fifty family members, who were murdered or "disappeared" by Saddam.

A few weeks earlier, this event, too, would have been impossible. For the ayatollah, it had been an elusive dream for over twenty years.

And yet, three months later, the dream became a nightmare. Saddam loyalists and Islamic terrorists with suspected ties to Al-Qaeda committed an atrocity against one of their fellow Muslims: in holy Najaf on August 29, after prayers ended, a massive car bomb was detonated outside Iraq's most sacred Shiite Muslim mosque, the Imam Ali Shrine. Eighty-three worshipers of Allah were killed, including the ayatollah.

The ayatollah's body had been blown into so many pieces that it was nearly impossible to identify his remains. Scattered bits of his clothing, jewelry, and flesh were collected by a clerical colleague, who brought them in a bag to the nearest hospital. He was buried in a coffin containing only his watch, pen, and wedding ring. Fifteen of his bodyguards perished with him in the explosion.[56]

Hakim had been returned to Iraq and protected by American soldiers—few of whom were Muslims—under strict orders from their Christian president. The ayatollah was murdered by his fellow Muslims, though at his funeral four days later his brother told 400,000 mourners that lax security by U.S. occupation forces was to blame for Hakim's death. The entire city and Shiite world grieved. Operation Iraqi Freedom had removed Saddam, but the War on Terror continued.

A VICTORY FOR DIVERSITY

Painful as the death of Hakim may have been, Iraqi Shiites were free at last—a change that had unexpected benefits. In July 2003, in a fierce firefight, U.S. forces killed Saddam's two sons, Uday and Qusay. Uday, a ferocious sadist and serial rapist who affectionately called himself "the wolf," had prominently displayed a photo of George W. Bush's twin daughters as one of his prized possessions.[57] According to one report, the informant who blew the whistle on the Hussein boys was a Shiite cleric.[58] A week later, another Shiite cleric, named Ibrahim al-Jafaari, a member of a political party banned under Saddam, was selected as the first person to serve on Iraq's interim governing council.[59]

The liberation of Iraq was a victory for persecuted minorities, and for diversity—particularly religious diversity. Among the freed Iraqis were Shiite/Shia and Sunni Muslims, as well as Christians, including Assyrian Othodox and Chaldeans. There were Kurds, Turkoman, and Marsh Arabs or Ma'dan. Aside from the Shiites, who constitute 60 to 65 percent of Iraq's population, all of these groups are Iraqi minorities.

In a sign of how much had changed and how quickly, on April 20, just a week and a half after Saddam's statue was toppled, Reverend Emmanuel Delly, once the bishop of Baghdad, sought Bush's help in devising a new Iraqi constitution that protected Christians. Delly pushed for the release of Christian schools and other property seized by Saddam's regime. On April 30, Iraq's Christian churches made a formal appeal to the Vatican for assistance in ensuring their rights in a constitution.[60] Just months earlier, they would have lost their tongues for making such overtures.

The irony was rich: it was said that Bush had an intolerant faith, a criticism leveled by individuals who hold an almost religiouslike commitment to diversity. And yet the Bible-thumping Bush brought religious freedom to these diverse Iraqi masses. And among those faiths, George W. Bush, the Texas Ranger who prays daily to Jesus, brought these children of Allah their first religious freedom in decades.

Without using the word *diversity*, Bush hailed just that in an April 28 speech before an electrified crowd of ethnic Iraqi Muslims in

Dearborn. "Whether you're Sunni or Shia or Kurd or Chaldean or Assyrian or Turkoman or Christian or Jewish," he said to loud cheers, rattling off different Iraqi faiths as he had done in Cincinnati six months earlier, "no matter what your faith, freedom is God's gift to every person in every nation."[61] His statement struck Amir Denha, editor-in-chief of the Chaldean *Detroit Times*, who exclaimed: "I've been here [in America] for almost forty years, and I've never heard an American president using our name—Chaldean. It was very historic."[62]

Bush spoke of the new freedoms of a Catholic from Basra named Tarik Daoud. He also talked of a Sunni from Basra named Najda Egaily, who had moved to the United States in 1998. In 1988, Najda's brother-in-law was executed for laughing at a joke about Saddam. Remarking on the liberation, she said, "We never believed that Saddam Hussein would be gone." The second that Bush read those words from Nadja, an audience member interrupted by shouting, "He's gone." The hall interrupted into chants of "U.S.A.! U.S.A.! U.S.A.!" Bush tried to cut back in: "Like Najda, a lot of Iraqis—a lot of Iraqis—feared the dictator, the tyrant, would never go away. You're right. He's gone." With that, another audience member interjected, "Because of you, Mr. President."[63]

Elated ethnic Iraqis jumped up and down laughing in elation. The president was interrupted by men rising to thank him. One was Jaleel al-Soweidi, a thirty-nine-year-old musician. Asked about the president, he replied with a grin: "My mom called me from Iraq last week. She told me to give Bush a kiss from her." Jaleel hugged him.[64] A presidential propagandist could not have contrived a better script. Bush had achieved a level of affection about which Saddam could only marvel.

A month after the liberation, the Universal Muslim Association of America held its Shiite national convention in Washington, D.C. The guest speaker was Deputy Defense Secretary Paul Wolfowitz, a driving force behind the Iraq war and bogeyman to doves. For the first time in twenty-six years, he told the convention, Shiite Muslims worldwide could observe their Arbaeen festival in Iraq. With those words, the room erupted in jubilation.[65]

THE UNSWAYED

Despite this liberation, many liberal Christians were unrepentant in their opposition to the war that enabled this freedom. A week after Saddam's statue fell, NCC's Bob Edgar said at the University of San Diego:

> President Bush has given us his vision. It is a vision of America as the world's Sheriff. We live in a town of outlaws, with unscrupulous gunslingers on all sides. We must shoot them before they shoot us. We can trust virtually no one. Perhaps the British can help watch our back in the Global Wild West, but ultimately we must rely on one thing and one thing only: our unrivaled military power, which gives us the ability to rain down "shock and awe" on our adversaries. The United Nations sits powerless and divided in the world's town hall; it is only useful to us if it stamps approval on our arrest warrants. Supposed allies such as France and Germany are cowardly and naïve. In President Bush's vision of the world, we, like the cowboys of old, must rely on ourselves. Our might makes right.[66]

Edgar's April 15 speech was the inaugural lecture in the Joan B. Kroc Distinguished Lecture Series at the University of San Diego's

Kroc Institute. Despite the jubilation of April 9, Edgar saw no reason to change his tune. He was not alone in what a conservative magazine had called "Anti-Liberation Theology."[67]

Similarly unmovable was International A.N.S.W.E.R. (Act Now to Stop War & End Racism), the group that organized massive antiwar protests. On April 9 no less, A.N.S.W.E.R. issued a press release announcing an April 12 antiwar rally in Washington. On the group's Web site that day, there were no pictures of the disgraced statue, nor any acknowledgment of the celebrations in Saddam's homeland.[68]

The unswayed included many non-Iraqi Arabs. "The majority of Muslims are . . . saddened by this war," said Ahmed Bedier on April 9, a spokesman for the U.S.-based Council on American-Islamic Relations. "This is not a just war."[69] His assessment was typical. Laith Alattar, a member of the U.S.-based Iraqi Forum for Democracy, concedes that most non-Iraqi Arabs were against the war: "All of the Arab population, most of them are just against this whole thing. They don't want to see liberation."[70]

It Was Intended

George W. Bush had hoped to unleash Iraqi religious freedom—long before the war. He had no qualms about an explosion of faith in Iraq, regardless of whether it was primarily Muslim. It didn't need to be Christian to meet his requirements. Like the people of Afghanistan, Iraqis experienced religious liberty for the first time in decades. The paradox was that the invasions of Iraq and Afghanistan would not have happened without September 11. It was that act of intolerant Islamic extremism, ordered by Osama bin Laden, that later enabled Bush to unshackle spiritual freedom in two of the religiously repressive nations he had singled out in the first months of his administration.

Shortly before Tomahawk cruise missiles began whistling through the Iraqi skies, Bush had given a sober evening press conference on March 6, 2003, where he was grilled by the media on the wisdom of the impending war. He told a reporter: "Iraq will provide a place where people can see that the Shia and the Sunni and the Kurds can get along in a federation." He was hopeful about what these predominantly non-Christians could do with freedom. "[Freedom] is God's gift to the world," he told the same reporter before a nationwide audience. He believed that Iraqi Muslims could be trusted with it.[71]

Seven weeks later, on April 24, the president spoke to workers at the army tank plant in Lima, Ohio:

> Many Iraqis are now reviving religious rituals which were forbidden by the old regime. See, a free society honors religion. A free society is a society which believes in the freedom of religion. And many Iraqis are now speaking their mind in public. That's a good sign. That means a new day has come in Iraq. When Saddam was the dictator and you spoke your mind, he would cut out your tongue and leave you to bleed to death in a town square. No fooling. That's how he dealt with dissidents.
>
> Today in Iraq, there's discussion, debate, protest, all the hallmarks of liberty. The path to freedom may not always be neat and orderly, but it is the right of every person and every nation. This country believes that freedom is God's gift to every individual on the face of the Earth.[72]

And in his pursuit of that goal in Iraq, it was Bush's own personal faith that had been attacked.

BEWARE THEOCRACY

The unleashing of this religious freedom is not without negatives. There is a distinct, ominous possibility that Saddam's brutal regime could be replaced not by kindly Jeffersonian democrats, but rigid Shiite imams who seek to establish a theocracy akin to that of their brethren next door in Iran, which, since 1979, has operated as an international poster child for repression and religious intolerance. Worse, if such did take place, a potential would exist for Iraq and Iran to join forces in a radical religious bloc that exports Shiite terror throughout the world. Over the past twenty-plus years, no country has funded more terrorism than Iran. Tehran remains the headquarters of radical Islamic fundamentalism. Might a post-Saddam Iraq join it?

The most popular figures in Iraq are Shiite holy men. If Iraq's next leader is a cleric, Bush must hope he is not of the Ayatollah Khomeini variety. His team hopes to head off the painful possibilities. Bush was later asked by NBC's Tim Russert about the prospect of Iraqis freely electing an "Islamic extremist regime." "They're not going to develop that," Bush replied categorically, with startling assuredness. He continued:

> And the reason I can say that is because I'm very aware of this basic law they're writing. They're not going to develop that, because right here in the Oval Office I sat down with Mr. [Adnan] Pachachi and [Ahmed] Chalabi and al-Hakim [brother of the slain ayatollah], people from different parts of the country that have made the firm commitment that they want a constitution eventually written that recognizes minority rights and freedom of religion.

I remember speaking to Mr. al-Hakim here, who is a fellow who has lost 63 family members during the Saddam reign. His brother was one of the people that was assassinated early on in this past year. I expected to see a very bitter person. If 63 members of your family had been killed by a group of people, you would be a little bitter.

He obviously was concerned, but he—I said, you know, "I'm a Methodist. What are my chances of success in your country, in your vision?" And he said, "It's going to be a free society where you can worship freely." This is a Shia fellow. And my only point to you is these people are committed to a pluralistic society.[73]

Bush's thinking is that such people so long on the receiving end of repression will not themselves become repressors, knowing intimately the longing for liberty. He cautioned Russert: "It's not going to be easy. The road to democracy is bumpy."

Needless to say, there are many who do not share the president's optimism.

The dominant form of government in the Middle East is *not* theocracy. The typical Middle East state is governed by a Muslim monarch who openly honors Islam. The Taliban was a theocracy, which has been replaced—with U.S. help—by a leadership much more hospitable to civil liberties. Sudan largely remains a theocracy, as is Iran, although Iran harbors a nascent democratic movement demanding political freedom. That said, the only thing less common than a Middle Eastern Muslim theocracy is a Middle Eastern Muslim democracy. In Iraq, Bush has set a literally unprecedented goal—a real long shot.

AFTER IRAQ—PRAYER AND CELEBRATION AT HOME

The Bush team was fully aware of the risks involved in its policy. For now, however, Saddam's vicious regime had been removed with surprisingly few U.S. combat deaths. The dire calamities predicted for American intervention had not transpired.

Two weeks after the Pentagon announced the cessation of major combat operations, Bush appeared before the annual White House Correspondents' Dinner—a gala black-tie evening of roasting and toasting. The president's speech at these functions is usually a comedy routine; everyone enjoys a hearty laugh. In 2001, Bush had presented a jovial slide show that featured self-deprecating childhood pictures of himself and the Florida governor, his brother Jeb.

In 2003, however, Bush used the occasion to pay tribute to two outstanding journalists whose young lives and brilliant careers were cut short by the war—NBC News correspondent David Bloom and *Atlantic Monthly* editor and *Washington Post* columnist Michael Kelly. Both left wives and small children behind, and both were also men of faith—Bloom a Protestant and Kelly a Catholic. Kelly had been raised Catholic. Bloom more recently had made a strong commitment to his religion. Bush spoke of their work and lives. In Bloom's case, he also spoke of faith, which, though unreported at the time by the major press, was pivotal to Bloom in his final moments.

Bush had a special feeling for Bloom's departure. Early in the Iraqi morning of April 5, Bloom huddled in a corner of a tank to check his phone messages. One had been sent by Jim Lane, a prayer partner and member of the advisory board for the Wilberforce Forum. Much like Bush, Bloom was doing a daily devotional from Oswald Chambers's *My Utmost for His Highest*. Lane read to Bloom from the

New Testament's Matthew 25: "Because of what the Son of Man went through, every human being can now get through into the very presence of God." Bloom absorbed the message, climbed out of the tank, walked a few steps, and collapsed. At age thirty-nine, this rising star and loving husband and father was dead from a pulmonary embolism—and was "ushered into the presence of God," as his friend and prominent Christian thinker Chuck Colson put it.[74]

The president finished his remarks at the Correspondents' Dinner by reading the last e-mail Bloom sent to his wife. Bloom had noted that there he was in Iraq on his fortieth birthday, a media celebrity with his face in nearly every household, and yet all that was really important to him was his wife, kids, and faith in Jesus. Bush used that word—Jesus—in reading the e-mail to the 2,700 journalists and their guests. Bush could identify with Bloom's recent spiritual commitment because he had been in a similar spot at the roughly forty-year mark in his own life, when Christianity became so central to him.

Bush also spoke of the exceptionally talented Michael Kelly. "We will remember them with admiration and affection," he said of the two journalists. "May God bless their souls." The audience came to its feet. "[The president] made me cry," said comedian Drew Carey, who had been the entertainer at the event the previous year. Former Secretary of State Madeleine Albright felt it was "appropriate" that Bush honored those who perished. "It was a different kind of dinner," she conceded.[75]

Bush had offered many such tributes to fallen heroes. He prayed with military families and sat for services in army chapels.[76] In a radio address, he singled out a twenty-two-year-old soldier from Mississippi named Henry Brown. He quoted a friend of the corporal: "[Henry] believed God was working through him and he was part of the plan. I guess part of the plan now is God calling his soldier home."[77]

Not long after combat operations ceased, Bush recognized the first Memorial Day since the war. He spoke at Arlington National Cemetery, where he memorialized a number of troops. He ended with an Army Ranger named Captain Russell B. Rippetoe, who was buried in Section 60 of the cemetery several weeks earlier. Rippetoe earned both the Bronze Star and Purple Heart in Operation Iraqi Freedom. Bush read the back of Rippetoe's dog tag, which was engraved with words from the book of Joshua.[78]

Amid the somberness, Bush took one occasion to cut loose. On May 1, 2003, he was scheduled to speak aboard the USS *Abraham Lincoln*. It was assumed that the president would arrive on the aircraft carrier in the traditional manner—via helicopter. But Bush loved to fly combat planes. It was in his blood from his Texas Air National Guard days.

The president entered via an SB-3B Viking, which he flew with two other pilots. He flew the aircraft himself for about one-third of the trip. The pilot asked if the president wanted to land the craft on the carrier—one of the most dangerous feats in aviation. Bush demurred with a smile. His confidence had not been boosted by his Q&A with the pilot. *What happens if the plane slides off the landing deck?* Bush asked. "At four seconds, we eject," said the pilot. "At five seconds, our parachutes open." This later prompted Bush's old friend, White House Communications Director Dan Bartlett, to quip that the president's choice of delivery was actually safer than a helicopter because in this case he had the ability to eject.[79]

MSNBC's Keith Olbermann noted that the president had skipped the appreciably safer route of announcing that combat was over from the White House, in favor of a venue that required his escort to perform a feat not unlike parking a car at a hundred miles an hour. While the landing was "a great moment," Olbermann noted, "he's the president and we have only one president."[80] Vice President Cheney nervously noted that George W. probably hadn't told his wife Laura what he was planning.

The plane skidded to a screeching halt on the small runway, a few feet from the ship's edge. A beaming Bush emerged in his bomber jacket, tucked his helmet under his left arm, and posed for pictures with the military. This was the kind of experience George W. Bush lived for; for a moment the humble Bush was replaced by a throwback to West Texas.

With the showy landing, Bush's cowboy talk was back. There were liberals who hated the landing. For each of those, there was a conservative who loved it.

Conservative Damon Wheeler wrote: "I am glad my president is a cowboy and a man close to God. Watch out Bin Ladens and Saddam Husseins of the world. He will get his man. Cowboys always do, you know."[81] "Great scene, great," raved Michael Ledeen in National Review, "who could ask for anything more?"[82] In a Wall Street Journal piece called "Hey, Flyboy," Lisa Schiffren, a Republican speechwriter working as a writer and mother in New York, gushed over Bush's sex appeal in his flight suit.[83]

From the left, Frank Rich of the New York Times dismissed the landing as Hollywood hype. "The Bush presidency," wrote Rich, "might well be the Jerry Bruckheimer presidency," referring to the producer of Hollywood features like Top Gun, Black Hawk Down, and Armageddon.[84] Some Democratic politicians were furious. Senator Robert Byrd (D-WV), who had harshly criticized Bush war policy, called the "spectacle" an "affront to the Americans killed or injured in Iraq."[85] Congressman Henry Waxman (D-CA) demanded a congressional investigation of the landing, requesting that the General Accounting Office do a study to determine how much money was spent. The office's comptroller general rejected the request, saying that such a study itself would cost too much: "In my view, it does not pass a cost-benefit test."[86]

Yet many liberals enjoyed the show. Bob Schieffer of the CBS *Evening News* praised the expressive aspect of the image Bush portrayed, drawing an analogy to Ronald Reagan's "great communicator" skills. "We saw some very powerful pictures tonight," said Schieffer. "I think this was a remarkable moment. I mean, it really was. . . . Here you have the president flying onto the aircraft carrier. The first president to fly on to an aircraft carrier in a fixed wing jet like he did, climbing out in that flight suit, looking very dashing. This whole day was quite an event." He continued, "We saw a little spontaneity today. We saw a little showmanship that we haven't seen in a long time in politics, and frankly, I think that's kind of good."[87]

MSNBC's Chris Matthews was effusive. The former aide to Speaker Tip O'Neill (D-MA) and speechwriter for Democratic presidents and presidential candidates, characterized the landing as a dare to Democrats hoping to challenge Bush's bid for two terms. According to Matthews, it was as if Bush were saying, "Try to do this. Look at me. Do you really think you've got a guy in your casting studio . . . who can match what I did today?" Matthews went on colorfully, finishing with a humble concession:

> Imagine Joe Lieberman in this costume, or even John Kerry. Nobody looks right in this role Bush has set. [Bush has] medium height, medium build, looks good in a jet pilot's uniform, has a certain swagger, not too literary, certainly not too verbal, but a guy who speaks plainly and wins wars. I think that job definition is hard to match for the Dems. . . .
>
> We're proud of our president. Americans love having a guy as

president, a guy who has a little swagger, who's physical. . . . Women like having a guy who's president. Check it out. Women like this war. I think we like having a hero as our president. It's simple. We're not like the Brits. We don't want an indoor prime minister type. . . . We want a guy as president.

And by the way, Democrats for years have made fun of Republicans, like Ike, who defeated the Nazis, and Ronald Reagan, who was probably the most evocative person for the World War II generation, and this guy. They always make fun of them for being simple. And guess what? They always win two terms, and they're always right.[88]

Matthews's statement was remarkable because he had predicted disaster in Iraq. He initially thought Bush was *not* right.

Lost in the landing hoopla was the substance of the speech that followed. Under a banner marked MISSION ACCOMPLISHED, Bush noted that major combat operations in Iraq had ended—a remark critics brought up each time another soldier was killed during the postwar occupation. Although major combat had in fact ceased, sporadic fighting continued through 2003 on a smaller scale. This was a big-picture speech that Bush ended by thanking those present and no longer present:

Those we lost were last seen on duty. Their final act on this Earth was to fight a great evil and bring liberty to others. All of you—all in this generation of our military—have taken up the highest calling of history. You're defending your country, and protecting the innocent from harm. And wherever you go, you carry a message of hope—a message that is ancient and ever new. In the words of the prophet Isaiah, "To the captives, 'come out'—and to those in darkness, 'be free.'" Thank you for serving our country and our cause. May God bless you all.[89]

The president had endeavored to close a day of purposeful ostentation with purposeful solemnity.

SADDAM'S CAPTURE

Though it looked like April 9, 2003, might go down as the best day of Bush's presidency, December 13 of that year brought equally joyous news: Saddam Hussein had been captured. On April 9, the Marines had chained a statue; now they chained the real thing. The deposed dictator was nabbed at 8:26 P.M. Baghdad time by U.S. troops combing the Iraqi countryside. The world awakened to the news at 7:00 A.M. Washington time on Sunday, December 14, as a grateful George W. Bush awakened to get ready for church at St. John's.[90] Three weeks earlier, he had stunned military personnel with a Thanksgiving Day visit to Baghdad: his eyes welled with tears when the room of surprised soldiers erupted in jubilation as he unexpectedly strolled in. Now, yet again, those boys were returning the favor: they had Saddam.

The man who constructed the "mother of all" palaces and mosques, and asked his men to fight the "mother of all battles" against Americans, had hidden in the mother of all "rat holes," as U.S. General Ray Odierno described the hideaway. Saddam had dug a hole adjacent to a farmhouse fifteen kilometers from Tikrīt.[91] "You had this leader in this exalted position and when they caught him he was living in a hole, like an animal," said Colonel Shane Deverill of Peachtree City, Georgia, one of those who captured Saddam.[92]

Over the years, Saddam had ordered countless Iraqis to fight to the death. During the Gulf War, he set up literal lines of fire to keep troops from retreating against the mightiest military in history. The penalty for surrender or refusing mandatory conscription was death. He asked Arab brothers to kill themselves as suicide bombers. Now, when it was his turn to fight, he hoisted his arms in the air, not even reaching for the pistol that sat in his holster. The guy who had tried to kill Bush's dad, all the while maiming and murdering numerous fellow Muslims, was handcuffed by soldiers under orders from the Texan, like a fugitive villain cornered and caught in Dodge City.

Not a single shot was fired. Colonel James Hickey said that U.S. Special Forces were mere seconds from pitching a grenade into Saddam's hole, but were stopped when the despot held up his hands. He identified himself in English and said he wanted to negotiate. "I am Saddam Hussein, I am the president of Iraq and I want to negotiate," he said from his pit. Bush's boys replied sarcastically, "President Bush sends his regards," and then led him away.[93] When asked his response to Saddam's gesture, Bush chuckled and counteroffered a two-word message: "Good riddance."[94]

It was fitting that Saddam was found hiding in a hole he had dug under a building, just as Juad Amir Sayed had done. That alone provided some measure of justice. Pol Pot had died peacefully in his sleep rather than beg for a spoonful of rice in a Cambodian killing field. Mao and Stalin did not perish like their tens of millions of subjects, with a gunshot to the head or with a wrenching stomach and emaciated frame. Saddam's countless torture victims could take comfort in the fact that he had suffered before his capture.

The press conference formally announcing the capture was an unforgettable spectacle. "Ladies and gentlemen," announced an emotional L. Paul Bremer III, administrator of the governing coalition,

"We got him." The room became positively electric when video footage of a bedraggled Saddam appeared on the overhead screen. The Iraqi reporters couldn't control their emotions; some could be heard wailing as they wept tears of joy. Also speaking at the press conference was Dr. Adnan Pachachi, the Iraqi serving as acting president of the governing council, who said that he would ask the council to declare the day a national holiday. "Allah is great," Pachachi said. "Allah is great." His council responded with a formal statement that read: "We thank God the tyrant has been arrested." An Iraqi reporter followed Pachachi by thanking the coalition forces and "the brother Americans" in the name of Allah. Among the other grateful Iraqi reporters was one who said he was so overwhelmed by happiness that he was too "confused" to formulate a question.[95]

The Iraqi press, made up of hundreds of newly emergent newspapers in the wake of Saddam's fall, now fully demonstrated to the world its newfound freedom. Iraqi writer Abd al-Hamid al-Sa'ih called Saddam's seizure the "mother of all arrests," writing: "His friends believed that he would resist like the knights until the last poisonous bullet in his conscience. But nothing of this sort happened." Iraqi and Arab writers focused on the dictator's refusal to battle his pursuers, calling him a coward, a hyena with no teeth, and noting that Saddam's sons and even grandson (who had been killed with Uday and Qusay) had fought more valiantly. An editorial in the Iraqi daily Al-Sabah said that the "beast," the "liar," and, plainly, the "Prince of Darkness," had met "an end suitable for criminals." The leading independent Iraqi daily, Al-Zaman, spoke for the country as a whole in its editorial entitled "The Fall of Saddam Is Complete and the Sun Has Returned to Shine on Iraq."[96] Abd al-Bassit al-Naqqash, the editor in chief of the daily Al-'Ahd Al-Jadid, asserted in an editorial:

There shall be no escape for the judgment of Allah on the wicked. Justice has caught the bloodsucker, the despot who has humiliated his people and relatives!!! We were notified yesterday, and in Karbala [the Shiite holy city] of all places . . . of the capture of Saddam Hussein. Guns began firing announcing happiness which exceeded the happiness of the 'Id [religious holiday] and exceeded the fall of the entire regime on April 9 . . . The entire population demonstrated against Saddam Hussein's terrorism. . . . It is the great Iraq and its people, Arabs and Kurds, Turkmen and other minorities, and all the monotheistic religions, against the unbelief, oppression, [and] despotism that were personified by Saddam Hussein. This is the clearest and most beautiful morning in my country, Mesopotamia. Be joyful, oh my brothers, be joyful.[97]

Jesus Christ recognized the need for civil law. Christians maintain that while their Redeemer forgives sins, his flock still must punish those mortals who transgress the bounds of morality and decency. During his press conference on Saddam's capture, President Bush noted that he had said many times that freedom is God's gift to all people, and that Saddam had "deprived" Iraqis of that gift.[98] Now the dictator would be permitted freedom of conscience and counsel. However, if Bush had his way, Saddam would be deprived of any hope of leaving a prison cell. To ABC's Diane Sawyer, Bush acknowledged that Saddam's fate ought to be decided by the Iraqi people. But the Texan proffered his own opinion: Saddam ought to be executed. Bush favored the same destiny for Saddam that Saddam had once sought for Bush's father.

Amazingly, not everyone was thrilled with Saddam's capture. The man who tapped into the anger against Bush, Vermont Governor Howard Dean, the front-runner for the Democratic presidential nomination, reacted with a notably nonjubilant speech in which he unsmilingly averred, "The capture of Saddam has not made America safer." The public disagreed: a Gallup poll taken just before Saddam's capture showed Bush leading Dean 50 to 46 percent in a race for the presidency, whereas the same poll just after the capture had Bush ahead by 60 to 37 percent.

Also disagreeing with Dean was Senator Joseph Lieberman (D-CN), another Democratic presidential aspirant. "Praise the Lord!" cheered Lieberman. "This is a day of glory . . . and it's a day of triumph and joy for anybody who cares about freedom and human rights and peace." That morning, Lieberman told NBC's Tim Russert: "If Howard Dean had his way, Saddam Hussein would still be in power today, not captured."[99] Lieberman's claim had the virtue of accuracy, a fact that Dean himself could not deny. Dean had opposed the entire operation, from start to finish, a point underscored the week before by Lieberman's former running mate, ex–Vice President Al Gore, in explaining his surprise endorsement of Dean.

It was a bad weekend for Dean: In a striking irony, *Newsweek* reacted to the capture of Saddam by bumping its planned cover story on the candidate for a feature on Saddam's capture.[100] Nevertheless, Dean continued to poll far ahead of the rest of the Democratic pack the following week.

A FEW DAYS AFTER SADDAM'S CAPTURE, GEORGE W. Bush got an early Christmas present from the most unlikely source. On December 19, Libyan dictator Moammar Kaddafi, the world's most-wanted terrorist throughout the 1980s, amazed the world by announcing that his nation would give up its weapons of mass destruction and related programs, even agreeing to full inspections of all "nuclear activities." The director-general of the International

Atomic Energy Agency, Mohammed el-Baradei, was thrilled, and said inspections could begin the next week.

Less than a week after Saddam was apprehended, Kaddafi had offered to do what Saddam wouldn't. For two decades, using sanctions and negotiations, the international community had tried to get Kaddafi to disarm, but he had refused.

This came on top of reports that North Korean despot Kim Jong II, whose regime Bush had dubbed "evil," had not been seen since October and was hiding somewhere with a supply of Hennessy cognac, of which he is the world's top purchaser, and a harem of blondes. According to reports, he was afraid of unmanned U.S. drone aircraft, which he supposed hovered silently in the North Korean night looking to kill him.

Some argued that Saddam's pursuit and ultimate capture caused Kim to cower and Moammar to cooperate. The timing was remarkable. Whatever the reason, as George W. Bush prepared to relax for his final Christmas before the 2004 presidential campaign, he could happily assess the state of the world since September 11: The world's worst dictator, Saddam, was under arrest, and its most misogynistic regime, the Taliban, was long gone. There were prospects for democracy in the most unlikely of places, Iraq and Afghanistan. There was now a multinational coalition of sixty nations involved in Iraq's postwar reconstruction.[101] Osama bin Laden was hiding in fear for his life, as was Kim Jong II. Moammar Kaddafi wanted to talk. There had been no major terrorist attacks in the United States. The number of terrorist attacks in 2002 had dropped by 44 percent and were at their lowest level since 1969, effectively the fewest in the entire era of modern terrorism.[102] The world was a better place. Domestically, a recession prolonged by the economic devastation of September 11 and wars in Afghanistan and Iraq was finally over. The economy was booming at a thirty-year record pace, sparked by a staggering 8.2 percent growth in the last quarter. The Dow had just surpassed 10,000. Not all was perfect: the deficit had exploded, eliminating the budget surplus of the Clinton era in a few short years. Job growth was still slow. Though in hiding, bin Laden had not been found, and neither had the Taliban's awful Mullah Omar. Worse, no Iraqi WMD had been found. For President Bush, however—and the Christian principles he had brought to the White House—it had been a year of righteous victories.

14.

2004

"George Bush is not my neighbor!"

> —*Vermont governor Howard Dean,*
> *January 2004*

"We are dealing with a messianic militarist . . . an unstable office-holder."

> —*Presidential candidate Ralph Nader on*
> *George W. Bush, April 2004*

Given all of the good news that greeted him at the end of 2003, George W. Bush might have expected 2004 to start on a high note. Unfortunately for the president, however, January 2004 marked the kickoff of a hotly contested election year. Though some of the Democratic pack seeking their party's presidential nomination lauded the recent accomplishments in Iraq, one who did not was the outspoken early front-runner, Vermont governor Howard Dean. More than any of his rivals for the nomination, Dean seemed not only to disagree with Bush but to harbor a personal anger toward the man. And it was that rather palpable sentiment that prompted a sixty-six-year-old Iowan to stand up at a Democratic debate on January 11 and ask Governor Dean a question.

As his campaign was traveling from the Northeast to the Midwest and South, Dean had been making overtures to Christian voters. An ABC News/*Washington Post* poll had just shown that 46 percent of Southerners said that a president should rely on his religious beliefs in making policy decisions. Dean, whom the sympathetic *New Republic* called "one of the most secular candidates to run for president in modern history," openly stated that he would begin to speak publicly about Jesus as he stumped in the South. And though there was no shortage of media coverage of Dean's gambit, neither the *New York Times* nor other secular publications excoriated the governor's deliberate exploitation of faith for strictly political purposes, even though it offended many liberals.[1]

The fifty-five-year-old Dean, a Congregationalist who, as the *Washington Post* put it, "rarely attends church services, unless it is for a political event," had left the Episcopal Church years earlier after a dispute over, of all things, a bike path. "I didn't think it was very Godlike," said Dean of his church committee's opposition to the construction of such a path which he favored. He said he now preferred being a Congregationalist because "there is almost no centralized authority structure." His wife and two children are Jewish, and the family does not attend church together. Dean's newfound enthusiasm for religious conversation led to some awkward moments on the campaign trail: Asked to name his favorite book from the New Testament, Dean cited the "allegory" of "the Book of Job," a book from the *Old* Testament.[2]

In early January, Dean called Jimmy Carter and asked if he could attend church services with the former president at the Maranatha

Baptist Church in Georgia—an excellent photo op. When Dean claimed that Carter had extended the invitation, however, Carter set the record straight: "I did not invite him," Carter explained, "but I'm glad he came."[3]

Now, during a question-and-answer session in Oelwein, Iowa, sixty-six-year-old Dale Ungerer confronted Dean with an appeal to the Christian virtues of charity and "love thy neighbor" that George W. Bush preached. Accusing Dean of acting "crass," he challenged the candidate to start treating the president in a more neighborly way. "Please tone down the garbage," urged Ungerer, invoking the Bible: "You should help your neighbor and not tear him down." Dean pointed his finger at the senior citizen and ordered, "You sit down!" To raucous applause from the hall of Democrats, he informed the Iowan: "George Bush is not my neighbor! . . . It is time not to put up [with] any of this 'love thy neighbor' stuff."[4]

It was typical behavior for Howard Dean—behavior that culminated in his infamous outburst after the Iowa caucuses a few days later, which doomed his chances and paved the way for Massachusetts senator John F. Kerry to run away with the Democratic nomination.

Though it fizzled early, Howard Dean and his Bush-bashing campaign set the tone for 2004. For various reasons—the war in Iraq chief among them—George W. Bush was suddenly attracting a level of hate from liberal Democrats unseen since the Nixon years. In that same January, when the Democratic website MoveOn.org sponsored a grassroots call for anti-Bush advertisements, they received—and briefly posted on their site—two ads comparing Bush to Adolf Hitler. One ad began with Hitler delivering a speech, before morphing into Bush. Another mingled Nazi and Bush images, using the tag line "What were war crimes in 1945 is foreign policy in 2003."[5]

Also in January, Senator Ted Kennedy (D-MA) maintained his role as the Bush administration's most dogged critic in the U.S. Senate. In a speech to the Center for American Progress at the Mayflower Hotel in Washington, D.C., Kennedy pressed his argument that the war in Iraq had been launched for political purposes. Referring to it as the "Iraq card," Kennedy charged that the president and his "extremist" and "reckless" administration had "brazenly" imposed their agenda on the rest of the world "at the expense of the truth." The Bush White House, charged Kennedy, "is breathtakingly arrogant" and "vindictive and mean-spirited." The senator predicted that the war in Iraq "could well become one of the worst blunders in more than two centuries of American foreign policy. We did not have to go to war. Alternatives were working. . . . And this war never should have happened." The November election, said the senator from Massachusetts, "cannot come too soon."[6]

As Kennedy spoke, Bush's popularity continued the slide that had begun with the president's pursuit of war in Iraq. The Texan was not helped when in late January chief weapons inspector David Kay reported that no stockpiles of weapons of mass destruction had been found in Iraq, although he emphasized that inspectors had discovered intent and infrastructure—a clear indication that the Iraqis had the capability to ramp up WMD production. Kay said that records indicated that in 2001 and 2002 Saddam and his sons had inquired as to when WMD production could begin again. Iraq had retained its WMD programs, and remained capable of "rapid reconstitution" of WMD assembly, particularly biological and chemical arms. Nonetheless, no actual WMD had been found; only in May did the first actual weapons begin to surface.[7]

Bush's loss was John F. Kerry's gain. A week after Kay's disclosure, on the night of February 3—known in election-speak as Super

Tuesday—Senator Kerry swept five of seven states in the latest Democratic primary battleground. A jubilant Kerry celebrated with a message to President Bush: "Like father, like son: One term and you're done." But the day was bittersweet for Kerry: That afternoon, a Catholic bishop in Missouri said he would deny Kerry, a pro-choice Catholic, Holy Communion if he tried to receive the Eucharist in the bishop's diocese. It was a sign of further troubles ahead for Kerry.

APRIL 2004: CHAOS IN FALLUJAH AND NAJAF

The outlook for Iraq at the start of 2004 was grand: a compromise had been reached to turn over control of the country from the U.S.-led interim governing coalition to a civilian government by June 30, and the United States helped Iraqis craft the most liberal constitution in all of the Middle East, featuring a bill of rights that would make any Westerner beam, including full religious freedom. Like Americans, Iraqis were now regularly being polled on a regular basis and from every conceivable angle. A major poll done by ABC News in March found Iraqis optimistic and looking forward to choosing their own leaders; indeed, they cited specific individuals for whom they planned to vote for president.[8]

One individual who did not register among the favorites was Muqtada al-Sadr, a young Shiite cleric and vicious demagogue. It was al-Sadr and a group of extremist followers in the holy city of Najaf, plus a pro-Saddam/Baathist insurgency (largely Sunni)—joined by foreign terrorists—in the city of Fallujah, that made Iraq a bloodbath for U.S. troops in April. This was an unwelcome development for a president and Pentagon that had a year earlier declared an end to major combat operations.

The al-Sadr situation was particularly vexing for the Bush admin-istration, for reasons that were deeply engrained in the nation's his-tory of religious factionalism. Iraq's liberation had freed the nation's Shiites, and polls showed that the vast majority of them were thrilled with the fact—with the exception of al-Sadr's minority faction, which would wreak havoc on fellow Shiites and U.S. soldiers alike in the weeks to come. Al-Sadr, a fringe figure looking to be Shiite dicta-tor for all of Iraq, was a top suspect in the shocking assassination of Iraq's most beloved Shiite cleric, the Ayatollah Mohammed Baqr al-Hakim. He was also wanted for the murder of Ayatollah Abdul Majid al-Khoei, another rival in his scheme for supreme power. Al-Sadr and his acolytes had been perpetuating violence for a year when the frus-trated American-led coalition decided to shut down a local newspa-per that served as al-Sadr's propaganda organ. With that move, al-Sadr declared war on Americans. Once U.S. troops moved in, he fled to a mosque, using it as a shield to protect himself from the bul-lets of coalition forces.

As al-Sadr holed up, thousands of his supporters threatened to un-leash all-out war on U.S. forces if they pursued the cleric. "You Ameri-cans, do not fall into a quagmire and storm Najaf," warned one al-Sadr supporter, Sheikh Nasser al-Saedi, "[or] rivers of your blood will flow." He shouted defiantly: "We killed the American dream. [They] will not take over this country. You do not understand what martyrdom means."[9] Both the sheikh and al-Sadr had bought the line of the in-ternational left: America was in Iraq not to remove Saddam, build democracy, and leave, but, rather, to pillage the nation for its oil. Ironically, the sheikh spoke in Baghdad's Sadr City, named after al-Sadr's father, who (along with al-Sadr's two older brothers) was gunned down by Saddam's henchmen in 1999. (The irony that Sadr City was formerly called Saddam City—and that the renaming was made possible by the U.S. liberation—was apparently lost on al-Sadr and his acolytes.)

The ugly war with al-Sadr in Najaf immediately followed the mutilation of four U.S. security contractors by a Saddamist mob in Fallujah, a city west of Baghdad. About 1,300 U.S. Marines and Iraqi security troops sealed off the city and fell into nasty street fighting with an insurgency of 1,500 hardened Saddam loyalists, including elite Republican Guard units and members of Saddam's secret service; these Saddamists were joined by foreign jihadists, including Al-Qaeda fighters.[10] Coalition commanders referred to the process of removing the loyalists as a "de-Baathization" of Iraq.

Worse, Islamic fanatics in April began taking hostages. Militants nabbed a French journalist named Alex Jordanov. Jordanov's captors repeatedly pushed him, "Is Jesus the son of God?" (Muslims believe Jesus was a prophet but not the son of God.) They reminded him: "You are facing twelve Islamists. There is no room for a mistake." There was one acceptable answer. Jordanov, who was eventually released, did not divulge his response.[11]

This witches' brew of kidnapping and killing was not sitting well at home. In Washington, Senator Robert Byrd (D-WV) dubbed the Bush intervention in Iraq "unwarranted" and a "blunder," calling the president too "stubborn" to admit the fact. "It is staggeringly clear that the administration did not understand the consequences of invading Iraq," said Byrd, who ominously added that from Iraq he could hear "echoes of Vietnam." Ted Kennedy stepped forward to say that he, too, sensed another Vietnam.[12] The press joined the chorus: When President Bush held a prime-time press conference in the East Room on April 13, the first question compared Iraq with Vietnam.

This sentiment prompted *Washington Post* columnist Charles Krauthammer to opine: "There is no cure for the Vietnam syndrome.

It will only go away when the baby-boom generation does, dying off like the Israelites in the desert, allowing a new generation, cleansed of the memories and the guilt, to look at the world clearly again."[13]

Two days after the president's April 13 press conference, Senator John F. Kerry accused Bush of excessively fixing the nation's attention on terror and manipulating security fears for political gain. "Home base for George Bush, as we saw to the nth degree in the press conference, is terror," said Kerry. "Ask him a question, he's going to terror."[14]

Actually, Bush would have been thrilled to change the subject. A few days before the press conference, the country had received fabulous news: Job growth was finally catching up to overall economic growth. In the largest job gain in four years, nonfarm payrolls jumped 308,000, well above expectations. Manufacturing activity was at a sixteen-year high.[15] Yet Bush was not asked about the economy once during the entire press conference; instead the media focused exclusively on terror and security.

Nonetheless, George W. Bush's resolve was unshaken. He had expected tough times in Iraq. He interpreted the new Iraqi attacks as an attempt to stifle democracy and prevent the June 30 transfer of power—which was indeed the objective of al-Sadr, the Saddamists, and Al-Qaeda. "America's objective in Iraq," Bush stated, "is firm: We seek an independent, free, and secure Iraq. . . . We're changing the world. And the world will be better off and America will be more secure as a result of the actions we're taking."[16]

The president also told the press that he did not make decisions based on polls. That was clear: As Bush held firm on Iraq, his popularity dipped to an all-time low, with the election just months away. At 86 percent in the polls after September 11, Bush was at half that mark by May 2004. The economy was growing like it hadn't in decades, but the war—which Senator Kennedy claimed was "made up in Texas" to help the president politically—was taking a toll on Bush's once-solid chances of reelection.

In all, April 2004 would feature the deadliest fighting for American GIs since the fall of Baghdad a year earlier. By the time the body bags were tallied up, the number of U.S. casualties for April alone was 126. The total since the war began was 736.[17]

Even some of the president's supporters were now turning. At the end of April, retired four-star general William E. Odom, a Republican who once headed the National Security Agency, served as a deputy national security adviser, and now teaches at Georgetown and Yale, said that staying the course in Iraq was untenable and that the president's vision of reordering the Middle East by building a democracy in Iraq was a pipe dream. He advised removing American troops "from that shattered country as rapidly as possible." "[W]e have failed," judged Odom. "[T]he issue is how high a price we're going to pay—less by getting out sooner, or more by getting out later."[18]

Amid all of this, the 9/11 Commission held hearings in Washington in April, exploring whether the Bush administration bore any responsibility for the September 11 massacre[19]—a suggestion that the president's supporters (and many nonsupporters) found outlandish and offensive. National Security Adviser Condoleezza Rice testified dramatically before the commission, and the president testified in private. A flurry of anti-Bush books hit the shelves, many of them soaring to the top of the New York Times bestseller list, from former adviser Paul O'Neill's story (as told to reporter Ron Suskind) in The Price of Loyalty, published in January, to books by former Bush and Clinton terrorism adviser Richard Clarke and even former Nixon White House counsel John Dean—who judged Bush's presidency "worse than Watergate."[20]

In mid-April, the latest book, by renowned journalist Bob

Woodward, was characterized as damaging to Bush, despite the fact that it painted a hands-on, sensible president leading the nation in wars in Afghanistan and Iraq. (In fact, the book was so fair and generally constructive that the Bush White House recommended it.) In an innocuous exchange in the book, Woodward asked Bush whether he had consulted his father before going to war in Iraq. Rather than consulting his earthly father, Bush casually replied, he appealed to his "higher father"—an action common in America since the nation's first president, General George Washington, had knelt in the snow of Valley Forge on the eve of battle.[21] When this exchange was reported, presidential candidate Ralph Nader declared of Bush: "We are dealing here with a basically unstable president. . . . We are dealing with a messianic militarist. . . . Talk about separation of church and state: It is not at all separated in Bush's brain, and this is extremely disturbing."[22]

Of course, not everyone disliked Bush, including his troops. The Associated Press reported on April 23 that U.S. soldiers had reenlisted at rates that exceeded the retention goals set by the Pentagon.[23] And Rabbi Shmuley Boteach wrote in the *Jerusalem Post*:

> I not only support President Bush, I revere him. At a time when so many other world leaders want to paint September 11 as a terror attack, President Bush saw it for what it was: a clash of civilizations, a war to the death between two systems, one open, democratic, and respectful of human life; the other oppressive, tyrannical, and deeply contempt[uous] of human life.
>
> Bush understands that the only way to defeat such a grave threat is by tumbling the dominoes that support terror one by one, even if he becomes the most criticized man on Earth for doing so. . . . Perhaps there is something redeeming about being the most powerful yet most vilified man on Earth.

Boteach quoted Edmund Burke: "All that is necessary for evil to triumph is for good men to do nothing." Bush's leadership, the rabbi proclaimed, "burns with virtue and blazes with uprightness"; the president "protects the innocent and punishes the wicked, assails tyranny and upholds democracy, and puts the fear of God into cold-hearted killers."[24]

SHOWDOWN: JOHN F. KERRY VS. GEORGE W. BUSH

Early in 2004, in the political comeback of the season, Massachusetts senator John F. Kerry, whose candidacy had seemed moribund just weeks earlier, surged ahead of the Democratic pack and ran away with the primaries. The Democratic Party had its man: a Vietnam War veteran long regarded as presidential timber. *National Journal* rated Kerry the most liberal member of the Senate (unlike Governor Bill Clinton, who in 1992 had a reputation as a moderate Democrat). The strategy of Republicans was to portray Kerry as a waffler; they hoped to suggest that his flip-flopping was too risky for a wartime president.

In comparison to Bush, Kerry's religious faith received much less scrutiny. And yet Kerry's personal religious beliefs were much more controversial than Bush's. Kerry is a Roman Catholic—and a very liberal Catholic, whose views were often at odds with those of his church. Groups like Catholics Against Kerry have been organized to oppose his bid for the presidency.

At home in Boston, Kerry attends not a conventional parish church but instead a kind of theological institute on Beacon Hill called the Paulist Center, which even the *New York Times* describes as a nontraditional, New Age–oriented church.[25] The center, which from the outside does not look like a church, is a home for wayward Catholics who disagree with church teachings. It has long been a hotbed for far-left Catholics, including those who in the 1970s and 1980s held to liberation theology, which played a central role in the Marxist uprisings in Central America. The center awards an annual Social Justice Award, beginning with the first two recipients in 1974 and 1975, labor activist Dorothy Day and antiwar activist Bishop Thomas Gumbleton, founder of Pax Christi USA, which strongly opposed the 2003 war in Iraq. The Paulist Center operates outside the oversight of the Boston diocese.

In the first half of 2004, as Kerry came under increased scrutiny, questions were raised about his spiritual life and background that troubled many Catholics. U.S. Catholic League president William Donohue issued a statement questioning whether Kerry's divorce from Julia Thorne was annulled, and whether Kerry and his second wife Teresa Heinz-Kerry were married in a Catholic Church.[26] Kerry also occasionally misidentified Catholic figures and statements; in one instance, he stated that "My oath privately between me and God was defined in the Catholic church by Pius XXIII and Pope Paul VI in the Vatican II." There is no Pope Pius XXIII.[27]

In March 2004, Kerry received the Eucharist—the Catholic sacrament of Holy Communion—while attending Mass during an Idaho ski trip. When he arrived to Mass quite late wearing a ski suit, his staff dismissed his tardiness and inappropriate dress by explaining: "It was just a media-op. . . . We set it up with some reporters that we knew were going to be there." But the website Catholic Exchange protested Kerry's appearance, under the headline "It's a Sacrament, Senator! Not an Opportunity for a Photo Shoot." Joseph M. Starrs, director of the Crusade for the Defense of Our Catholic Church, called the incident "disgusting."[28] In April, Kerry seemed to make another misstep, taking communion in an African Methodist Episcopal church; Catholicism teaches that Catholics should not take communion in non-Catholic churches, where the consecration of the elements served during communion does not take place.

Where Kerry differs most markedly from the Church and its teachings, however, is in his position on abortion and other social issues. Kerry is not passively pro-choice on abortion; he is a champion of the cause. At the 2003 NARAL Pro-Choice America Dinner, where he described pro-lifers as "the forces of intolerance," Kerry boasted that his maiden speech as a freshman senator had been in support of Roe v. Wade.[29] In 1994, he argued for taxpayer funding of abortions, calling for abortions to be performed in every hospital and for it to become a part of mainstream medical training. At one point he even seemed to suggest that religious institutions need to forswear those "intolerant" believers that fight legalized abortion. Kerry stated:

> The right thing to do is to treat abortions as exactly what they are—a medical procedure that any doctor is free to provide and any pregnant woman free to obtain. Consequently, abortions should not have to be performed in tightly guarded clinics on the edge of town; they should be performed and obtained in the same locations as any other medical procedure. . . . [A]bortions need to be moved out of the fringes of medicine and into the mainstream of medical practice. And by the same token, if our children are to be safe from the danger of fanaticism, tolerance needs to be spread out of the mainstream churches, mosques, and synagogues, and into the religious fringes.[30]

Deal Hudson, editor of the influential Catholic publication *Crisis*, has written that while Kerry describes himself as "personally opposed" to abortion, few senators have worked so hard not only to keep abortion legal but to actively promote and expand the procedure. Hudson maintains that Kerry's actual promotion of abortion would be akin to him saying, "I personally oppose watching television, and it's about time we get a television in every home."[31]

With Kerry, Democrats were nominating the most fiercely pro-choice individual ever to receive a major party nomination for president—a fact that greatly disturbed the Catholic Church, which has worked as steadfastly as any institution to slow abortion. To the church, nothing would be more aggravating than to watch its progress on abortion reversed by no less than a Catholic president.

Of course, there are many pro-choice Catholics. Why pick on Kerry? The Church has its reasons. The Roman Catholic Church has recently begun to favor some type of sanction against pro-choice politicians—most prominently in its January 2003 "Doctrinal Note on Some Questions Regarding the Participation of Catholics in Political Life," which put new emphasis on the Catholic politician's responsibility to uphold Catholic beliefs concerning the sanctity of human life. Kerry is seeking the presidential nomination at a time when pro-choice Catholics are being held to new standards. In the 1980s, when Governor Mario Cuomo of New York was a front-runner for the Democratic nomination, the church had not yet addressed the issue in detail. In addition, the Church pointed out a major difference between John Kerry and the typical lay Catholic: as a senator and potential president, Kerry wields enormous influence. He can impact abortion far more than can those in the pews.

Indeed, while many liberals complained that pro-life politicians use a "litmus test," selecting judges based on their position on abortion, John Kerry said openly that he would impose just such a litmus test himself, appointing only pro-choice judges to the Supreme Court.[32]

On April 23, 2004, Kerry was the featured speaker at a massive abortion rights rally in Washington, D.C. An estimated half-million marchers carried signs that read "Stop Bush's War on Women," "If Only Barbara Bush Had Choice," "Barbara Chose Poorly," and "Pro-Life is to Christianity as Al-Qaeda is to Islam." Congresswoman Maxine Waters (D-CA) took to the podium to tell George W. Bush to "go to hell." Abortion doctor George Tiller referred to Bush, Dick Cheney, Donald Rumsfeld, and John Ashcroft as "the four horsemen of the apocalypse." A number of pro-choice religious groups were in attendance, including the Religious Coalition for Reproduction Choice, Catholics for a Free Choice, and Christian Dykes for Choice. Francis Kissling of Catholics for Free Choice called the gathering a "sacred place . . . the place to be, not the churches." In similar language, another speaker, Barry Lynn of Americans United for the Separation of Church and State, described the protest as a "hallowed space." One speaker denounced the religious right as the "religious Reich"; another spoke of the "Bush/Satan administration." A female rabbi spoke about being "pro-God, pro-choice."[33]

Kerry's speech kicked off the rally and brought the house down. Three weeks earlier, Kerry had taken time out from his campaign to make a rare appearance on the Senate floor and vote against a bill that would make it a crime to harm a fetus during an assault on the mother—a bill supported by the president and two-thirds of Kerry's fellow senators. The bill offered a landmark extension of legal rights to the unborn.[34] He also joined a Senate minority in voting against a ban on the horrific procedure known as partial-birth abortion, which he likewise perceived as an obstacle to legalized abortion.[35]

That weekend, the candidate's wife, Teresa Heinz-Kerry, expressed her view on abortion in an interview with *Newsweek*. While reaffirming her pro-choice beliefs, she conceded that she believes that abortion is "stopping the process of life." "I ask myself," said Heinz-Kerry, "if I had a 13-year-old daughter who got drunk one night and got pregnant, what would I do. Christ, I'd go nuts." Asked if he shares his wife's view, Kerry told *Newsweek*: "I do not know the answer to that. We've never—she's never had to vote."[36]

As Kerry prepared to address the rally, Cardinal Francis Arinze, speaking from the Holy See, presented *Redemptionis Sacramentum*, a Vatican declaration stating that priests must deny communion to pro-abortion Catholic politicians. The document restated the church's position that anyone knowingly in "grave sin" must go to confession before lining up for communion to ingest the consecrated bread and wine that Catholics consider the literal body and blood of Jesus Christ. Arinze said that "unambiguously pro-abortion" Catholic politicians are "not fit" to receive the sacred elements.[37] The Vatican had spoken. It was now up to American bishops to decide whether to carry out the policy.

As the campaign heated up, a number of Catholic archbishops suggested, or stated flatly, that if John Kerry presented himself for communion in their diocese he would be turned away.[38] These included Archbishop Raymond L. Burke of St. Louis, Archbishop Alfred C. Hughes of New Orleans, and even Archbishop Sean O'Malley of Boston—Kerry's home diocese.

John F. Kerry will be the third Catholic nominated by a major party for president, following Democrats Al Smith in 1928 and John F. Kennedy in 1960. In Kennedy's case, there was concern—particularly among evangelical Protestants—that a President Kennedy would look to the Pope for guidance in affairs of the state. In 2004—ironically, including among evangelicals who find value in Pope John Paul II's social and moral teachings—there was concern that a President Kerry would take *no* advice from the Pope. Kennedy's candidacy inspired fears that he would be too religious, a Catholic first and a president second. Kerry's candidacy has caused some to fear that he would be too nonreligious—not influenced by the Church at all. Catholic George Neumayr has taken this concern one step further, raising the possibility that, under Kerry, "the most anti-Catholic presidency in American history [would be] occupied by a Catholic."[39] The world's most politically powerful Catholic, in other words, would stand against the Church on abortion, euthanasia, stem cell research, and a number of other core issues.[40]

Throughout the first half of 2004, the polls found Kerry and Bush in a dead heat for the White House. Catholics were one group that might have been expected to make the difference in that narrow gap, by voting overwhelming for the Catholic candidate. And yet just the opposite may transpire: Not only may Kerry fail to receive a huge majority of Catholic votes over Bush, he may not win the majority at all—and he seemed unlikely to win over the many white, middle-aged Catholics who attend Mass weekly or more. The 2004 election may be decided by committed Catholics who vote for a Protestant over a Catholic because they perceive the Protestant as more friendly to Catholic concerns. Just as Al Gore lost in 2000 by losing his home state of Tennessee, Kerry could lose in 2004 by failing to carry one of his core constituencies. On religious grounds, then, John F. Kerry may be the strangest presidential candidate—Democrat or Republican—that the electorate has witnessed. Should Kerry win the presidency, the nation may experience another peculiar development: a Catholic president denied communion in certain areas of the country.

Kerry himself may have been sensitive to these concerns; apparently eager to shift the spotlight to his rival, twice during the spring of 2004 Kerry questioned George W. Bush's faith. In a March 7 speech at a Mississippi church, Kerry charged that Bush does not practice the compassionate conservatism he preaches. The senator pointed to James 2:14: "What good is it, my brothers, if a man claims to have faith but has no deeds?" Neither the *New York Times* nor liberals in general protested Kerry's use of the New Testament to judge the president's Christian commitment—or his alleged inability to meld church and state. Undeterred, Kerry leveled the accusation again on March 28, speaking at the New Northside Baptist Church in St. Louis, aiming James 2:14 at "our present national leadership." A spokesman for the Bush campaign called Kerry's remarks "a sad exploitation of scripture for political attack."[41]

IRAQI POWs AND NICK BERG

As if April had not been bad enough for American troops in Iraq, it was succeeded by May's sorry images of U.S. military personnel mistreating Iraqi prisoners of war at the Abu Ghraib detention facility inside Iraq. Though the extent of physical torture the Iraqi detainees suffered was unclear, a number of sadomasochistic military personnel certainly humiliated them, stripping them naked and placing them in embarrassing sexual positions—all the while stupidly filming their dirty deeds. The pictures, which included the images of American military men and women relishing the situation, exploded on to the media and Internet. A few sick, nonprofessional soldiers—whose crimes had been exposed by fellow troops—had thereby caused immense harm to the U.S. effort to win the hearts and minds of not just the Iraqi and Arab people but also Americans and the global community at large. They had produced a public-relations disaster for the Coalition effort—and, much worse, a major moral disappointment.

For conservatives who celebrate the image of the citizen-soldier simply doing his duty, the prisoner abuse was a rude wake-up call.

And yet there were undoubtedly more troops in Iraq who could quote Jefferson and Adams than the variety who posed in bondage with a bullwhip—a perverse GI version of a Madonna video. The situation was indeed the classic case of a few bad apples rotting the whole barrel. Critics exploited the photographs for political purposes, and tried to extend the tentacles all the way to the Oval Office.

In response, there were calls for Secretary of Defense Donald Rumsfeld to resign, including (predictably) from the *New York Times*. Members of the Congressional Black Caucus threatened to withhold war appropriations until Rumsfeld stepped down, and even suggested that President Bush should be impeached if his secretary of defense did not fall on his sword.

The president condemned the abuse as "appalling," and apologized to the world for the behavior of his fellow Americans. He gave two interviews to Arab television in which he made the critically important distinction that this mistreatment of Iraqi POWs and the torture and killing of Iraqis under Saddam was ordered from the top, whereas these unacceptable actions by Americans were not dictated by their commander in chief and would not be tolerated. Those responsible would be punished in the most severe terms.[42] Senator Ted Kennedy was quick to step in and tell the people of the world that the president of the United States was misleading them. "Shamefully," said Kennedy, "we now learn that Saddam's torture chambers reopened under new management: U.S. management."[43]

On the day that Kennedy spoke, Islamists exacted a measure of payback. Claiming they were reacting to the U.S. abuse of Iraqi detainees, a group of Al-Qaeda operatives in Baghdad—mimicking the actions of Al-Qaeda operatives in Pakistan in 2002 with *Wall Street Journal* reporter Daniel Pearl—released video that showed the beheading of a 26-year-old American named Nick Berg from West

Chester, Pennsylvania, there in Iraq as a private citizen lending a hand to the nation's postwar reconstruction. As Bush continued to seek forgiveness—the Christian ethic—these Muslims sought justice by the edge of a sword.

Yelling "Allah Akbar!" or "God is great!," the killers sawed off Berg's head. According to estimates, the beheading lasted thirty to sixty seconds; Berg's screaming was halted only by the severing of his vocal cords. The video was streamed online for the world to absorb in horror. Unlike the pictures of Iraqi POWs, splashed on the front pages of every newspaper, the Berg video was too graphic to air. Even the boldest radio talk shows—frustrated by the media's non-stop, weeks-long coverage of the Iraqi prisoner-abuse scandal while barely covering the Berg execution beyond the day's wires—would play only the audio portion of the beheading. Some talk-show hosts posted still pictures of the execution on their website. Few to none linked to the grisly raw video.

The beheading brought perspective to the Abu Ghraib scandal: the humiliation of the POWs was intolerable mistreatment, the action against Nick Berg an unspeakable atrocity. The Berg beheading made it abundantly clear that the war on terror was being fought in Iraq.

Not everyone interpreted it that way. Rather than interpreting his son's beheading as vindication of the Bush war on Islamic terror, Nick Berg's father blamed the murder squarely on the president. "My son died for the sins of George Bush and Donald Rumsfeld," said Michael Berg in a May 13 press conference. "This administration did this." Berg, a member of the radical antiwar group International A.N.S.W.E.R., posed a shocking moral equivalence between Al-Qaeda and the Bush team: "The Al-Qaeda people are probably just as bad as they are," Berg conceded, were *possibly* as bad as the Bush

White House; he wasn't completely sure.[44] Even Hezbollah, the Shi-ite terrorist group founded in Iran after the Khomeini revolution, had blamed Al-Qaeda instead of Bush.[45]

As Michael Berg accused President Bush of sinful behavior, out west yet another Roman Catholic bishop was directing an edict at the eternal soul of Senator John F. Kerry. Bishop Michael J. Sheridan of Colorado Springs issued a stern pastoral letter saying that Catholics who vote for politicians who advocate legal abortion, euthanasia, or stem-cell research should be denied communion. "Anyone who pro-fesses the Catholic faith with his lips while at the same time publicly supporting legislation or candidates that defy God's law makes a mockery of that faith and belies his identity as a Catholic," wrote Sheridan. Charging that Catholics whose vote diametrically opposes church teaching "jeopardize their salvation," Sheridan said that the coming election was "critical" because of the progress that had been made in slowing abortion. For the first time since the Supreme Court legalized the procedure in 1973, he pointed out, the number of abor-tions was declining. "We cannot allow the progress that has been made to be reversed by a pro-abortion president, Senate, or House of Representatives," wrote the bishop. Abortion, said Sheridan, "trumps all other issues."[46]

Only a few days before Sheridan's letter, Archbishop John J. Myers of the Newark, New Jersey, diocese released a five-page statement ti-tled "A Time for Honesty," in which he wrote that Catholic politi-cians who support abortion rights should not seek communion. In response, New Jersey's pro-choice governor, Democrat James Mc-Greevey, said he would respect the archbishop's request and not seek the Eucharist at Mass.[47] McGreevey's action raised an obvious ques-tion: Would John F. Kerry do the same?

As the stage was set for November, and George W. Bush's race against John F. Kerry, it was increasingly clear that religious faith would be very much a part of the debate. It was also obvious that the race was up for grabs: On May 9, John Zogby, the only major pollster to predict that Al Gore would win the popular vote in 2000, issued his forecast for 2004: "John Kerry will win the election. . . . [T]his race is John Kerry's to lose."[48]

15.

The Mountaintop

"Events aren't moved by blind change and chance. Behind all of life and all of history, there's a dedication and purpose, set by the hand of a just and faithful God."

—*George W. Bush, February 2003*[1]

"The moments on the mountaintop are rare and meant for something in God's purpose."

—*Oswald Chambers, My Utmost for His Highest*[2]

Historians will have ample opportunity to assess the failures and successes of George W. Bush. On a personal, spiritual basis, Bush admits that he remains a sinner in need of constant redemption. He knows his faults: He has a propensity for foul language, for example, though he never takes his Lord's name in vain.[3] Forgiveness can be a struggle. And as a sinner, he must always tap into that Christian-based humility; it reminds him that he is not always right and that many of those who disagree with him likewise love America. He also strives to rein in that natural tendency to swagger. "We will kick his ass," Bush said privately of Saddam in 2003, just as he had said of bin Laden and al Qaeda (behind closed doors) in 2001.[4]

"His faith has tamed him," writes biographer Peter Schweizer, "but not completely."[5] Indeed, not completely. Brother Bush is a work in progress.

It may take years, decades, or perhaps generations, before we can fully grasp President George W. Bush's legacy. Was Iraq's liberation and Saddam's capture the high-water mark of the Bush presidency? Or his victory over the Taliban? It is treacherously easy to overestimate the wins of the moment, as well as the losses. Historical perspective comes only with patience and time.

The Bush administration hopes to make a historic and permanent change for the better in the Middle East, a difficult area in which to build a legacy. The Middle East has been a black hole for presidents. Few left the region a better place. Consider two recent examples: Jimmy Carter and Ronald Reagan.

Despite the fact that the grand achievement of his presidency involved the Middle East—the Camp David Accords—Carter's presidency was severely hampered by events in the region. An OPEC energy crisis and two late 1979 events within weeks of each other— the taking of American hostages in Tehran and the Soviet invasion of Afghanistan—ultimately put the final nail in the coffin of his presidency.

Reagan's presidency saw the closing of the Cold War. He accomplished more with the Soviet Union than any of his predecessors. In foreign policy, his eight years produced extraordinary accomplishments—except in the Middle East. Until his final days,

Reagan lamented the worst disaster of his tenure, the 1983 suicide bombing of American barracks in Beirut.

The Middle East is the cradle of civilization, the home of biblical holy lands, of Moses, Christ, and Muhammad. It is the birthplace of three of the world's most dominant religious faiths. And it has been the ruin of foreign policies and presidencies.

And yet, in a roughly three-year period, George W. Bush achieved indisputable change in the region. Unparalleled for a president, he *may* have set the foundation for Arab-Muslim democracy—a concept previously nonexistent in the region.

Against those odds, Bush may have laid the ground for Middle East democracy in the two most unlikely places: the Taliban's Afghanistan and Saddam's Iraq. Nowhere were women more repressed than in Afghanistan under the Taliban. Nowhere were humans generally more repressed than in Iraq under Saddam. Between the two, Saddam was the biggest destabilizer in the world's most unstable neighborhood.

How did Bush achieve this? In both cases, by force—military force unleashed in reaction to September 11.

THE AGE OF LIBERTY

In the academic field of international relations, one of the few practical debates concerns the matter of "democratic peace." It is widely, if not universally, recognized that democracies rarely fight one another. Consequently, to the extent that the hostile Middle East becomes more democratic, it may become more peaceful. And to the extent that such a peace endures—still very much an open question—Bush may have sowed the seeds of it in Afghanistan and Iraq.

George W. Bush's most far-reaching address was delivered in November 2003 to the National Endowment for Democracy. In it was the germ of his hopeful legacy. The president that day reminded the crowd that in the early 1970s the nations of the world included only forty democracies. As the twentieth century ended, there were 120. "And I can assure you," he said to applause, "more are on the way." In little more than a generation, Bush said, the world had witnessed the quickest advance of freedom in democracy's history. Historians will search for explanations for this occurrence. And yet, Bush contended, we already know some of the reasons they will cite. "It is no accident that the rise of so many democracies took place in a time when the world's most influential nation [America] was itself a democracy," he said. After World War II, Bush reported, the United States made military and moral commitments in Europe and Asia that protected free nations from aggression and created conditions for new democracies to flourish. Now, in the Middle East, under his administration, America would seek to do so again.[6]

That progression of liberty, said the Texan, is "a powerful trend" that, if not defended, could be lost. "The success of freedom," said Bush, "rests upon the choices and the courage of free peoples, and upon their willingness to sacrifice." Because the United States and its allies were steadfast, Germany and Japan became democratic nations that no longer threatened the world. Bush then explicitly affirmed his belief in democratic peace: "Every nation has learned, or should have learned, an important lesson: Freedom is worth fighting for, dying for, and standing for—and the advance of freedom leads to peace." "And now," he continued, thinking of the Middle East, "we must apply that lesson in our own time. We've reached another great turning point—and the resolve we show will shape the next stage of the world democratic movement." He continued:

In many nations of the Middle East—countries of great importance—democracy has not yet taken root. And the questions arise: Are the peoples of the Middle East somehow beyond the reach of liberty? Are millions of men and women and children condemned by history or culture to live in despotism? . . . I, for one, do not believe it. I believe every person has the ability and the right to be free.

Some skeptics of democracy assert that the traditions of Islam are inhospitable to representative government. This "cultural condescension," as Ronald Reagan termed it, has a long history. After the Japanese surrender in 1945, a so-called Japan expert asserted that democracy in that former empire would "never work." Another observer declared the prospects for democracy in post-Hitler Germany are, and I quote, "most uncertain at best." . . . Seventy-four years ago, the *Sunday London Times* declared nine-tenths of the population of India to be "illiterates not caring a fig for politics." . . . Time after time, observers have questioned whether this country, or that people, or this group, are "ready" for democracy—as if freedom were a prize you win for meeting our own Western standards of progress.

Seeing the Islamic nations of the Middle East as no exception, Bush contended that "in every region of the world, the advance of freedom leads to peace." The "freedom deficit" in the Middle East had to be changed; doing so would change not just the region but the world. He conceded that while democracy is not perfect and not the path to utopia, it is "the only path to national success and dignity." Importantly, he added that democratic governments in the Middle East "will not, and should not, look like us." They should reflect their own cultures and traditions; they could be constitutional monarchies, federal republics, or parliamentary systems. Equally significant, Bush urged that "working democracies always need time to develop—as did American democracy." America must be "patient" with those nations at different stages of the journey.

In the most controversial parts of the address, Bush claimed: "It should be clear to all that Islam . . . is consistent with democratic rule." For doubters, he singled out examples of democratic progress in predominantly Muslim countries—Turkey, Indonesia, Senegal, Albania, Niger, and Sierra Leone. He said that Muslim men and women were good citizens of India and South Africa, of the nations of Western Europe, and of the United States. According to Bush, more than half of all Muslims live under "democratically constituted governments," and they succeed in democratic societies "not in spite of their faith, but because of it." Here again, one might be hard-pressed to find a more passionate advocate for Islam among Western leaders. Speaking of Islam's alleged relation to liberty on a more theological level, Bush asserted: "A religion that demands individual moral accountability, and encourages the encounter of the individual with God, is fully compatible with the rights and responsibilities of self-government." He identified signs of democratic progress in Morocco, Bahrain, Oman, Qatar, Yemen, Kuwait, and Jordan.

If such countries become twenty-first-century democracies, historians will struggle to explain how impossible democracy's prospects once seemed in these nations, and thus how boundless was Bush's optimism. His assessment may have been more far-fetched than Ronald Reagan's predictions about the end of communism in the early 1980s, to which Bush referred in this speech. Speaking specifically of Reagan's June 1982 Westminister Address, as well as Woodrow Wilson's Fourteen Points and Franklin Delano Roosevelt's Four Freedoms, Bush concluded: "The advance of freedom is the calling of our time; it is the calling of our country. . . . We [Americans] believe that liberty is the design of nature; we believe that liberty is the direction of history. . . . This is, above all, the age of liberty."

He finished by stamping his blessing on the work of all champions of liberty at the National Endowment for Democracy: "May God bless your work."

The speech's revolutionary sentiments were not new for Bush. Since the first days after September 11, he had argued that what the terrorists hated most was freedom. A week after September 11, he promised: "We're going to lead the world to fight for freedom."[7] He told Bob Woodward: "I truly believe that out of this [September 11] will come more order in the world—real progress to peace in the Middle East."[8]

George W. Bush assigned himself the role of catalyst. A year after September 11, and more than a year before his National Endowment for Democracy speech and invasion of Iraq, in its sweeping National Security Strategy the Bush administration had promoted the spread of democracy to nations held hostage to despots. This objective, Bush said with hope, could bring long-term peace to regions like the Middle East. In a parallel not lost upon Bush, John Lewis Gaddis noted that by seeking to spread democracy everywhere, the president appeared to be trying to finish the job Woodrow Wilson had started a century earlier.[9] "The world," writes Gaddis, "quite literally, must be made safe for democracy, even those parts of it, like the Middle East, that have so far resisted that tendency."[10] In July 2001, in his Proclamation 7455 marking Captive Nations Week, Bush had declared: "The 21st century must become the 'Century of Democracy.'"

OSAMA'S DOING, BUSH'S CHOICE

How might Bush achieve that vision? September 11 handed him the opportunity. If a democratic Middle East should one day take shape—unimaginable as the prospect might seem—which individual will have helped facilitate that better world, aside from George W. Bush? One answer, Osama bin Laden.

Prior to bin Laden's attack on the United States that Tuesday morning, Bush was content to talk about education and faith-based organizations. He hoped to be remembered for compassionate conservatism, not some unforeseen war on terror. He would have left turning points in American history to historians like Jay Winik, who found the great lessons of American history buried deep in the past.

A rout of radical Islamic terror, and defeat of dictatorship in Afghanistan and Iraq, was not what Osama had in mind. Nor did he expect a steady dismantling of his Al-Qaeda network, or a life on the run. It's hard to believe that he envisioned his acts unleashing a wave of democratic freedom in the Middle East—as Bush hoped they would.

Friend and foe can debate whether the president's reaction was for the best. Neither can dispute that he seized the moment, that he chose how to react. Bush put it this way: "This is a testing time for our country. . . . We face an ongoing threat of terror. One thing is certain: we didn't ask for these challenges, but we will meet them. I say that with certainty."[11]

One common mistake Bush's accusers make is to assume that Bush is manipulated by string pullers: neoconservatives, the Iraq hawks, Bill Kristol and the *Weekly Standard*, and an "evil axis" of Paul Wolfowitz, Richard Perle, and Donald Rumsfeld. One anti-Semitic sliver within the left, reaching into the ivory tower, has complained that a purported Jewish conspiracy is enveloping the president. Yet Bush and those around him concur that he is his own man—his own biggest influence. Ivo Daalder, a former Clinton NSC member who is now a fellow at the Brookings Institution, is no fan of Bush. Still, as he acknowledged at Princeton University, "George Bush is an agent

of his own making. This is a man who is in control. This is not a revolution of an administration. This is a revolution of one man."[12]

Writing in the London Times, presidential watcher Tim Hames
groped for an analogy. Is Bush another Wilson? Is he somehow Roose-
veltian? No, says Hames. If Bush bears comparison with any modern
American president, it is with Harry S Truman. Truman, as Hames
points out, was a slightly accidental president mocked by elites. Like
Bush, Truman found himself suddenly faced with globe-altering de-
velopments: the end of World War II, the advent of the bomb, the superpower confrontation. Looking into the eye of a storm that would
stir for decades, he was obliged to lay the groundwork for a long war
with many pauses and disappointments. "[Truman] had to shape foreign policy on the hoof," averred Hames, "invent institutions at
home and abroad to match new circumstances, set precedents and
draw lines in the sand."[13]

Any analogy has imperfections, but this is a keen one. Like Truman, Bush built new bureaucracies to handle new realities, such as
a Department of Homeland Security; sought massive defense ex-
penditures; and enunciated grand new national-security doctrines.
Truman established containment and NSC-68; Bush initiated preemption and his NSS. As Hames noted, it was Truman, the man
from Independence, who claimed that a statesman is a politician
who has been dead ten or fifteen years. "It was certainly a decade after [Truman] left the White House before his approach was universally appreciated," Hames wrote. "Much the same will be true for
Mr. Bush."

Historian Richard Brookhiser perceives an intriguing analogy
between Bush and Sam Houston. "Time will judge Bush," wrote
Brookhiser in The Atlantic. Like the story of Sam Houston leaving
Austin, Bush's story "is hopeful: virtue temporarily unrecognized."[14]

The legacy of both Bush and Houston will spring from them having pursued what they felt was right, despite the most vitriolic protests. Like cowboys of conviction, they stuck to their guns. And, like Houston, Bush's summit may lay ahead.

SEARCHING FOR THE MOUNTAINTOP

Where is the mountaintop for George W. Bush? The Texan perceives his calling as ongoing. He expects more battles; other outlaws remain. He has not claimed final victory, and has repeatedly warned that the war on terror will be long. He maintains a firm resolve to push toward that peak.

Where is that apex? Bush may not have even a vague idea. Mortals are constrained by human limitation, and can only plan so much. Major events are rarely foreseen. As a student of history, Bush knows that. As the September 11 president, who spent the morning of September 10 thinking about taxes, he is keenly aware of the unexpected challenges of history. And that fact makes the final pages of his prepresidential memoir quite interesting:

> This is a unique moment in history. A generation after the success-ful struggle against an evil empire, a new generation of American leaders will determine how American power and influence are used. This is still a world of terror and missiles and madmen. . . . Peace is not ordained, it is earned. Building a durable peace . . . requires firmness with regimes like North Korea and Iraq. . . .
>
> America must not retreat within its borders. Our greatest ex-port is freedom, and we have a moral obligation to champion it throughout the world.[15]

Bush is now the American leader determining how that power and influence are used at a unique moment in history, with nations like North Korea and Iraq. He seems aware that he can only know and plan so much: It gets cloudy as a sojourner approaches the summit. That is where that devout faith comes into play. There lies that "Charge to Keep," of which he reminds himself via the painting that has hung in his office since Austin. Not knowing his final destination, he trusts God to move him in the right direction. He wrote in those same memoirs: "I build my life on a foundation that will not shift. My faith frees me. . . . Frees me to enjoy life and not worry about what comes next. I've never plotted the various steps of my life." He says: "I live in the moment, seize opportunities, and try to make the most of them."[16]

This thinking is consistent with Oswald Chambers in *My Utmost for His Highest*:

> Each morning as you wake, there is a new opportunity. . . . God does not tell you what He is going to do next. . . . A life of faith is not a life of one glorious mountaintop experience after another, but it is a life of day-in and day-out consistency; a life of walking without fainting. Living a life of faith means never knowing where you are being led. But it does mean knowing the One who is leading.[17]

By his own account, George W. Bush looks to God for guidance on a daily basis—to plot his steps, to pick that purpose. That purpose, he says, will be his duty to meet. As he said in his presidential inaugural, "We are not this story's author, who fills time and eternity with His purpose. Yet His purpose is achieved in our duty."

It is a common message for Bush. One of his lesser-known, but more amusing and telling, speeches was a brief commencement address he made at Yale University, his alma mater, in May 2001. Making fun of his notorious garbling of syntax, he quipped: "Everything I know about the spoken word, I learned right here at Yale." Amid the laughs, he turned serious, recalling life after Yale:

> When I left here, I didn't have much in the way of a life plan. I knew some people who thought they did, but it turned out that we were all in for ups and downs, most of them unexpected. Life takes its own turns, makes its own demands, writes its own story, and along the way, we start to realize we are not the author. We begin to understand that life is ours to live but not to waste and that the greatest rewards are found in the commitments we make with our whole hearts—to the people we love and to the causes that earn our sacrifice.[18]

Bush has not shied away from perceiving God's hand in the struggles of other peoples, leaders, and nations at previous points in history. On June 15, 2001, at Warsaw University, he spoke of Poland's battle against the twentieth century's two most vicious totalitarianisms—Nazi fascism and Soviet communism. The world had witnessed the character of the Polish people, he said, "and the hand of God in [their] history." The Polish people, said Bush, had spurned totalitarianism "armed only with their conscience and their faith."[19]

But Bush went further in his speech. He noted that more than a half century ago, standing where he stood, all that could be seen in Warsaw was a desert of ruins, bricks upon bricks, rubble on rubble. The city had been razed by Nazis and then betrayed by Soviets. Not far from that same spot was the only monument that survived. "It is the figure of Christ falling under the cross and struggling to rise," said Bush. "Under him are written the words: 'Sursum corda'—'lift up your hearts.'" With that hope, he said, Poland rose again; Europe stood again. "And, together," he requested, "let us raise this hope of freedom for all who seek it in the world. God bless." With that, he left the podium.

George W. Bush sees God's hand guiding history; as it guided Poland then, he believes that it will guide America now.

God's Plan

President Bush believes that God has a plan for him. He has said that he could not be president if he didn't believe in a "divine plan that supersedes all human plans."[20] Before the inauguration, the president-elect sat for an interview with *Time*. "I believe things happen for a reason," he said of the messy election that made him president. "It is a unique moment, and I intend to seize it. . . . I view it as a very positive opportunity."[21]

In the opening weeks of his presidency, when the nation had been shaken by a disputed election, observers were asked about the new president's opportunities. Walter Dean Burnham, a University of Texas political scientist, remarked: "I think he'll find himself with limited opportunities, given the times and divisions."[22] At the time, Burnham's assessment was reasonable. The events of September 11, of course, proved otherwise. Speaking of September 11, Michael Duffy wrote in *Time*: "Bush didn't rise to meet history but that history fell to him."[23]

Even as God charts his ultimate course, the president has taken pains to lay out his own vision. His trust in God's guidance appears to extend to a basic confidence in the measures his administration has taken. Many people talk about faith, but Bush appears to be walking by faith. "I recognize that a walk is a walk," he says, "it's a never-ending journey."[24] When his evangelical supporters hail him for "walking the walk," they may not know the degree to which that is the case.

AS THE INVASION OF IRAQ APPROACHED, THE PRES-sure on Bush was acute. Some critics questioned his very faith, his very understanding of God. Just a few weeks before the first Toma-hawks were unleashed, he spoke to a packed room at the National Prayer Breakfast at the Washington Hilton. He acknowledged those fellow spiritual warriors who were present, and spoke of the current challenge and time of "testing." He talked of how he appreciated the prayer he felt from the nation. At 8:20 A.M., he ended his brief re-marks with this common sentiment:

> We can . . . be confident in the ways of Providence, even when they are far from our understanding. Events aren't moved by blind change and chance. Behind all of life and all of history, there's a dedication and purpose, set by the hand of a just and faithful God. . . . We pray for wisdom to know and do what is right.[25]

It is fitting to finish this story with a final line from Bush's most cherished hymn. "Through many dangers, toils, and snares, I have al-ready come," wrote the authors of "Amazing Grace," " 'Tis grace hath brought me safe thus far, and grace will lead me home." In his life and presidency, Bush has endured many such toils and snares—from Robin and the bottle to Osama and Saddam. Some carried embarrass-ment, some the most bitter of criticism; one simply brought pain. George W. Bush is certain that he has overcome these adversities with God's help. He is confident that God's grace will continue to carry him—eventually all the way home.

NOTES

PREFACE

1. George W. Bush, "Remarks in Acceptance Speech at Republican Convention," Philadelphia, August 3, 2000.
2. George W. Bush, A Charge to Keep: My Journey to the White House (New York: Harper-Collins, 2001), pp. x and 45.

CHAPTER 1

1. Ibid., p. 8.
2. Quoted in Bill Minutaglio, First Son: George W. Bush and the Bush Family Dynasty (New York: Random House, 1999), p. 45.
3. Quoted in George Lardner Jr. and Lois Romano, "A Sister Dies; a Family Moves On," Washington Post, July 26, 1999.
4. Bush, A Charge to Keep, pp. 14–15.
5. The interview was with the Washington Post on May 11, 1999, in Austin, TX. See: "In His Own Words: 'I Remember the Sadness,'" Washington Post, July 26, 1999. Also see: Lardner Jr. and Romano, "A Sister Dies; a Family Moves On."
6. George H. W. Bush, All the Best, George Bush (New York: Drew Book/Scribner, 1999), p. 102; George H. W. Bush with Victor Gold, Looking Forward (New York: Bantam, 1987), p. 69; and Minutaglio, First Son, p. 43.
7. George H. W. Bush, All the Best, George Bush, p. 102.
8. Barbara Bush, Barbara Bush: a Memoir (New York: Drew Book/Scribner, 1994), p. 42; and George H. W. Bush, Looking Forward, p. 69.
9. Barbara Bush, Barbara Bush: a Memoir, p. 44.
10. Robin was born December 20, 1949; she died on Columbus Day in October 1953.

11. Though only twenty-eight, her friends remember her hair changing color. Lardner Jr. and Romano, "A Sister Dies; a Family Moves On."

12. Lardner Jr. and Romano, "A Sister Dies; a Family Moves On."

13. Barbara Bush, *Barbara Bush: a Memoir*, p. 46.

14. George H. W. Bush, *All the Best, George Bush*, pp. 81–82 and 96. Also see the very moving account by Bush on pages 449 and 592. Also: George H. W. Bush, *Heartbeat* (New York: Scribner, 2001), pp. 270–271; and George H. W. Bush, *Looking Forward*, p. 69.

15. Bush, *A Charge to Keep*, p. 15; and Barbara Bush, *Barbara Bush: a Memoir*, p. 46.

16. "In His Own Words: 'I Remember the Sadness.' "

17. Quoted in: Lardner Jr. and Romano, "A Sister Dies; a Family Moves On."

18. Minutaglio, *First Son*, p. 63.

19. Bush, *A Charge to Keep*, p. 15.

20. In his memoir, the first chapter begins with Mark Craig's sermon and Bush's "calling." The second chapter, which starts the narrative chronology of his life, begins with Robin in the first sentence.

21. The date was September 6, 1993. Source: Barbara Bush, *Reflections* (New York: Scribner, 2003), p. 27.

22. Lois Romano and George Lardner Jr., "Bush: So-So Student but a Campus Mover," *Washington Post*, July 27, 1999, p. A1.

23. George H. W. Bush, *Heartbeat*, p. 286.

24. Source: Original December 30, 1993, fund-raising letter.

25. Lardner Jr. and Romano, "A Sister Dies; a Family Moves On."

26. Bush, *A Charge to Keep*, p. 16.

27. George H. W. Bush, *Looking Forward*, p. 27.

28. Bush's move out of the Episcopal church is symptomatic of the exodus over the last forty years. According to various accounts, membership is now around 2.3 million, a drop of 33 percent since the mid-1960s.

29. He told this to a group of kids in an Arkansas school. President George W. Bush, "Question-and-Answer Session at Lakewood Elementary School in North Little Rock, Arkansas," March 5, 2001.

30. Bush, *A Charge to Keep*, p. 18.

31. Ibid., pp. 15–16.

32. Ibid., pp. 16–17.

33. See: Lardner Jr. and Romano, "A Sister Dies; a Family Moves On."

34. Bush, *A Charge to Keep*, p. 19.

35. Ibid., p. 8.

36. Ibid., pp. 6–7.

37. See: Lardner Jr. and Romano, "A Sister Dies; a Family Moves On"; and Barbara Bush, *Barbara Bush: a Memoir*, p. 47.

38. See: Lardner Jr. and Romano, "A Sister Dies; a Family Moves On."

39. Frank Bruni, "Senior Bush's Loss Set Course for Son's Candidacy," *The New York Times*, December 26, 1999.

40. Bush, *A Charge to Keep*, p. 19.

41. This journalist, Howard Fineman, also reported that Bush used the deacon position to

engineer pranks more than to minister to the flock. I could not confirm this. Fineman, "Bush and God."

42. Information provided by Phillips Academy archivist Ruth Quattlebaum, September 9, 2003.

43. Phillips Academy Yearbook, 1964, p. 56. Pages provided by Quattlebaum.

44. Bush, A Charge to Keep, p. 21.

45. Ibid., p. 20.

46. Lois Romano and George Lardner Jr., "Bush: So-So Student but a Campus Mover," p. A1.

47. David Maraniss and Ellen Nakashima, "Gore's Grades Belie Image of Studiousness," Washington Post, March 19, 2000, p. A1.

48. Bush, A Charge to Keep, pp. 48–49.

49. Lois Romano and George Lardner Jr., "Bush: So-So Student but a Campus Mover," p. A1.

50. Ibid.

51. Interview with George W. Bush, "George W. Bush: Running on His Faith," U.S. News & World Report, December 6, 1999.

52. See: Minutaglio, First Son, pp. 149–151; and George Lardner Jr. and Lois Romano, "At Height of Vietnam, Bush Picks Guard," Washington Post, July 28, 1999, p. A1.

53. See: Minutaglio, First Son, pp. 149–151; and George Lardner Jr. and Lois Romano, "At Height of Vietnam, Bush Picks Guard," p. A1.

54. George Lardner Jr. and Lois Romano, "At Height of Vietnam, Bush Picks Guard," p. A1.

55. Minutaglio, First Son, pp. 149–151; and George Lardner Jr. and Lois Romano, "At Height of Vietnam, Bush Picks Guard," p. A1.

56. Bush, A Charge to Keep, pp. 58–59; Minutaglio, First Son, pp. 149–151; and George Lardner Jr. and Lois Romano, "At Height of Vietnam, Bush Picks Guard," p. A1.

57. Bush, A Charge to Keep, p. 59.

58. Ibid.

59. Ibid., pp. 60–61.

60. George Lardner Jr. and Lois Romano, "At Height of Vietnam, Bush Picks Guard," p. A1.

61. Bush, A Charge to Keep, pp. 56–57.

62. This saying has also been attributed to the early church father Saint Augustine.

CHAPTER 2

1. Bush, A Charge to Keep, p. 139.

2. Charles Bradbury, History of Kennebunk Port from Its First Discovery by Bartholomew Gosnold (Kennebunk, ME: James K. Remich, 1837), pp. 30–31, 40–41, 58–59; and Kenneth Joy, The Kennebunks: "Out of the Past" (Freeport, ME: Bond Wheelwright Co., 1967).

3. Bush, A Charge to Keep, p. 136.

4. Ibid.

5. See: interview with Steven Waldman of Beliefnet; and "George W. Bush: Running on His Faith," U. S. News & World Report, December 6, 1999."

6. J. Lee Grady, "PLUS: God and the Governor," interview with George W. Bush, *Charisma*, August 29, 2000.

7. Governor George W. Bush, "Address to the Second Baptist Church," Houston, TX, March 7, 1999.

8. Bush, *A Charge to Keep*, p. 19.

9. Today, Evans is secretary of commerce in the Bush administration. He married Susie Evans, George's old elementary-school friend. Don went to the University of Texas at Austin when Bush headed to Yale.

10. Bush, *A Charge to Keep*, p. 136.

11. Minutaglio, *First Son*; and Lois Romano and George Lardner Jr., "Bush's Life-Changing Year," *Washington Post*, July 25, 1999, p. A1.

12. Bush, *A Charge to Keep*, p. 182.

13. Lois Romano and George Lardner Jr., "Bush's Life-Changing Year," p. A1.

14. Bush, *A Charge to Keep*, pp. 132–133.

15. Among others, quoted in: Dave Boyer, "Bush Sees Reagan Traits in Self," *Washington Times*, November 1, 2000.

16. Quoted by Frum, *The Right Man* (New York: Random House, 2003), p. 283.

17. Quoted by Howard Fineman, "Bush and God," *Newsweek*, March 10, 2003.

18. On the first page of her latest book, Barbara Bush begins by saying that she hoped all of her children would believe in God. Barbara Bush, *Reflections* (New York: Scribner, 2003), p.1. Also see: "George W. Bush: Running on His Faith," *U.S. News & World Report*, December 6, 1999.

19. Bush wrote this in a July 29, 1982, letter to A. Bartlett Giamatti. The letter is published in George H. W. Bush, *All the Best, George Bush*, pp. 319–320.

20. Laura Bush quoted in Tony Carnes, "A Presidential Hopeful's Progress," *Christianity Today*, October 2, 2000.

21. Bush, *A Charge to Keep*, p. 137.

22. Ibid.

23. See: Lee Strobel, *The Case for Christ* (Grand Rapids, MI: Zondervan, 1998), pp. 132–134.

24. Bill Keller, "God and George W. Bush," *The New York Times*, May 17, 2003.

25. Ibid.

26. J. Lee Grady, "PLUS: God and the Governor," Interview with George W. Bush.

27. Interview with George W. Bush, "George W. Bush: Running on His Faith."

28. Bush told this to a friend named Mark Leaverton, who was interviewed on "The Jesus Factor," *Frontline*, PBS, 2004.

29. Ibid.; and Bush, *A Charge to Keep*, p. 137.

30. Bush, *A Charge to Keep*, pp. 137–138.

31. Ibid., p. 137.

32. On this, see: Minutaglio, *First Son*, pp. 217–228 and 288–290.

33. See: Bush, *A Charge to Keep*, p. 4; and Minutaglio, *First Son*, p. 264.

34. Interview with Brian Berry, July 1, 2003.

35. Interview with Brian Berry, June 18, 2003.

36. Barbara Bush, *Reflections*, p. 27.

37. See: Minutaglio, *First Son*, pp. 290–300.
38. Bush, *A Charge to Keep*, pp. 42–43.
39. See: Minutaglio, *First Son*, p. 300. Graham would swear in Jeb Bush as Florida governor in 1999. Barbara Bush, *Reflections*, p. 260.
40. Transcript of January 1995 inaugural address.
41. Bush, *A Charge to Keep*, pp. 44–45.
42. Ibid., p. 45.
43. Governor George W. Bush, "Speech at the Dedication of the Power Center's Jesse H. Jones Ballroom," Houston, July 8, 1997. Transcript provided by the Texas State Archives Commission. Bush used the anecdote again on March 7, 1999, when speaking to the Second Baptist Church in Houston.
44. As governor, Bush used the same story on March 7, 1999, at the Second Baptist Church in Houston.
45. Quoted in: Bush, *A Charge to Keep*, p. 10.
46. Governor George W. Bush, "Address to the Second Baptist Church."
47. Interview with George W. Bush, "George W. Bush: Running on His Faith."
48. Tony Carnes, "A Presidential Hopeful's Progress," *Christianity Today*, October 2, 2000; and Bush, *A Charge to Keep*, p. 153.
49. Tony Carnes, "A Presidential Hopeful's Progress"; and Bush, *A Charge to Keep*, p. 154.
50. Slater interviewed for "The Jesus Factor," *Frontline*, PBS, 2004.
51. Bush, *A Charge to Keep*, p. 148.
52. Ibid.
53. Tony Carnes, "A Presidential Hopeful's Progress."
54. Bush, *A Charge to Keep*, pp. 161–162.
55. Tony Carnes, "A Presidential Hopeful's Progress."
56. On the love theology, also see: President George W. Bush, "Remarks to Employees of Sears Manufacturing Company," Davenport, IA, September 16, 2002.
57. Interview with Marvin Olasky, February 7, 2003.
58. Bush, *A Charge to Keep*, p. 236.
59. President George W. Bush, "Remarks by the President at the National Hispanic Prayer Breakfast," Capitol Hilton, Washington, D.C., May 16, 2002, p. 2. He also uses this rhetoric in his prepresidential memoirs.
60. Interview with Marvin Olasky, February 5, 2003.
61. Quoted in Laurie Goodstein, "Puts His Faith in Providence," *The New York Times*, February 9, 2003.
62. Hanna Rosin and Terry M. Neal, "Texas Prison Uses 'Christ-Centered' Agenda," *Washington Post*, November 27, 1999, p. A1.
63. Ibid.
64. Sources: Governor George W. Bush, "Address to the Second Baptist Church"; and Bush, *A Charge to Keep*, pp. 214–216.
65. President George W. Bush, "Remarks on Faith-Based Initiative in Tennessee," Opryland, Nashville, February 10, 2003.
66. Quoted in Joe Loconte, "Leap of Faith," *National Review*, July 12, 1999, pp. 40–41.
67. See: Ibid.

68. President George W. Bush, "Remarks in Commencement Address at University of Notre Dame," South Bend, IN, May 21, 2001.

69. Material from the section that follows was provided primarily by Don Browning and Tom Brown; both now residents of Phoenix, Arizona, each man was close to those who experienced the tragedy.

70. Interview with Don Browning, April 1, 2004.

71. Ibid.

72. Ibid.

73. Ibid.

CHAPTER 3

1. Richard Brookhiser, "Close-Up: The Mind of George W. Bush," *The Atlantic*, March 2003.

2. Bush, *A Charge to Keep*, p. 46.

3. Dr. Paul Vickery, an expert on Marquis James, is a source for some of this information.

4. Bush, *A Charge to Keep*, p. 43.

5. This is evident throughout the *Presidential Documents*.

6. On this occasion, he neglected to note that Houston was also governor of Tennessee, which he usually acknowledges. President George W. Bush, "Remarks at East Literature Magnet School in Nashville," Nashville, September 17, 2002.

7. President George W. Bush, "Remarks on Presenting the National Teacher of the Year Award," Washington, D.C., April 23, 2001.

8. President George W. Bush, "Remarks on the Unveiling of the President's Portrait in Austin, Texas," Austin, January 4, 2002.

9. Marquis James, *The Raven: A Biography of Sam Houston* (New York: Blue Ribbon Books, 1929), p. 157.

10. Ibid., p. 130.

11. Among other spots, he said this in Alamogordo, NM, on October 28, 2002, in Denver, CO, on October 28, 2002, and in Las Cruces, NM, on August 24, 2002.

12. President George W. Bush, "Remarks to the Cattle Industry Annual Convention and Trade Show," Denver, February 8, 2002.

13. The date was December 5, 2002.

14. James, *The Raven*, p. 412.

15. Ibid., p. 175.

16. Richard Brookhiser, "Close-Up: The Mind of George W. Bush."

17. James, *The Raven*, p. 157.

18. Ibid.

19. Ibid.

20. Ibid., pp. 186 and 207.

21. Ibid., pp. 281 and 385.

22. Richard Brookhiser, "Close-Up: The Mind of George W. Bush."

23. Source: Tony Carnes, "A Presidential Hopeful's Progress."

24. James, *The Raven*, pp. 64–67.

25. Quoted by Brookhiser, "Close-Up."

26. James, *The Raven*, p. 121.

27. Ibid., pp. 119–120, 124, and 385–386.

28. Ibid., pp. 203–204.

29. Ibid., p. 81.

30. Ibid., p. 381.

31. Ibid., pp. 365–367.

32. Ibid., p. 385.

33. Ibid.

34. Ibid., pp. 385–386.

35. Ibid., pp. 401–402.

36. Ibid., pp. 422–423.

37. Ibid., pp. 432–433. Aside from these references by James, almost nothing has been written on Sam Houston's faith. One of the only works was a tableau produced by three Texas women—Caroline Moore, Dorothy Leeper, and Bonnie Thorne—to mark the anniversary of the First Baptist Church in Huntsville, TX, that Houston attended. They published the tableau in a short 1997 manuscript titled *Sam Houston: A Man Who Knew and Loved God*. Their research reveals that a comprehensive work on Houston's faith begs to be written.

CHAPTER 4

1. J. Lee Grady, "PLUS: God and the Governor," Interview with George W. Bush, *Charisma*, August 29, 2000; and Bush interview with the *Catholic Digest*, "George W. Bush: 'We Want the American Dream to Touch Every Willing Heart,'" *Catholic Digest*, August 11, 2000.

2. Bush tells this story in: Bush, *A Charge to Keep*, pp. 1–13.

3. See Jakes featured on *The Spirituality of George W. Bush*, documentary by Thirteen WNET New York, January 19, 2001.

4. Pederson and Land were interviewed on "The Jesus Factor," *Frontline*, PBS, 2004.

5. Mansfield, *The Faith of George W. Bush*, p. 109. In a December 5, 2003, interview on CBN's *The 700 Club*, Mansfield went a bit further with his observations on this episode, saying that Bush sensed that his country was "about to go through a horrible trauma." A couple of lines later, Mansfield spoke about September 11. This led some to say that Bush had sensed a tragedy like 9/11 before it happened.

6. Interview with George W. Bush, "George W. Bush: Running on His Faith," *U.S. News & World Report*, December 6, 1999.

7. There are also Christians who believe Jews are dealt with differently than non-Jews who don't accept Christ.

8. Bush has been criticized for once remarking (as governor) that only those who accept Christ go to heaven—a Christian belief that Christian politicians avoid discussing.

9. Cited in Tony Carnes, "A Presidential Hopeful's Progress," *Christianity Today*, October 2, 2000; and Carl M. Cannon, "Bush and God," *National Journal*, January 2, 2004.

10. Quoted in Michael Novak, *On Two Wings* (San Francisco: Encounter Books, 2002), p. 29.
11. Questions from New Hampshire Republican debate moderator Tim Russert to George W. Bush, January 6, 2000. Transcribed by the Media Research Center (MRC).
12. MSNBC's coverage of the New Hampshire Republican debate, January 6, 2000. Transcribed by MRC.
13. MSNBC's coverage of the New Hampshire Republican debate, January 6, 2000. Transcribed by MRC.
14. Brian Williams to *Newsweek*'s Howard Fineman, January 6, 2000, MSNBC's *The News with Brian Williams*. Transcribed by MRC.
15. *Time*'s Margaret Carlson commenting on the South Carolina Republican debate, January 8, 2000, on CNN's *Capital Gang*. Transcribed by MRC.
16. Laurie Goodstein, "Puts His Faith in Providence," *The New York Times*, February 9, 2003.
17. Maureen Dowd, "Playing the Jesus Card," *The New York Times*, December 15, 1999.
18. Source: S. Robert Lichter, Daniel R. Amundson, and Linda S. Lichter, "Media Coverage of Religion in America, 1969–1998," Center for Media and Public Affairs, June 2000. This particular study found that 37 percent of the public attend a religious service weekly.
19. Source: S. Robert Lichter, Daniel R. Amundson, and Linda S. Lichter, "Media Coverage of Religion in America, 1969–1998."
20. The May 2003 study by William Scott Green and Curt Smith is titled "Religion in American Newspapers: A Critique and Challenge."
21. Michael Gove, "Thank God for Politicians Who Take Their Cue from Above," *London Times*, May 6, 2003.
22. Tony Karon, "W Goes to Finishing School," *Time*, June 13, 2001.
23. Quoted by Joseph Curl, "Liberals Concede, Defend, Double Standard," *Washington Times*, August 11, 2000.
24. Maureen Dowd, "Playing the Jesus Card."
25. Quoted by Joseph Curl, "Liberals Concede, Defend, Double Standard"; and Cannon, "Bush and God."
26. In 2002, as president, George W. Bush and his wife reported taxable income of $771,940, resulting in a total of $268,719 in federal income taxes paid by the Bushes. Of this, they contributed $69,925 to churches and charitable organizations.
27. Terry M. Neal, "Bush Moves to Define His Credo," *Washington Post*, July 23, 1999, p. A2.
28. Interview with George W. Bush, "George W. Bush: Running on His Faith."
29. Among others, see: J. Lee Grady, "PLUS: God and the Governor"; and Interview with Will Hall of the Baptist Press, the national news service of the Southern Baptist Convention, August 31, 2000.
30. Bush, *A Charge to Keep*, p. 184.
31. Ibid., pp. 136 and 138.
32. Interview with Brian Berry, June 18, 2003.
33. Interview with Brian Berry, July 1, 2003.
34. Joe Klein, "The Blinding Glare of His Certainty," *Time*, February 18, 2003.

35. Sources quoted on convention coverage by *The Newshour with Jim Lehrer*, PBS, August 3, 2000.

36. George W. Bush, "Remarks in Acceptance Speech at Republican Convention," Philadelphia, August 3, 2000; and "Bush, Other Speakers Give Convention a Methodist Presence," United Methodist News Service, August 4, 2000.

37. George W. Bush, "Republican Nomination Acceptance Speech," Philadelphia, August 3, 2000.

38. Quotes taken from analysis of the debate hosted on MSNBC by Brian Williams, October 11, 2000.

39. J. Lee Grady, "PLUS: God and the Governor."

40. These quotes were juxtaposed by the media at the time. They were posted by both NBC's *Meet the Press with Tim Russert* and ABC's *This Week* on November 19, 2000, amid the Florida recount fiasco.

41. Lois Romano and George Lardner Jr., "Bush's Life-Changing Year," *Washington Post*, July 25, 1999, p. A1.

42. Interview, "George W. Bush: 'We Want the American Dream to Touch Every Willing Heart,'" *Catholic Digest*, August 11, 2000.

43. Al Gore, quoted by *Newsweek*, November 20, 2000.

44. Bush interview with Will Hall of the Baptist Press, the national news service of the Southern Baptist Convention, August 31, 2000.

45. Interview with Brian Berry, July 1, 2003.

46. Bush, *A Charge to Keep*, p. 6.

CHAPTER 5

1. Barbara Bush, *Reflections*, p. 383.

2. Ibid., p. 261. Jeb Bush was sworn in with the same Bible during his second inauguration as governor of Florida in 2003.

3. Bush, *A Charge to Keep*, p. 40.

4. Quoted in Dave Boyer, "Bush Campaign Says It's in the Bag," *Washington Times*, November 6, 2000.

5. Bill Clinton received 44.9 million votes in 1992 and 47.4 million in 1996.

6. This incident is relayed by Bill Sammon, *At Any Cost* (Washington, D.C.: Regnery, 2001).

7. Ibid.

8. Ibid.

9. See: Ralph Z. Hallow, "Gore Used Race as His Card in Election," *Washington Times*, November 9, 2000.

10. Dave Boyer, "Bush Campaign Says It's in the Bag."

11. Data provided by the Associated Press on December 20, 2000.

12. "The Vote Tuesday, County by County," *USA Today*, November 9, 2000, p. 19A.

13. A study by *USA Today*, the *Miami Herald*, and Knight Ridder found that "Bush would have won a hand count of Florida's disputed ballots if the standard advocated by Al Gore had been used." Bush, claimed the study, would have won by 1,665 votes, more than triple his official 537-vote margin, "if every dimple, hanging chad and mark on

the ballots had been counted as votes." Source: Dennis Cauchon, "Newspapers' Recount Shows Bush Prevailed," *USA Today*, April 5, 2001.

14. See: Dave Boyer, "Bush Seeks a California Coup," *Washington Times*, October 31, 2000.

15. Audrey Hudson, "Jackson Predicts 'Explosion' If Gore Loses," *Washington Times*, December 12, 2000.

16. Nancy Gibbs, "Person of the Year: George W. Bush," *Time*, December 17, 2000.

17. Quoted in: Karen MacPherson and Rachel Smolkin, "Real Troupers: Crowds Brave Elements to Cheer or Protest," *Pittsburgh Post-Gazette*, January 21, 2001.

18. Quoted in James O'Toole, "Few Arrests of Generally Peaceful Demonstrators," *Pittsburgh Post-Gazette*, January 21, 2001.

19. MacPherson and Smolkin, "Real Troupers: Crowds Brave Elements to Cheer or Protest."

20. "100 Gather Downtown to Protest Against Bush," *Pittsburgh Post-Gazette*, January 21, 2001.

21. Frank Bruni, "Senior Bush's Loss Set Course for Son's Candidacy," *The New York Times*, December 26, 1999.

22. George H. W. Bush, speaking to the 99th Annual Meeting of the Manufacturers' Association of Northwest Pennsylvania, June 30, 2004, Erie, Pennsylvania.

23. The speech was written by Michael Gerson, a Wheaton College graduate and conservative Christian. Bush did not talk to Gerson about the address until just six weeks before the swearing-in ceremony, when he arrived in Washington as president-elect in mid-December. They chatted briefly in Washington, D.C., and then more extensively for two hours aboard the plane back to Texas. Bush stressed the two themes he wanted to emphasize in the address—healing the divide and a compassionate conservative presidency. Bush and aides tinkered with Gerson's initial draft. Source: Fred Barnes, "The Real George W. Bush," *Weekly Standard*, January 29, 2001. This is Bush's style. "He would do a lot of striking [of words]," remembers campaign manager Brian Berry from the first gubernatorial days. "He questions things all the time, on and off paper. He writes questions all over documents." Interview with Brian Berry, July 1, 2003.

24. Fineman interviewed by Brian Williams of MSNBC, January 20, 2001.

25. "United Methodist Pastor Gives Inaugural Benediction," United Methodist News Service, January 22, 2001.

26. James O'Toole, "Few Arrests of Generally Peaceful Demonstrators."

27. Nancy Gibbs, "Person of the Year: George W. Bush."

28. See comments by Walter Isaacson on NBC's *Meet the Press with Tim Russert*, December, 17, 2000.

29. Richard Cohen, "Gore Can't Heal the Hurt," *Washington Post*, November 24, 2000.

CHAPTER 6

1. Among others, see: President George W. Bush, "Remarks by the President at the National Hispanic Prayer Breakfast," Washington, D.C., May 16, 2002; and President George W. Bush, "Remarks via Satellite to the 2002 Southern Baptist Convention," June 11, 2002.

2. President George W. Bush, "The President's News Conference," February 22, 2001.

3. President George W. Bush, "Proclamation 7403—National Day of Prayer and Thanksgiving," January 20, 2001.

4. "United Methodist Pastor Gives Inaugural Benediction," United Methodist News Service, January 22, 2001. Note: Craig had also spoken at the Republican convention in August 2000.

5. Among others, see: President George W. Bush, "Remarks by the President at the National Hispanic Prayer Breakfast"; and President George W. Bush, "Remarks via Satellite to the 2002 Southern Baptist Convention."

6. President George W. Bush, "Remarks by the President at the National Prayer Breakfast," Washington, D.C., February 7, 2002.

7. Judy Keen, "President's Faith Is a 'Great Comfort' to Him," USA Today, May 18, 2001, p. A6.

8. Paul Kengor, "Our Chinese Chess Match: We Need More Leverage," Pittsburgh Post-Gazette, April 8, 2001.

9. See commentary on: Hardball with Chris Matthews, MSNBC, April 11, 2001; and The News with Brian Williams, MSNBC, April 11, 2001.

10. This was reported at the time by NBC News' Campbell Brown on The News with Brian Williams, MSNBC, April 11, 2001.

11. This was reported by Fred Barnes, "A Pro-Life White House," Weekly Standard, January 1/8, 2001, p. 13.

12. Kenneth L. Connor, "The Born Alive Act: a Win for Humanity," Pittsburgh Post-Gazette, August 5, 2002. Arkes is also Ney Professor of Jurisprudence and American Institutions at Amherst College.

13. Governor George W. Bush, "Address to the Republican Convention," August 3, 2000.

14. Jerry Falwell, "Our Pro-Life President," Falwell Confidential, November 6, 2003.

15. This event was held on January 21, 2004, and broadcast live by Eternal World Television Network.

16. Dobson speaking on Larry King Live, CNN, August 9, 2001.

17. The press conference was held at the National Press Club in Washington, D.C., on August 10, 2001. It was broadcast live by C-SPAN.

18. Alan Keyes speaking during interview with Jeff Greenfield, CNN, August 9, 2001.

19. The press conference was held at the National Press Club in Washington, D.C., on August 10, 2001. It was broadcast live by C-SPAN.

20. President George W. Bush, "Remarks by the President on Human Cloning Legislation," Washington, D.C., April 10, 2002.

21. "Establishment of White House Office of Faith-Based and Community Initiatives," Executive Order, January 29, 2001.

22. President George W. Bush, "Remarks in Commencement Address at University of Notre Dame," South Bend, IN, May 21, 2001.

23. President George W. Bush, "The President's News Conference," February 22, 2001.

24. See: President George W. Bush, "Remarks by the President at the National Hispanic Prayer Breakfast"; and President George W. Bush, "Remarks via Satellite to the 2002 Southern Baptist Convention."

25. President George W. Bush, "Remarks by the President in Commencement Address at the University of Notre Dame," p. 3.

26. President George W. Bush, "Remarks by the President via Satellite to the Southern Baptist Convention 2002 Annual Meeting."

27. President George W. Bush, "Remarks in Commencement Address at University of Notre Dame."

28. Ibid.

29. President George W. Bush, "President's Radio Address," June 28, 2003.

30. President George W. Bush, "Executive Order 13279—Equal Protection of the Laws for Faith-Based and Community Organizations," December 12, 2002.

31. President George W. Bush, "Remarks at the White House Conference on Faith-Based and Community Initiatives in Philadelphia," Philadelphia, December 12, 2002.

32. Dean said this in an interview with *Jewish Week*. James D. Besser, "Dean Does Damage Control," *Jewish Week*, October 3, 2003.

33. President George W. Bush, "State of the Union Address," January 28, 2003.

34. Michael Kelly, "We Can Save 10 Million Lives," *Washington Post*, February 5, 2003, p. A23.

35. President George W. Bush, "Remarks by the President on Global HIV/AIDS Initiative," Washington, D.C., April 29, 2003.

36. Ibid.

37. President George W. Bush, "Interview on *Meet the Press with Tim Russert*," February 8, 2004.

38. "Bush Signs AIDS Plan; Tells Europe to Follow Suit," Reuters, May 27, 2003; and "Bush to Sign Global AIDS Bill," Associated Press, May 27, 2003.

39. President George W. Bush, "Remarks by the President to the Corporate Council on Africa's U.S.–Africa Business Summit," Washington, D.C., June 26, 2003.

40. Bush, *A Charge to Keep*, p. 236.

41. Fred Barnes, "A 'Big Government Conservatism,'" *The Wall Street Journal*, August 15, 2003.

42. Rich Lowry, "The President Keeps His Distance," *Washington Post*, August 10, 2003, p. B1.

43. The Christian gospel says that of all the gifts God gave humanity, the greatest is love. This is clear throughout the New Testament, where Christ also indicates that loving God and one's neighbor sums up the Old Testament. He called those two commands— love God and love thy neighbor—the greatest commandments of the law. He called the love commandment a "new commandment." Christ essentially said that people will know that Christians are Christians by the love Christians show. A reading of the Bible reveals that love is the foundation of both the Old and New Testaments. Among these, see: 1 Corinthians 13:13, Luke 10:26, Matthew 22:37–40, and John 13:34–35, 14:15, and 23. In 1 Corinthians, it is Paul who uses the "gift" language, which was easily an appropriate conclusion based on Christ's own teachings.

44. Bush, *A Charge to Keep*, p. 8.

45. President George W. Bush, "Message on the Observance of Easter," April 13, 2001.

46. President George W. Bush, "Message on the Observance of Christmas 2001," December 20, 2001.

47. President George W. Bush, "Message on the Observance of Easter 2002," March 27, 2002.

48. President George W. Bush, "Message on the Observance of Easter 2003," April 17, 2003.

49. President George W. Bush, "Remarks at the National Fallen Firefighters Memorial in Emmitsburg, Maryland," October 7, 2001.

50. President George W. Bush, "Remarks to the Fourth National Summit on Fatherhood," June 7, 2001.

51. Joe Klein, "The Blinding Glare of His Certainty," *Time*, February 18, 2003.

52. President George W. Bush, "Remarks by the President at the National Prayer Breakfast," Washington, D.C., February 7, 2002.

53. President George W. Bush, "Remarks at the National Religious Broadcasters' Convention," Nashville, February 10, 2003.

54. President George W. Bush, "Remarks via Satellite to the 2002 Southern Baptist Convention."

55. See: David Frum, *The Right Man* (New York: Random House, 2003), pp. 103–104.

56. President George W. Bush, "Press Conference," July 30, 2003.

57. Bush, *A Charge to Keep*, pp. 138–139. Bush shared this experience with congregants at the Second Baptist Church in Houston on March 7, 1999.

58. President George W. Bush, "Remarks at the National Prayer Breakfast," February 1, 2001.

59. President George W. Bush, "Remarks to Catholic Leaders," March 23, 2001; President George W. Bush, "Remarks at the Dedication of the Pope John Paul II Cultural Center," March 23, 2001; President George W. Bush, "Interview with Foreign Journalists," July 17, 2001.

60. President George W. Bush, "The President's News Conference with Prime Minister Silvio Berlusconi," Rome, Italy, July 23, 2001.

61. President George W. Bush, "Remarks in Address to Faculty and Students of Warsaw University," Warsaw, Poland, June 15, 2001.

62. President George W. Bush, "Radio Address by the President to the Nation," April 14, 2001. Bush calls Easter "the most important event of the Christian faith." See: President George W. Bush, "Presidential Message: Passover," and "President's Easter Message," Washington, D.C., April 17, 2003.

63. These include: Passover Observance (April 6, 2001), Proclamation of Jewish Heritage Week (April 9), Observance of National Days of Remembrance of Holocaust (April 19), remarks to the American Jewish Committee (May 3), Observance of Rosh Hashanah (September 17), Observance of Yom Kippur (September 26), Hanukkah Observance (December 7), and Menorah Lighting Ceremony (December 10).

64. President George W. Bush, "Remarks on Lighting the Hanukkah Menorah," December 10, 2001.

65. President George W. Bush, "Interview with Print Journalists," May 29, 2003.

66. For an excellent analysis of this, see: Robert J. Lieber, "The Neoconservative-Conspiracy Theory: Pure Myth," *Chronicle of Higher Education*, May 2, 2003, p. B14.

67. Horowitz's online publication is FrontpageMagazine.com. One of the more insidious examples of leftist hysteria (from academia) came via a December 2002 letter signed by over a thousand academics recommending that the Bush administration intervene to

communicate to the Israeli government that it would not tolerate any attempt by Israel to employ the "fog of war" in Iraq as a pretext to conduct an "ethnic cleansing" campaign against Palestinians. This petition was underscored and denounced by Martin Kramer of the History News Network. Lo and behold, such a campaign never transpired. See: Martin Kramer, "The Petition Middle East Scholars Would Rather Forget," *History News Network*, April 25, 2003.

68. David Frum, *The Right Man*, pp. 249–253.
69. Comments by Sharon during an October 16, 2002, press conference in Washington, D.C.
70. President George W. Bush, "Remarks on the Space Shuttle Columbia," February 1, 2003.
71. President George W. Bush, "Remarks by the President at the National Hispanic Prayer Breakfast."
72. President George W. Bush, "Remarks by the President at the National Prayer Breakfast."
73. Quoted by David L. Greene, "Bush Turns Increasingly to Language of Religion," *Baltimore Sun*, February 10, 2003.
74. See: Nancy Gibbs, "Person of the Year: George W. Bush," *Time*, December 17, 2000.
75. Bush, *A Charge to Keep*, pp. 48–49.
76. President George W. Bush, "Remarks at the Independence Day Celebration," Philadelphia, PA, July 4, 2001.
77. President George W. Bush, "President Bush Speaks at Goree Island in Senegal," Goree Island, Senegal, Africa, July 8, 2003.
78. Tony Carnes, "The Bush Doctrine," *Christianity Today*, April 25, 2003.
79. Ibid.
80. President George W. Bush, "Interview with Print Journalists," Washington, D.C., May 29, 2003.
81. President George W. Bush, "Remarks to the American Jewish Committee," Washington, D.C., May 3, 2001.
82. President George W. Bush, "Proclamation 7455—Captive Nations Week, 2001," July 12, 2001.

CHAPTER 7

1. President George W. Bush, "Remarks Following a Meeting with the National Security Team," Washington, D.C., September 12, 2001.
2. Jay Winik, *April 1865: The Month That Saved America* (New York: HarperCollins, 2001).
3. This description was provided by Bush's brother, Florida governor Jeb Bush, who had spoken to Bush that September 10. George told Jeb about the book. Source: "Interview with Jeb Bush," *Hannity & Colmes*, Fox News, June 2, 2003.
4. Winik, p. xiii.
5. Ibid., pp. xiv–xv.
6. Ibid., pp. 34–36.
7. President George W. Bush, "Remarks for National Day of Prayer," Washington, D.C., May 1, 2003.
8. The two buildings actually housed up to fifty thousand. Fortunately, after the 1993 attacks, occupants had been instructed in how to evacuate the buildings in an emer-

gency. Also, the terrorists struck before 9:00 A.M., when many were still on their way to work. Most of those below the floors hit were able to escape.

9. The bill also allows schools to teach competing interpretations of the theory of evolution.

10. President George W. Bush, "Remarks on the Terrorist Attack on New York City's World Trade Center," Sarasota, FL, September 11, 2001.

11. Quoted in Bob Woodward, *Bush at War* (New York: Simon & Schuster, 2002), p. 15.

12. Bob Woodward and Dan Balz, "A Day of Anger and Grief," *The New York Times*, September 14, 2001.

13. Greenfield and Williams speaking on, respectively, CNN and MSNBC, September 11, 2001.

14. On this, see the interesting material in Woodward, *Bush at War*, pp. 28, 46, 55–56, and 172.

15. President George W. Bush, "Address to the Nation on the Terrorist Attacks," Washington, D.C., September 11, 2001.

16. The country learned later that Flight 93 crashed at 10:10 A.M. It left Newark en route to San Francisco.

17. Reported by David S. Broder, "Echoes of Lincoln," *Washington Post*, September 23, 2001.

18. Lance Morrow, "The Case for Rage and Retribution," *Time*, September 14, 2001.

19. President George W. Bush, "Remarks by the President at a Townhall Meeting," Ontario, CA, January 5, 2002.

20. President George W. Bush, "Address to the Nation on the Terrorist Attacks."

21. President George W. Bush, "Remarks Following a Meeting with the National Security Team," Washington, D.C., September 12, 2001.

22. Quoted in Sammon, *Fighting Back* (Washington, D.C.: Regnery, 2002), pp. 193–194.

23. President George W. Bush, "Remarks to Police, Firemen, and Rescueworkers at the World Trade Center Site," New York City, September 14, 2001.

24. Howard Fineman, "A President Finds His True Voice," *Newsweek*, September 24, 2001.

25. Secretary of State Colin Powell was asked about Saddam's silence during a September 13, 2001, press conference. Powell said he was not surprised, as the "despicable" Saddam himself was a terrorist.

26. Quoted in Howard Fineman, "Bush and God," *Newsweek*, March 10, 2003.

27. Among others, see: President George W. Bush, "Remarks on War on Terror," Atlanta, November 2, 2002.

28. President George W. Bush, "Remarks to a Special Session of the German Bundestag," Berlin, Germany, May 23, 2002.

29. President George W. Bush, "Remarks at National Day of Prayer," February 2002; and President George W. Bush, "Remarks via Satellite to the 2002 Southern Baptist Convention," June 11, 2002.

30. President George W. Bush, "Remarks at a Reception for Senatorial Candidate John Sununu," Manchester, NH, October 5, 2002. Also see: President George W. Bush, "Remarks on War on Terror," Atlanta, November 2, 2002; and "Remarks in Bentonville, Arkansas," November 4, 2002. The man who said, "Let's roll," was Todd Beamer, a devout Christian. His wife Lisa, whom he met when they were undergrads at Wheaton College, wrote a book titled *Let's Roll*. The bestseller was a testimony to Todd's life and their shared faith.

31. Charles R. MiVille, "Bush's Faith Factor," *Family News in Focus*, October 2, 2001.

32. Interview with Brian Berry, July 1, 2003.

33. And after September 11, Bush would turn to his faith, through prayer, for, in his words, "wisdom and resolve, for compassion and courage, and for grace and mercy."

34. See: Bill Sammon, *Fighting Back*, pp. 159–160; and Woodward, *Bush at War*, pp. 66–67.

35. Sammon, *Fighting Back*, p. 161.

36. Ibid., p. 158.

37. President George W. Bush, "Remarks at the National Day of Prayer and Remembrance Service," National Cathedral, Washington, D.C., September 14, 2001.

38. Sammon, *Fighting Back*, p. 162.

39. Ibid., pp. 165–166. Bob Woodward writes that rather than a patting on the arm, Bush's father squeezed his hand. Woodward, *Bush at War*, p. 67.

40. Woodward, *Bush at War*, pp. 67–68.

41. Ibid., p. 67.

42. Source: Tony Carnes, "Bush's Defining Moment," *Christianity Today*, November 12, 2001, pp. 38–40.

43. Ibid.

44. This was reported by Brian Williams, *The News with Brian Williams*, CNBC, September 20, 2001.

45. President George W. Bush, "Address to a Joint Session of Congress and the American People," U.S. Capitol, Washington, D.C., September 20, 2001.

46. Howard Kurtz, "Bush Speech Wins Critics, Wins Praise," *Washington Post*, September 21, 2001.

47. David S. Broder, "Echoes of Lincoln," *Washington Post*, September 23, 2001.

48. Jim Hoagland, "Putting Doubts to Rest," *Washington Post*, September 23, 2001.

49. Sidey speaking on *The News with Brian Williams*, CNBC, September 20, 2001.

50. Gergen speaking on *Hardball with Chris Matthews*, MSNBC, September 20, 2001.

51. Gerald Posner, "I Was Wrong About Bush," *The Wall Street Journal*, September 25, 2001.

52. "U.S. Leaders React," CNN.com, September 20, 2001.

53. Quoted in Kurtz, "Bush Speech Wins Critics, Wins Praise."

54. "Congressional Reaction to Bush," Associated Press, September 20, 2001.

55. Gergen speaking on *Hardball with Chris Matthews*, MSNBC, September 20, 2001.

56. Delay speaking on Fox News Channel, September 20, 2001.

57. "U.S. Leaders React," CNN.com, September 20, 2001.

58. President George W. Bush, "Remarks by the President on the Jobs and Growth Plan," Indiana, May 13, 2003.

59. Among others, see: Diane West, "Bush and Muslims," *Washington Times*, October 31, 2003.

60. He said this in an interview on NBC. Graham provided a detailed explanation to his statement in an interview on the *Hannity & Colmes* show, Fox News, August 5, 2002.

61. See: "Hurrah for Franklin Graham," *World*, December 1, 2001; and Bob Jones, "Speaking Frankly," *World*, December 7, 2002.

62. Quoted by Nicholas D. Kristof, "Giving God a Break," *The New York Times*, June 10, 2003.

63. Robertson interviewed on the *Hannity & Colmes* show, Fox News, September 18, 2002.

64. President George W. Bush, "Message for Ramadan," November 15, 2001.

65. Quoted in Deborah Sontag, "The Erdogan Experiment," *The New York Times Magazine*, May 11, 2003.

66. Howard Fineman, "Bush and God," *Newsweek*, March 10, 2003.

67. Nicholas D. Kristof, "Giving God a Break."

68. Jim Hoagland, "Putting Doubts to Rest."

69. President George W. Bush, "Remarks at the Islamic Center of Washington, D.C.," Washington, D.C., September 17, 2001.

70. President George W. Bush, "Remarks Following a Meeting with Congressional Leaders and an Exchange with Reporters," September 19, 2001.

71. President George W. Bush, "Address to a Joint Session of Congress and the American People," U.S. Capitol, Washington, D.C., September 20, 2001.

72. President George W. Bush, "President Hosts Iftaar Dinner," Washington, D.C., November 19, 2001.

73. Wolfowitz spoke on November 30, 2001. Powell spoke on November 29, 2001.

74. President George W. Bush, "Remarks to Department of State Employees," October 4, 2001.

75. President George W. Bush, "Remarks at Parkside Hall," San Jose, CA, April 30, 2002.

76. President George W. Bush, "President Calls for New Palestinian Leadership," Rose Garden, Washington, D.C., June 24, 2002.

77. President George W. Bush, "President George W. Bush Holds Roundtable with Arab and Muslim-American Leaders," Afghanistan embassy, Washington, D.C., September 10, 2002.

78. President George W. Bush, "Remarks by President George W. Bush on U.S. Humanitarian Aid to Afghanistan," Presidential Hall, Dwight David Eisenhower Executive Office Building, Washington, D.C., October 11, 2002.

79. President George W. Bush, "Remarks at an Iftaar Dinner," November 7, 2002.

80. President George W. Bush, "Remarks by President George W. Bush in a statement to reporters during a meeting with UN Secretary General Kofi Annan," Oval Office, Washington, D.C., November 13, 2002.

81. President George W. Bush, "Press Conference by President Bush and President Havel of Czech Republic," Prague Castle, Prague, Czech Republic, November 20, 2002. Karen Hughes, a Bush adviser since the Austin days, notes that the president "has gone to great lengths to make it clear" that the war on terror and war in Iraq (which he saw as the same) were not about religion; they were not part of a religious war. Quoted by David L. Greene, "Bush Turns Increasingly to Language of Religion," *Baltimore Sun*, February 10, 2003. Reporting in the *Baltimore Sun*, Greene noted that soon after the September 11 attacks, Bush once spoke of leading a "crusade" against terrorism (he did so on September 16), which puzzled and angered Islamic leaders, who said that Muslims might construe such language as signaling a religious war against their faith. Ari Fleischer, the president's spokesman, quickly said that Bush "would regret if anything like that was conveyed." In fact, Bush never used the term again. Bush definitely rectified any such mistake. "In speaking of terrorism and of America's confrontation with

Iraq," agreed Greene, after conceding the initial "crusade" remark, "Bush typically goes out of his way to clarify that the enemies are terrorists and outlaw regimes, not Muslims." On this, also see: Woodward, *Bush at War*, p. 94.

82. "Bush Visits Islamic Center to Celebrate Eid al-Fitr," U.S. Department of State, December 5, 2002.

83. President George W. Bush, "Remarks by the President on Eid Al-Fitr," Islamic Center of Washington, D.C., December 5, 2002.

84. Ibid.

85. "Bush Visits Islamic Center to Celebrate Eid al-Fitr."

86. President George W. Bush, "Interview with Print Journalists," May 29, 2003.

87. While the examples offered here are many, they constitute merely a sample of Bush's many presidential statements in support of Islam.

88. President George W. Bush, "Remarks at the White House Conference on Character and Community," June 19, 2002.

89. Discussion with Paul C. Kemeny, June 27, 2003.

90. President George W. Bush, "Proclamation 7427—National Volunteer Week, 2001," April 16, 2001.

91. President George W. Bush, "Message on the Observance of Eid al-Adha," March 6, 2001.

92. Governor George W. Bush, "Address to the Republican Convention," August 3, 2000.

93. Governor George W. Bush, "Address to the Second Baptist Church," Houston, March 7, 1999.

94. President George W. Bush, "Remarks at the National Prayer Breakfast," Washington, D.C., February 6, 2003.

CHAPTER 8

1. President George W. Bush, "State of the Union Address," January 29, 2002.

2. See: Michael Kelly, "A Presidential Blast from the Past," *Washington Post*, February 27, 2002.

3. President George W. Bush, "Conversation with Reporters," September 17, 2001; and David E. Sanger, "Bin Laden Is Wanted in Attacks, 'Dead or Alive,' President Says," *The New York Times*, September 18, 2001.

4. Quoted by Alex Johnson, "Bush: Anti-terror Effort Going Well," MSNBC.com, October 11, 2001.

5. Quoted by Joseph Curl, "Bush Tells Taliban: 'No' Means 'No,'" *Washington Times*, October 15, 2001.

6. "Bush Speaks of Facing 'Full Wrath' of United States," Associated Press, September 17, 2001.

7. President George W. Bush, "Address to the Nation on Homeland Security," Atlanta, November 8, 2001.

8. President George W. Bush, "Remarks to the United Nations General Assembly," New York City, November 10, 2001. Also see: Bush, "The President's Radio Address," October 6, 2001.

9. President George W. Bush, "Remarks on Humanitarian Aid to Afghanistan," October

11, 2002; and Bush, "Remarks to the United Nations General Assembly," November 10, 2001.

10. Bush, "Remarks to the United Nations General Assembly."

11. President George W. Bush, "Remarks on Humanitarian Aid to Afghanistan."

12. President George W. Bush, "Address to the Nation on Homeland Security."

13. President George W. Bush, "Address to a Joint Session of Congress and the American People," U.S. Capitol, Washington, D.C., September 20, 2001.

14. Bush, "Remarks to the United Nations General Assembly."

15. Woodward, Bush at War, pp. 130–131.

16. Bush, "Remarks to the United Nations General Assembly."

17. This data is provided by Freedom House, by the UN High Commissioner for Refugees, and by the U.S. Department of State.

18. President George W. Bush, "Proclamation 7517—Religious Freedom Day," January 15, 2002.

19. "International Religious Freedom Report 2002," U.S. Department of State.

20. President George W. Bush, "Remarks on War on Terror," Atlanta, November 2, 2002.

21. President George W. Bush, "Remarks on Humanitarian Aid to Afghanistan."

22. Gore said this in an interview with Barbara Walters. Cited in: Dan Balz, "Gore Calls 2000 Verdict 'Crushing,' Assails Court," Washington Post, November 15, 2002, p. A1.

23. Poll results reported on Fox News Channel, October 17, 2001.

24. Bush told Bob Woodward that he "loathed" Kim Jong Il. See Bush at War. On the two- to three-million figure, see: Barbara Crossette, "North Korea Appears to Be Emerging from Years of Severe Famine," New York Times, August 20, 1999.

25. "Yes, They Are Evil," editorial, Washington Post, February 3, 2002.

26. On this, see: Michael Kelly, "As Good as Doctrine Gets," Washington Post, February 13, 2002, p. A27.

27. Jonathan Freedland, "Patten Lays into Bush's America," The Guardian, February 9, 2002.

28. See: Michael Kelly, "A Presidential Blast from the Past."

29. President George W. Bush, "Remarks in Address to Faculty and Students of Warsaw University," Warsaw, Poland, June 15, 2001.

30. Interview with George W. Bush, "George W. Bush: Running on His Faith," U.S. News & World Report, December 6, 1999.

31. Bush interview with Will Hall of the Baptist Press, the national news service of the Southern Baptist Convention, August 31, 2000.

32. President George W. Bush, "The President's News Conference with President Kim Dae-jung of South Korea," Seoul, South Korea, February 20, 2002.

33. President George W. Bush, "Remarks and a Question-and-Answer Session at Tsinghua University," Beijing, China, February 22, 2002.

34. Woodward, Bush at War, pp. 119–120.

35. President George W. Bush, "Remarks to Community and Religious Leaders in Moscow," Moscow, Russia, May 24, 2002.

36. President George W. Bush, "Remarks and Exchange with Reporters Following a Tour of the Choral Synagogue in St. Petersburg," St. Petersburg, Russia, May 26, 2002.

CHAPTER 9

1. Garry Wills, "With God on His Side," *The New York Times*, March 30, 2003.
2. President George W. Bush, "Remarks by the President at a Townhall Meeting," Ontario, CA, January 5, 2002.
3. President George W. Bush, "Remarks by the President at the National Hispanic Prayer Breakfast," Capitol Hilton, Washington, D.C., May 16, 2002, p. 3.
4. Dobson speaking on his *Focus on the Family* daily radio show, May 9, 2001.
5. This took place in February 2003. The account was relayed to me by Janet Parshall, a member of that executive committee, who was there. Interview with Janet Parshall, February 14, 2003.
6. President George W. Bush, "Remarks by the President at the National Prayer Breakfast," Washington, D.C., February 6, 2003. The Columbia exploded on February 1, 2003. Also see: Bush, "Remarks at a Memorial Service for Crew of the Space Shuttle Columbia," Houston, February 4, 2003.
7. Conversation with Pastor Jean Gomola, March 6, 2003.
8. Data provided by CNN via CNN's exit-polling service, November 2000.
9. Carl Cannon makes a similar point in examining not the 2000 vote but the overall breakdown among registered Democrats and Republicans generally. Cannon, "Bush and God."
10. Data provided by CNN via CNN's exit-polling service, November 2000.
11. Ryan Lizza, "Bush's Strategy for 2004: the Catholic Vote," *Pittsburgh Post-Gazette*, April 29, 2001.
12. Daniel Henninger, "The Nonreligious Left," *The Wall Street Journal*, October 17, 2003.
13. Bush interview with Will Hall of the Baptist Press, the national news service of the Southern Baptist Convention, August 31, 2000.
14. James Dobson's comments on *Focus on the Family* daily radio program, January 24, 2003.
15. Interview with Marvin Olasky, February 5, 2003.
16. Quoted in Laurie Goodstein, "Puts His Faith in Providence," *The New York Times*, February 9, 2003.
17. President George W. Bush, "President Bush Discusses Faith-Based Initiative in Tennessee," Opryland Hotel, Nashville, February 10, 2003, p. 2.
18. Interview with Janet Parshall, February 14, 2003.
19. Dana Milbank, "Bush Links Faith and Agenda in Speech to Broadcast Group," *Washington Post*, February 10, 2003.
20. Interview with Reverend Louis P. Sheldon, February 6, 2003.
21. President George W. Bush, "Remarks to the American Jewish Committee," May 4, 2001.
22. On this, see: Charles Krauthammer, "When Liberals Get Religion," *Washington Post*, September 8, 2000, p. A33.
23. Letters published in *The New York Times* on May 20, 2003.
24. Quoted by Joseph Curl, "Liberals Concede, Defend, Double Standard," *Washington Times*, August 11, 2000.
25. Jonathan Chait, "Blinded by Bush-Hatred," *Washington Post*, May 8, 2003, p. A31.
26. John H. Adams, "'Condi' Rice: Presbyterian with Faith, Political Mettle," *The Presbyterian Layman*, Vol. 33, No. 6, November/December 2000, p. 16.

27. Condoleezza Rice, "Let Us Once Again Recommit Ourselves to Those Values Which Define Us," *New Visions Commentary*, April 2002. For a profile of Rice and her faith, see the cover story by Sheryl Henderson Blunt, "The Unflappable Condi Rice," *Christianity Today*, September 2003, pp. 43–48.

28. Arthur M. Schlesinger Jr., "Good Foreign Policy a Casualty of War," *Los Angeles Times*, March 23, 2003.

29. Howard Fineman, "Bush and God," *Newsweek*, March 10, 2003.

30. Kenneth T. Walsh, "A Sunday Service in the Air," *U.S. News & World Report*, May 19, 2003, p. 32.

31. Michael Gove, "Thank God for Politicians Who Take Their Cue from Above," *London Times*, May 6, 2003.

32. David Frum, *The Right Man* (New York: Random House, 2003), pp. 3–4.

33. Jack Beatty, "In the Name of God," *The Atlantic*, March 5, 2003.

34. Garry Wills, "With God on His Side."

35. This was the assessment of a May 20, 2003, letter to the editor by a C. W. Griffin of Honolulu.

36. David Frum, *The Right Man*, pp. 17–18.

CHAPTER 10

1. President Bill Clinton, "Remarks at the Full Gospel A.M.E. Zion Church," Temple Hills, MD, August 14, 1994.

2. President Bill Clinton, "Remarks at the New Hope Baptist Church," Newark, NJ, October 20, 1996.

3. Quoted by Rachel L. Swarns and Diane Cardwell, "Democrats Try to Regain Ground on Moral Issues," *The New York Times*, December 6, 2003.

4. Washington's first inaugural address was April 1789. His farewell address was September 1796.

5. On this, see: Novak, *On Two Wings*, pp. 5–24.

6. Quoted by William J. Federer, *America's God and Country: Encyclopedia of Quotations* (Coppell, TX: Fame Publishing, 1994), pp. 697–698; Peter Marshall and David Manuel, *The Glory of America* (Bloomington, MN: Garborg's Heart n' Home, 1991), pp. 2–3; and Gary DeMar, *The Untold Story* (Atlanta: American Vision, 1993), pp. 60 and 121.

7. See: Alexander and Juliette George, *Woodrow Wilson and Colonel House* (New York: Dover Publications, 1964); and James David Barber, *The Presidential Character* (Englewood Cliffs, New Jersey: Prentice-Hall, 1985).

8. It is instructive that when *Encyclopedia Americana* gave Link just a few short pages to sum up the life of Wilson, he chose to include these remarks on Wilson's faith—it was that important a factor in his life.

9. Quoted in Conrad Cherry, *God's New Israel: Religious Interpretations of American Destiny* (Englewood Cliffs, NJ: Prentice-Hall, 1972), p. 288.

10. Quoted in DeMar, *The Untold Story*, p. 60; and Gabriel Sivan, *The Bible and Civilization* (New York: Quadrangle/The New York Times Book Co., 1973), p. 178.

11. Franklin Delano Roosevelt, "Second Inaugural Address," January 20, 1937.

12. The special edition was printed by the National Bible Press in Philadelphia. Cited in Federer, *America's God and Country*, pp. 538–539.

13. See: Ibid.; Gary DeMar, *The Biblical Worldview* (Atlanta: American Vision, 1993), p. 12; and Larry Witham, " 'Christian Nation' Now Fighting Words," *Washington Times*, November 23, 1992, p. A1.

14. Franklin Delano Roosevelt, "Fourth Inaugural Address," January 20, 1945.

15. Quoted in Paul Johnson's, *A History of the American People*, p. 792.

16. David McCullough, *Truman*, pp. 596–597.

17. See: Harry S Truman, *Years of Trial and Hope* (New York: Doubleday, 1956), p. 161; Zvi Ganin, *Truman, American Jewry, and Israel, 1948–1948* (New York: Holmes, 1979), p. 157; and McCullough, *Truman*, pp. 599, 607, and 620.

18. Ibid., p. 618.

19. Get exact source from Johnson, *History of the American People*, p. 819, footnote 233.

20. See: David McCullough talk in Robert Wilson, ed., *Character Above All*. (New York: Touchstone Books, 1997).

21. John F. Kennedy, "Inaugural Address," January 20, 1961.

22. Hillary Rodham Clinton, *Living History* (New York: Simon & Schuster, 2003), pp. 22, 167–168, 480, and 494.

23. Hillary Rodham Clinton, *It Takes a Village* (New York: Simon & Schuster, 1996), pp. 174–178.

24. Hillary Rodham Clinton, *Living History*, pp. 21–22.

25. Senator Al Gore, *Earth in the Balance: Ecology and the Human Spirit* (New York: Houghton-Mifflin, 1992), pp. 163, 238–265, 269, 272–274, 282–283, and 293–294. Also see: Paul Kengor, *Wreath Layer or Policy Player? The Vice President's Role in Foreign Policy* (Lanham, MD: Lexington Books, 2000), pp. 241–245.

26. Joseph I. Lieberman with Michael D'Orso, *In Praise of Public Life* (New York: Simon & Schuster, 2000), pp. 102, 114–115, 140–141, 145, 150–151, and 153.

27. The quotes in this paragraph come from Rachel L. Swarns and Diane Cardwell, "Democrats Try to Regain Ground on Moral Issues," *New York Times*, December 6, 2003.

28. "Religion and Politics: Contention and Consensus," survey by the Pew Research Center and Pew Forum on Religion & Public Life. The survey of 2,002 adults was conducted June 24 to July 8.

29. Cannon, "Bush and God."

30. Researchers at the University of Massachusetts did a content analysis of the first forty-nine inaugurals. Only about 10 percent lacked reference to a deity in some form. In total, they found 150 references to a deity. Cynthia Toolin, "American Civil Religion From 1789 to 1981: A Content Analysis of Presidential Inaugural Addresses," *Review of Religious Research*, Vol. 25, No. 1, September 1983, p. 41.

    Most presidents mention God, in some form—some use words like *Almighty Being* or *Divine Providence*—in their inaugural. Professors Michael E. Bailey and Kristin Lindholm write that George Washington used his first inaugural to symbolically "take the nation to church." Modern presidential inaugurals, they state, have moved beyond the political into "the poetical and divine." Michael E. Bailey and Kristin Lindholm,

"Tocqueville and the Rhetoric of Civil Religion in the Presidential Inaugural Addresses," *Christian Scholar's Review*, Spring 2003, Vol. 32, No. 3, p. 259.

31. A search was done on the words "Jesus," "Jesus Christ," and "Christ." This is not a flawless research design. The search engine for the *Presidential Documents* does not make a distinction between when the president himself utters those words in a speech and if, say, they are listed in another way, such as a presidential speech transcript that ends with a note that the president was introduced by Pastor John Doe, Reverend of the Church of "Christ," Peoria, Illinois. Thus, we dug into each statement and tried to isolate those speeches in which the president himself mouths the word "Christ." (Without digging into each statement, the count total was obviously much higher: 208 for Clinton's eight years and 77 through Bush's first years.)

  Another constraint is that while the *Presidential Documents* purport to be a collection of every presidential statement, they occasionally miss a speech. For example, George W. Bush's May 2003 speech at the White House Correspondents Dinner, in which he mentioned Jesus, is not listed. The references to Christ tabulated here are taken strictly from the *Presidential Documents* count. While this method thus misses certain statements, it would also miss certain references by Clinton. In other words, any such errors should not unfairly skew the study in one direction or the other.

32. Quoted by Joseph Curl, "Liberals concede, defend, double standard," *Washington Times*, August 11, 2000.

33. In 1993, he made three references, in 1995 four, in 1997 two, and in 1999 five.

34. President Bill Clinton, "Remarks in a Discussion at the Ministers' Leadership Conference," South Barrington, IL, August 11, 2000.

35. President Bill Clinton, "Remarks at a Reception for Congressional Candidate Terry L. Lierman," July 26, 2000.

36. President Bill Clinton, "Remarks to African American Religious Leaders," New York City, October 31, 2000.

37. President Bill Clinton, "Remarks to the Congregation of Alfred Street Baptist Church," Alexandria, VA, October 29, 2000.

38. President Bill Clinton, "Remarks to the Congregation of Shiloh Baptist Church," Washington, D.C., October 29, 2000.

39. President Bill Clinton, "Remarks at the Metropolitan Baptist Church," Washington, D.C., December 12, 1997.

40. President Bill Clinton, "Remarks at the Metropolitan Baptist Church," Newark, NJ, October 8, 1997.

41. President Bill Clinton, "Remarks at the New Hope Baptist Church."

42. In Fruitland, TN, in August (1996) and in Greeleyville, SC, in June. In a January 15, 1996, commemorative service for Martin Luther King Jr. in Atlanta, which included a U.S. senator, a mayor, the governor, three members of Congress, and White House staff, Clinton spoke about foreign policy (Bosnia specifically) and the federal budget. He quoted Genesis and one of the books of Corinthians.

43. President Bill Clinton, "Remarks to Senior Citizens at St. Monica's Episcopal Church," Washington, D.C., January 5, 1996.

44. President Bill Clinton, "Remarks at the Full Gospel A.M.E. Zion Church."

45. President Bill Clinton, "Remarks at the Bethel A.M.E. Church," New York City, September 25, 1994.

46. President Bill Clinton, "Remarks to the Convocation of the Church of God in Christ," Memphis, November 19, 1993.

47. He spoke at memorial services in 1995 and 1996 for, respectively, the late Secretary of Defense Les Aspin and the late civil rights figure Barbara Jordan. Both talks were outstanding. Clinton showed an excellent command of Scripture.

48. Importantly, my argument here is not about legality. Whether such campaigning would be considered a violation of Federal Election Commission guidelines is an issue that I'm not qualified to judge.

49. One was a memorial service in Landover, MD, honoring Martin Luther King Jr. The other came in Atlanta in June 2002. Another came on January 15, 2004, in Atlanta.

50. The Atlanta appearance featured a push for his faith-based programs. President George W. Bush, "Remarks at St. Paul A.M.E. Church," Atlanta, June 21, 2002.

51. Four came in 2000, six in 1996, and two in 1994.

52. "New Davis Committee Radio Ad Features Pres. Clinton," press release by the Governor Gray Davis Committee, October 31, 2002. Davis had been appearing in churches for at least a year up until the recall.

53. "Clinton Stumps for Davis," CNN.com, September 15, 2003. The *Sacramento Bee* reported: "Former President Bill Clinton will begin his long-awaited trip to help Gov. Gray Davis fight off the recall election by joining Davis at church services Sunday in south-central Los Angeles, aides to the governor said." The church talk was actually the start of Clinton's campaign swing for Davis; the kickoff took place in a house of worship. "Clinton to Start Campaign Swing for Davis Sunday," *Sacramento Bee*, September 10, 2003.

54. Adam Nagourney, "Mrs. Clinton Preaches to the Party Faithful," *The New York Times*, pp. A1 and B5. Also see: Maggie Haberman, "Mass Appeal as 'Sister' Hillary Tours Churches," *New York Post*, p. 7.

55. Gebe Martinez, "Gore Turns to Labor Unions and Blacks for Late Support," *Detroit News*, October 30, 2000; Patricia Montemurri, "Gore Goes Full Bore to Sweep Michigan, He Scours State for Support, Reaches Out to Blacks, Arabs," *Detroit Free Press*, October 30, 2000; and Bill Sammon, "An Impassioned Plea," *Washington Times*, October 30, 2000.

56. Ann McFeatters, "Head to Head, Neck and Neck," *Pittsburgh Post-Gazette*, November 5, 2000.

57. Gore believed that Byrd's death should be classified a "hate crime"; Bush opposed the idea of a separate category of crimes, insisting that any murder is a hate crime and, moreover, that any murderer ought to be considered for the death penalty.

58. James O'Toole, "Candidates Blitz Pittsburgh," *Pittsburgh Post-Gazette*, November 5, 2000; Ralph Z. Hallow, "Gore Used Race as His Ace Card in Election," *Washington Times*, November 9, 2000; and Marisol Bello, "Gore Appeals to Pittsburgh's Black Voters," *Pittsburgh Tribune-Review*, November 5, 2000.

59. Ibid.

60. Katharine Q. Seelye and Kevin Sack, "Gore Rallies Base," *The New York Times*, November 6, 2000.

61. Andrew Cain, "Gore Curbs Attacks on Bush," *Washington Times*, November 6, 2000.

62. Quoted by Joseph Curl, "Liberals Concede, Defend, Double Standard," *Washington Times*, August 11, 2000.

CHAPTER 11

1. And yet, "despite some problems," Gaddis wrote, "the Bush strategy is right on target with respect to the new circumstances confronting the United States and its allies in the wake of September 11." See: John Lewis Gaddis, "A Grand Strategy of Transformation," *Foreign Policy*, November/December 2002.

2. *The National Security Strategy of the United States of America*, The White House, September 2002. On this, also see: President George W. Bush, "Remarks at the Graduation Exercise of the U.S. Military Academy," West Point, NY, June 1, 2002.

3. Douglas Jehl, "U.S. Convinced Iraqi Saboteurs Plotted to Kill Bush," *The New York Times*, May 8, 1993.

4. Stephen Hubbell, "Kuwait Tries Iraqis Charged in April Plot to Assassinate Bush," *Christian Science Monitor*, June 7, 1993.

5. On Gore's role, see: Paul Kengor, *Wreath Layer or Policy Player? The Vice President's Role in Foreign Policy* (Lanham, MD: Lexington Books, 2000), pp. 225–226.

6. Kenneth T. Walsh, "A Vice President Who Counts," *U.S. News & World Report*, July 19, 1993.

7. Martin Fletcher and Ben Macintyre, "UN Accepts Clinton Evidence That Iraq Plotted to Kill Bush," *London Times*, June 29, 1993.

8. Bush is widely alleged to have used the phrase "SOB." While that is not unlikely and not contested here, and fits with Bush's temperament and colorful language, I was only able to confirm this statement: "This is the guy who tried to kill my dad," Among others, see: John King, "Bush calls Saddam 'the guy who tried to kill my dad,'" CNN.com, September 27, 2002.

9. "Iraq VP Suggests Bush-Saddam Duel," Associated Press, October 3, 2002.

10. Among others on this, see: Woodward, *Bush at War*, p. 316.

11. Con Coughlin, *Saddam: King of Terror* (New York: HarperCollins, CCC Imprint, 2002), pp. 3–4.

12. Coughlin, p. 4. Also on Saddam's life, see the work of biographer Amatzia Baram, who has written or spoken of Saddam in books, articles, and public appearances.

13. Dyer cites Isaiah 13:19 and Revelation 18:21. Charles H. Dyer, *The Rise of Babylon* (Wheaton, IL: Tyndale, 1991).

14. The exact figure on the total plotters has been reportedly differently. It is usually reported as twenty-one or twenty-two.

15. Quoted by Garry Wills, "With God on His Side," *New York Times*, March 30, 2003.

16. Ibid.

17. He said the same at a prayer breakfast in Houston on August 20, 1992. See: George H. W. Bush, *Heartbeat*, pp. 20–21, 210, and 286–287.

18. See: Ann Clwyd, "See Men Shredded, Then Say You Don't Back War," *London Times*, March 18, 2003.

19. A group of four Iraqi women shared examples with ABC's Barbara Walters on the television program *20/20* on March 21, 2003. See: "A Worthy Cause: Women Who Know of Saddam's Brutality Say This War Is Just," ABCNews.com, March 21, 2003. Their stories were consistent with human rights reports.

20. Maryam Elahi and Adam Kushner, researchers for the group Physicians for Human Rights in Iraq, interviewed one young man who experienced this fate. In the operating room, the anesthesiologist said to him: "You shouldn't have left the army. If I could leave the hospital now, I would, but it is surrounded so you cannot run away. I am sorry about this." When he awoke, his wrists were handcuffed to the bed, and he was informed that his ears were gone. That night, he unwrapped the gauze from his head, looked in the mirror, and wept. He said he felt "very sad, angry and destroyed." He noticed a hunk of gauze in his pocket. He grabbed and opened it. His ear was inside. Maryam Elahi and Adam Kushner, "Doctors with 'Dirty Hands,'" *Washington Post*, June 8, 2003.

21. Rumsfeld Pentagon briefing, April 9, 2003.

22. The possible exception is that Saddam may have stopped stockpiling WMDs after 1998. As of this writing, that issue is in dispute among David Kay, George Tenet, and the Bush administration. Kay concluded that Iraq seems to have stopped stockpiling after 1998, though it retained WMDs intent and capability.

23. This information (made public in the mid to late 1990s) was personally shared with me by David Kay, UNSCOM chief, in 1998. Kay disclosed the information in speeches and media appearances at the time.

24. One of the sources for this information was an Iraqi defector named Sabah Khodada, a captain in the Iraqi army from 1982 to 1992. He and another high-level defector were interviewed by *The New York Times*, the BBC, and PBS's documentary series *Frontline*. In the mid-1990s, Khodada worked at Salman Pak. He described this supersensitive center there, separated from the rest of the camp, under the direct control of Saddam himself, where these non-Iraqi terrorists were trained on the 707. Khodada, who was interviewed by the FBI, noted, "I think the American government should have pictures of this camp from the air." He drew a map of the camp and its location. Space Imaging, which operates a civilian surveillance satellite, procured photographs from April 25, 2000. The imagery revealed pictures not merely of the camp but also of the 707. The defector's story checked out. The publication *Aviation Week & Space Technology* reported these facts in its January 7, 2002, issue. Excerpts from Khodada's gripping interview ran in newspapers around the world, including November 11 and 12 features in, respectively, Britain's *Guardian* ("The Iraqi Connection") and in *The New York Times* ("Defectors Cite Iraqi Training for Terrorism"). A full transcript of his interview with *Frontline* was posted on PBS's Web site, from where, through the magic of the Internet, it received mass circulation around the world.

25. Some of the best work on Saddam's Al-Qaeda connection has been done by Jeffrey Goldberg in *The New Yorker*, who has done exhaustive research, particularly his February 10, 2003, piece "The Unknown." From *The New York Times* op-ed page, William Safire has done impressive investigation. *The New York Sun* has done commendable work, as have reporter Bill Gertz in his book *Breakdown* and former NSC staffers Daniel Benjamin and Steven Simon in their book *The Age of Sacred Terror*.

26. The most intriguing work on this has been done by Stephen F. Hayes for *The Weekly Standard*.

27. In a speech to the Chicago Council on Foreign Relations, Condoleezza Rice stated un-equivocally that there was no proof of such a connection. On the other hand, there have been many articles that speak of private conversations and memos from high-level Bush officials believing there was a link.

28. Among others, see: President George W. Bush, "The President's News Conference," December 15, 2003.

29. Arnaud de Borchgrave, "Lucky Break for Jordan," United Press International, March 21, 2003. See: Clwyd, "See Men Shredded, Then Say You Don't Back War," March 18, 2003.

30. Joseph wrote an op-ed piece on his experiences. The piece was posted by UPI and widely circulated in late March 2003. These quotes are taken from his op-ed and separate interview with UPI. Source: Arnaud de Borchgrave, "Lucky Break for Jordan."

31. "Ousting Saddam Hussein 'Was Worth Hardships Endured Since Invasion,' Say Citizens of Baghdad," Gallup Organization, September 24, 2003.

32. Daniel Pepper, "I Was a Naïve Fool to Be a Human Shield for Saddam," *London Telegraph*, March 23, 2003.

33. "Gallup Poll of Baghdad: Execution as a Weapon of Mass Destruction," Gallup Organization, December 9, 2003.

34. See: Philip Smucker, "Iraq Builds 'Mother of All Battles' Mosque in Praise of Saddam," *London Telegraph*, July 29, 2001; Rajiv Chandrasekaran, "Attitudes Altered in Iraq," *Washington Post*, September 22, 2002; David Blair, "Saddam Has Koran Written in His Blood," *London Telegraph*, December 14, 2002; Marvin Olasky, "Iraq: the Unstated Assumption," *World*, February 11, 2003; and Marvin Olasky, "Saddam, Terrorists, and Islam," *World*, March 8, 2003.

35. See: "Iraqi Christians Want Rights Guaranteed," Associated Press, April 30, 2003; "Human Rights in Saddam's Iraq," U.S. Department of State, 2002; "Christian Agencies Call for Protection of Religious Minorities in Post-war Iraq," Christian Solidarity Worldwide, June 16, 2003; "Annual Report of the U.S. Commission on International Religious Freedom," May 2003; "Endless Torment: the 1991 Uprising in Iraq and Its Aftermath," Human Rights Watch, June 1992; "Iraq's Brutal Decrees: Amputation, Branding, and the Death Penalty," Human Rights Watch, June 1995; and "Night Visions in Iran & Iraq," *The Voice of the Martyrs*, October 2003.

36. Ibid.

37. That figure was cited by the United Nations since at least the mid-1990s and was still being cited in the days up to Operation Iraqi Freedom.

38. Walter Russell Mead, "Deadlier Than War," *Washington Post*, March 12, 2003.

39. Among conservatives, there were influential just-war writings by Pope John Paul II's biographer George Weigel, Princeton's Robert George, the University of Texas's J. Budziszewski, and Chuck Colson, as well as the pages of *First Things* or *World* magazine.

40. David Earle Anderson, "Not a Just or Moral War," *Sojourners*, January/February 2003.

CHAPTER 12

1. "Ad to Bush: Let Jesus Change Your Mind," Religious News Service, December 7, 2002.
2. "Remarks of Jim Winkler, General Secretary of the United Methodist General Board of Church & Society," Dirksen Senate Office Building, February 26, 2003.
3. Laurie Goodstein, "Puts His Faith in Providence," *The New York Times*, February 9, 2003.
4. Dana Milbank, "Bush Links Faith and Agenda in Speech to Broadcast Group," *Washington Post*, February 10, 2003.
5. George W. Bush, "Remarks at the National Religious Broadcasters' Convention," Nashville, February 10, 2003.
6. Howard Fineman, "Bush and God," *Newsweek*, March 10, 2003.
7. Martin E. Marty, "The Sin of Pride," *Newsweek*, March 10, 2003.
8. Michelle Cottle, "God and Monsters," *The New Republic*, March 7, 2003.
9. President George W. Bush, "Interview with Tom Brokaw of NBC News," April 24, 2003.
10. Interview with Brian Berry, June 18, 2003.
11. Quoted in Goodstein, "Puts His Faith in Providence."
12. Interview with Janet Parshall, February 14, 2003.
13. Quoted by Dana Milbank, "For Bush, War Defines Presidency," *Washington Post*, March 9, 2003.
14. *Los Angeles Times* and NBC television broke the Boykin story in October 2003.
15. Robert J. Lieber, "The Neoconservative-Conspiracy Theory: Pure Myth," *Chronicle of Higher Education*, May 2, 2003, p. B14.
16. Nicholas D. Kristof, "The Stones of Baghdad," *The New York Times*, October 4, 2002.
17. Chris Matthews, "To Iraq and Ruin," *San Francisco Chronicle*, August 25, 2002.
18. Quoted in David Earle Anderson, "Not a Just or Moral War," *Sojourners*, January/February 2003.
19. Ibid.
20. Jim Wallis, "Disarm Iraq . . . Without War," *Sojourners*, November/December 2002.
21. Jim Wallis, "The Lessons of War," *Sojourners*, May/June 2003.
22. Jim Wallis, "Disarm Iraq . . . Without War."
23. Jim Wallis, "Is Bush Deaf to Church Doubts on Iraq War?" *Boston Globe*, December 9, 2002.
24. "NCC 2002 General Assembly: Resolution 'After September 11, 2001: Public Policy Considerations for the United States of America,'" November 16, 2002.
25. The ad was paid for by a group called Religious Leaders for Sensible Priorities, chaired by Edgar. "Ad to Bush: Let Jesus Change Your Mind," *Religious News Service*, December 7, 2002.
26. Jan Nunley, "Five Years On, Griswold Calls Church to God's Mission of Reconciliation, Love," Episcopal News Service, January 16, 2003.
27. Ibid.
28. Material taken from March 24, 2003, press release announcing the antiwar rally. Press release titled, "Nobel Peace Laureate Maguire, US Bishop to Lead Action Wednesday in DC."
29. Quote taken from March 24, 2003, press release.

30. Gary Kohls, "US President Professes Too Much," *Catholic New Times*, March 16, 2003.

31. To be fair, not all were so presumptuous. Some were careful enough to know they shouldn't make the same mistake they were ascribing to their subject. Martin Marty wisely emphasized that the president's critics were obliged to check whether their own convictions were wrong or misguided. Still, many did make the mistake. Martin E. Marty, "The Sin of Pride."

32. Norman Mailer, "We Went to War Just to Boost the White Male Ego," *London Times*, April 29, 2003.

33. For the record, the NSS document does not use words like *world domination* or *empire*; that is obviously Bellah's interpretation. See: Robert N. Bellah, "Righteous Empire," *Christian Century*, April 4, 2003.

34. Full text of letter is published in: Mark Tooley, "UM Bishop Seems to Liken Bush to Saddam and Bin Laden," *Institute on Religion and Democracy*, December 18, 2002.

35. Quoted in David Earle Anderson, "Not a Just or Moral War."

36. "Remarks of Jim Winkler, General Secretary of the United Methodist General Board of Church & Society," Dirksen Senate Office Building, February 26, 2003.

37. Quoted in Laurie Goodstein, "Puts His Faith in Providence."

38. The religious left was noisy in the 1980s, protesting Ronald Reagan's Cold War policies. It was hardly unusual to hear a nuclear-freeze bishop or pro-Sandinista pastor speak out not only against Reagan but for Christ Himself. Some of these individuals went so far as to claim that Jesus was not only anti-Reagan but pro-communism. There is a vast record of such material that begs to be chronicled in a full-length book. Mona Charen documented some examples in her *Useful Idiots* (Regnery: Washington, D.C., 2003).

    This religious left, with the same methods applied to a different cause, was quite visibly and audibly on display throughout the period leading up to and including the war in Iraq.

39. The letter to Giamatti is published in George H. W. Bush, *All the Best, George Bush*, pp. 319–320.

40. Data reported by Mark O'Keefe, "Church Leaders' Anti-war Message Fails in the Pews," Religious News Service, April 16, 2003.

41. Ibid.

42. Ibid.

43. Peggy Noonan has also made this comparison to Eisenhower and Kennedy. See: Peggy Noonan, "The Anti-Ikes," *The Wall Street Journal*, February 24, 2003.

44. Jimmy Carter, "The Troubling New Face of America," *Washington Post*, September 5, 2002.

45. Jimmy Carter, "Just War—or a Just War?," *The New York Times*, March 9, 2003.

46. This claim was very odd: Such bipartisanship is illusory at best, as Carter himself experienced in his own administration and then witnessed for eight years in the foreign policy of his successor, not to mention what he watched under presidents Richard Nixon and Gerald Ford, Republicans who preceded him and whose foreign policy Carter and his Democratic Party had run against. In fact, all of these men and their parties opposed one another's foreign policy.

47. At the time, the Bush administration had about as many supporters on the UN Security Council as opponents, and was assembling a coalition of some forty nations.

48. For example, when Ronald Reagan mentioned Jesus Christ in a January 1984 speech to the National Religious Broadcasters, the *Times* denounced him. Reagan presented the speech, complained the *Times*, "not while worshiping in his church but in a Washington hotel. . . . You don't have to be a secular humanist to take offense at that display of what, in America, should be private piety. . . . It's an offense to Americans of every denomination, or no denomination, when a President speaks that way." The *Times* noted that Reagan was, after all, "the President of a nation whose Bill of Rights enjoins Government from establishing religion, aiding one religion, even aiding all religions." This was 1984, but the *Times* has remained consistent in this thinking. If anything, the *Times* editorial board is more liberal today than it was in 1984. Editorial, "Sermon on the Stump," *The New York Times*, February 3, 1984.

49. Michael Gove, "Thank God for Politicians Who Take Their Cue from Above," *London Times*, May 6, 2003.

50. Governor George W. Bush, "Address to the Second Baptist Church," Houston, TX, March 7, 1999. These are points also made by Michael Novak in his *On Two Wings*, pp. 39–42.

51. President George W. Bush, "President Delivers Remarks on the National Day of Prayer," Washington, DC, May 1, 2003.

52. David Frum, "Iraq Will Test Bush's Spiritual Bond with Americans," *USA Today*, February 23, 2003.

53. The book has been in continuous print since 1935. A revised edition published ten years ago has sold more than two million copies. It has been published in forty languages. There are twenty-two books of sermons from Chambers. "Bush's Inspiration: Scottish Preacher He Reads Before Breakfast Every Day," *The Scotsman*, March 4, 2003.

54. David Wright of the University of Edinburgh states: "His books are good quality Christian devotional writings with a strong emphasis on practical, personal faith. I am impressed that President Bush finds time in his day to read writing of this quality." Source: "Bush's Inspiration: Scottish Preacher He Reads Before Breakfast Every Day."

55. "Bush's Inspiration: Scottish Preacher He Reads Before Breakfast Every Day."

56. On the protests and protesters, see pieces by Michael Kelly, "Marching with Stalinists," and "Immorality on the March," *Washington Post*, January 22 and February 19, 2003.

57. Howard Kurtz, "Bush's Moment of Fate," *Washington Post*, March 10, 2003; and Andrea Mitchell speaking on the *Imus in the Morning Show*, MSNBC, February 26, 2003.

58. Quoted in Howard Kurtz, "Bush's Moment of Fate."

59. For instance, a March 11–12, 2003, Fox News/Opinion Dynamics poll showed 71 percent supporting the use of U.S. military force to disarm Saddam, and 20 percent opposed.

60. The number thirty or forty-five depended on the level of support, which ranged from a vocal/open thirty nations to a more quiet/discreet fifteen nations.

61. "Powell: 30 Nations in Coalition," Associated Press, March 18, 2003.

62. Doggett said this in an official statement issued from his office. Quoted by Jonathan Wright, "30 Governments Back U.S. Stance on Iraq," Reuters, March 19, 2003.

63. Thomas Friedman, "D-Day," *The New York Times*, March 19, 2003. Also see: Anne Applebaum, "Blair in Agony," *Washington Post*, March 19, 2003.

64. See: President George W. Bush, "President's News Conference," December 15, 2003. He would make the point again in his January 20, 2004, State of the Union Address, and Democratic leader Representative Nancy Pelosi (D-CA) would again charge unilateralism in her same-night response to Bush's address.

65. Kennedy made this remark on September 18, 2003. For a stinging counterresponse, see: Charles Krauthammer, "Ted Kennedy, Losing It," *Washington Post*, September 26, 2003, p. A27.

66. Chambers, *My Utmost for His Highest*, pp. 10/1 and 10/4.

67. The vote on exhausting all diplomatic means was 396 to 217. See: Glenn Frankel, "Parliament Backs Blair on Action Against Baghdad," *Washington Post*, March 19, 2003; and Matthew Tempest, "Parliament Gives Blair Go-ahead for War," *The Guardian*, March 18, 2003.

68. President George W. Bush, "Remarks by the President in Address to the Nation," March 17, 2003.

69. "Walter Cronkite Criticizes President Bush's 'Arrogance' over Iraq," Associated Press, March 19, 2003.

70. Zachary Coile, "Rep. Stark Blasts Bush on Iraq War," *San Francisco Chronicle*, March 19, 2003.

71. Arthur M. Schlesinger Jr., "Good Foreign Policy a Casualty of War," *Los Angeles Times*, March 23, 2003.

72. This incident was widely reported at the time. For the initial source, see: Matthew Continetti, "Professor Mogadishu," *National Review Online*, March 31, 2003.

73. Nedra Pickler, "Kerry Doesn't Shy from Anti-Bush Comment," Associated Press, April 4, 2003.

74. See: Jim Dwyer, "Cheers and Smiles for U.S. Troops in a Captured City," *The New York Times*, April 2, 2003; and news reports on MSNBC, April 3, 2003.

75. President George W. Bush, "Press Conference on Iraq," Washington, D.C., March 6, 2003.

76. Bush speaking in El Paso, TX, on March 15, 2003. Bush clip was aired on MSNBC, March 18, 2003.

77. Jay Lindsay, "Prayer Warriors' Do Their Bit to Back Bush, Troops in Iraq," Associated Press, April 12, 2003.

78. The poll was done by Fox News/Opinion Dynamics. It was conducted March 11–12, 2003. It sampled nine hundred registered voters nationwide and had a margin of error of plus/minus 3 percent.

79. President George W. Bush, "President Delivers Remarks on the National Day of Prayer," Washington, D.C., May 1, 2003.

80. Bush, *A Charge to Keep*, pp. 8–9.

81. From this period, the *Presidential Documents* reveal such statements from Bush on November 11, 2002, and, from 2003, the following dates: February 3 and 17 (twice), March 3, May 5, April 28 (twice), June 9, and July 4.

82. Carl Cannon seemed to allude to a similar conclusion in his "Bush and God."

83. Less than a month before the first missile volley into Baghdad, David Frum wrote a piece for *USA Today* in which he pondered the question of how a president like Bush contemplates a decision such as whether to send troops into Iraq. Frum noted that some presidents think ideologically, whereas others are guided purely by pragmatism. But Bush, he said, belongs in a "very different" category—"he's a leader who thinks in terms of morality and faith." David Frum, "Iraq Will Test Bush's Spiritual Bond with Americans," *USA Today*, February 23, 2003.

84. Garry Wills, "With God on His Side," *New York Times*, March 30, 2003.

85. The source insisted on anonymity. He responded by email on May 11, 2004.

86. Letter to Paul Kengor from Dan Bartlett, The White House, June 2, 2004.

87. Woodward, *Plan of Attack*, p. 379.

88. President George W. Bush, "Interview with Tom Brokaw of NBC News," April 24, 2003.

89. President George W. Bush, "State of the Union Address," January 28, 2003.

90. Bush said something similar in an earlier speech to a Hispanic religious gathering. He was speaking of prayer and its relationship to America. Iraq was not on his mind on this occasion. "Since America's founding, prayer has reassured us that the hand of God is guiding the affairs of this nation," said Bush, to applause. "We have never asserted a special claim on His favor, yet we've always believed in God's presence in our lives." Bush, "Remarks at the National Hispanic Prayer Breakfast," May 16, 2002.

91. Oswald Chambers, *My Utmost for His Highest* (Grand Rapids, MI: Discovery House, 1995), p. 1–2.

92. There were reports by noncredible sources, usually Bush-hating Web sites. Among nonpartisan sources, one report that was rejected by the White House came from a Middle East news source—Haaretz. As characterized by a reporter from the White House press corps, Haaretz reported in June 2003 that Palestinian Prime Minister Abbas "suggested" that Bush told him "that God spoke to him about Al Qaeda and . . . Saddam." The reporter asked White House press secretary Ari Fleischer if the report was "a stretch." "It's beyond a stretch," replied Fleischer in his July 1, 2003, briefing. "It's an invention. It was not said." This did not stop the quote from gaining a life of its own on Bush-bashing Web sites. The full quote attributed to Bush is this: "God told me to strike at al Qaida and I struck them, and then he instructed me to strike at Saddam, which I did, and now I am determined to solve the problem in the Middle East." For an example of a left-wing source employing this quote, see: Chris Floyd, "The Revelation of St. George," *Moscow Times*, June 30, 2003.

93. Duffy cited no sources, no background, no context, and offered no follow-up. His statement was made almost in passing. Michael Duffy, "Marching Along," *Time*, September 1, 2002.

94. Dana Milbank, "For Bush, War Defines Presidency," *Washington Post*, March 9, 2003.

95. Prime Minister Tony Blair, "Address to the U.S. Congress," Washington, D.C., July 18, 2003.

96. David Frum, "Iraq Will Test Bush's Spiritual Bond with Americans."

CHAPTER 13

1. Juad's story was published in the *London Telegraph*. Details and quotes that follow were taken from that report. "Juad Celebrates 'Return to the World' After 21 Years Hiding from Saddam," *London Telegraph*, May 21, 2003.

2. Nicholas D. Kristof, "The Man with No Ear," *The New York Times*, June 27, 2003.

3. Ellen Knickmeyer and David Crary, "Jubilant Iraqis Swarm Streets of Baghdad," Associated Press, April 9, 2003; and Ellen Knickmeyer and Hamza Hendawi, "Marines Help Iraqis Topple Saddam Statue," Associated Press, April 9, 2003.

4. The most conspicuous exception was the BBC, which opted to cover an earthquake in India as the statue tumbled.

5. Andrew Clennell, "Crowd Egged Me On, Says Marine in Statue Stunt," *London Telegraph*, April 11, 2003.

6. Mike Allen, "Bush, Cheney Declare Vindication of War Policy," *Washington Post*, April 9, 2003; and John Daniszewski, "Iraqis Cheer as Baghdad Falls," *Los Angeles Times*, April 10, 2003.

7. President George W. Bush, "Interview with Tom Brokaw of NBC News," April 24, 2003.

8. Knickmeyer and Hendawi, "Marines Help Iraqis Topple Saddam Statue."

9. Quotes recorded by on-site observer Henry Payne, the editorial cartoonist for the *Detroit News* in an April 11, 2003, piece.

10. Awad Nasir, "Thank You," *The Wall Street Journal*, May 8, 2003.

11. Ibid.

12. As reported by journalist David Shater, ITN (British television network), Fox News, April 9, 2003.

13. Anthony Shadid, "Hussein's Baghdad Falls," *Washington Post*, April 10, 2003; and Ellen Knickmeyer and Hamza Hendawi, "Iraqis Cheer Arriving U.S. Troops in Baghdad," Associated Press, April 9, 2003.

14. As reported by journalist David Shater, ITN (British television network).

15. Dexter Filkins and Jane Perlez, "Residents Blare Horns, Dance and Empty Government Offices," *The New York Times*, April 9, 2003.

16. Associated Press photograph, April 9, 2003.

17. Specifically, Gallup found that 67 percent thought they would be better off in five years, and Zogby found 71 percent. "Ousting Saddam Hussein 'Was Worth Hardships Endured Since Invasion,' Say Citizens of Baghdad," Gallup Organization, September 24, 2003; and "Zogby International Conducts 1st Scientific Survey of Iraq," Zogby International, September 10, 2003.

18. See: Brian Murphy, "Kurdish, U.S. Forces Seize N. Iraq Target," Associated Press, April 9, 2003; and "Kurds Celebrate Fall of Baghdad, Seize Strategic Mountain," Associated Press, April 9, 2003.

19. Karl Vick, "Iraq's Kurds Cheer News from Baghdad," *Washington Post*, April 9, 2003.

20. Described by reporter Steve Centanni, Fox News, April 9, 2003, 11:00 P.M. news broadcast. Also see: Donna Abu-Nasr, "Arabs Shocked, Relieved at Baghdad's Fall," Associated Press, April 9, 2003.

21. The unavoidable sign was broadcast by a number of cameras, including CNN.

22. "Iraqi-Americans Rejoice at Saddam Defeat," Associated Press, April 9, 2003; and Niraj Warikoo and Patricia Montemurri, "President Promotes Iraqi Democracy in State's Arab Community," *Detroit Free Press*, April 28, 2003.

23. Ibid.

24. Report was filed by KIRO-TV, Seattle, WA, April 9, 2003.

25. "Iraq Ambassador: 'The Game Is Over,'" Associated Press, April 9, 2003.

26. Rove asked ahead of time that no media be present. The college public-relations office, for the first time anyone could remember, telephoned local media to implore press people *not* to come. One disobedient Pittsburgh television crew had to be chased away. The event took place on the afternoon of April 9, 2003. I was present and spoke to Rove privately.

27. Karl Rove, speaking at Grove City College, April 9, 2003.

28. Howard Fineman, "A Big Win for Bush," *Newsweek*, April 9, 2003.

29. Statistics provided in *The New York Times*, April 20, 2003, p. B16.

30. Awad Nasir, "Thank You."

31. Quoted in: Jocelyn Gecker, "Saddam's Ouster Shifts Mood in France," Associated Press, April 11, 2003. No honest observer could deny the American president's unique victory. The assessment by House Minority Leader Nancy Pelosi (D-CA) seemed especially unfair. Just a day after the statue tumbled, Pelosi, who before the war had predicted "thousands of people killed on both sides," told reporters: "We could have probably brought down that statue for a lot less." The congresswoman might have been better served postulating that Saddam could have been *disarmed* for less, though that was eminently debatable. Yet it was completely unrealistic to assert that the statue would have tumbled short of unseating Saddam. Source: Pelosi made this remark on April 1, 2003, on CNBC's *Capitol Report*. The full quote was this: "There are other ways to go about [this war] than to have thousands of people killed on both sides."

32. Juad's story was published in the *London Telegraph*. Details and quotes that follow were taken from that report. "Juad Celebrates 'Return to the World' After 21 Years Hiding from Saddam," *London Telegraph*, May 21, 2003.

33. Juan O. Tamayo, "Baghdad Falls," Knight Ridder Newspapers, April 10, 2003; and Joseph Laconte, "Anti-Liberation Theology," *Weekly Standard*, May 5, 2003.

34. James Matise, "Grateful Iraqis Let Freedom Ring," *Albuquerque Tribune*, April 23, 2003.

35. Cassio Furtado, "Local Iraqis Call Regime's End a 'Miracle,'" *Tampa Tribune*, April 10, 2003.

36. Niraj Warikoo and Patricia Montemurri, "President Promotes Iraqi Democracy in State's Arab Community."

37. "Iraqi-Americans Happy to See Saddam's Reign Over," WABC, New York, April 9, 2003.

38. David Rohde, "'Let Them Arrest Him,' Tariq Aziz's Aunt Says," *The New York Times*, April 21, 2003.

39. Ibid.

40. James Meek, "You're Late. What Took You So Long? God Help You Become Victorious," *The Guardian*, March 22, 2003.

41. "Saddam's Birthday Marked Without Fanfare," Associated Press, April 28, 2003.

42. This was recorded by on-site observer Henry Payne, the editorial cartoonist for the *Detroit News* in an April 11, 2003, piece.

43. Steven Farrell, "Babylon Weeps as Grave of 10,000 Gives Up Secrets," *London Times*, May 14, 2003. Also see: "11,000 Feared Buried in Mass Grave in Iraq," Associated Press, May 14, 2003.

44. Robert Lane Greene, "Dubious Blame," *The New Republic*, May 20, 2003.

45. Scott Wilson, "Iraqis Killing Former Baath Party Members," *Washington Post*, May 20, 2003.

46. "Shiite Throng Begins Pilgrimage That Meant Death Under Saddam," Associated Press, April 20, 2003.

47. Ellen Knickmeyer, "Saddam's 'Shiite Thug' Is Captured," Associated Press, April 22, 2003.

48. Anthony Shadid, "A Tradition of Faith Is Reclaimed on Blistered Feet," *Washington Post*, April 23, 2003; and "Iraqi Shias Gather for Climax of Pilgrimage," Associated Press, April 22, 2003.

49. Barbara Slavin and Vivienne Walt, "As Iraqi Shiites Gain Clout, Will U.S. Interests Suffer?," *USA Today*, April 22, 2003.

50. "Shiites Hold Anti-American Demonstration," Associated Press, April 23, 2003.

51. Barbara Slavin and Vivienne Walt, "As Iraqi Shiites Gain Clout, Will U.S. Interests Suffer?"

52. Ellen Knickmeyer, "Saddam's 'Shiite Thug' Is Captured."

53. "Shiites Hold Anti-American Demonstration."

54. It was all too good to be true for some. "I still think that it is a dream," confided thirty-eight-year-old Ghassan Amari. "I think we'll wake up and realize it was an illusion." Anthony Shadid, "A Tradition of Faith is Reclaimed on Blistered Feet."

55. Stephen Farrell, "Foreign Forces Must Go, Insists Shia Ayatollah," *London Times*, May 12, 2003.

56. Anthony Shadid and Daniel Williams, "Bombing at Iraqi Shrine Appears Carefully Planned," *Washington Post*, August 31, 2003; Andrew Gray, "Thousands in Iraq Mourn Slain Shiite Muslim Cleric," Reuters, August 31, 2003; and "Car Bomb Explodes Outside Baghdad Police Headquarters," Associated Press, September 2, 2003.

57. "Saddam's Son Had Photos of Bush Twins," Associated Press, April 14, 2003.

58. This was reported by military analyst Colonel David Hunt on Fox News, among other sources.

59. This took place on July 31, 2003. The leadership position was rotated on a monthly basis.

60. "Iraqi Christians Want Rights Guaranteed," Associated Press, April 30, 2003.

61. Niraj Warikoo and Patricia Montemurri, "Bush Shares Hope for Iraqi Homeland," *Detroit Free Press*, April 29, 2003. Also see: Bush, "Address to the Nation on Iraq," Cincinnati, October 11, 2002.

62. Niraj Warikoo and Patricia Montemurri, "Bush Shares Hope for Iraqi Homeland."

63. President George W. Bush, "Remarks on Operation Iraqi Freedom," Dearborn, MI, April 28, 2003.

64. Niraj Warikoo and Patricia Montemurri, "Bush Shares Hope for Iraqi Homeland."

65. Stephen Schwartz, "Cheers for Wolfy," *New York Post*, May 31, 2003. The material that follows is taken from that article.
66. The Reverend Dr. Bob Edgar, "The Role of the Church in U.S. Foreign Policy Today," Inaugural Lecture in the Joan B. Kroc Distinguished Lecture Series, Joan B. Kroc Institute, University of San Diego, April 15, 2003.
67. See: Joseph Laconte, "Anti-Liberation Theology," *Weekly Standard*, May 5, 2003.
68. Jane Norman, "Harkin: Iraq War Ousted Paper Tiger," *Des Moines Register*, April 11, 2003.
69. Cassio Furtado, "Local Iraqis Call Regime's End a 'Miracle.'"
70. Andrew McCormack, "Bush Addresses Local Iraqi-Americans, War," *Michigan Daily*, April 29, 2003.
71. President George W. Bush, "The President's News Conference," Washington, D.C., March 6, 2003.
72. President George W. Bush, "Remarks to Employees at the Army Tank Plant," Lima, OH, April 24, 2003.
73. President George W. Bush, "Interview on *Meet the Press with Tim Russert*," February 8, 2004.
74. Chuck Colson, "Into the Very Presence of God," *BreakPoint with Charles Colson*, April 17, 2003.
75. Susie L. Oh, "President Bush, Ray Charles headline event," Medill News Service, April 26, 2003.
76. See: President George W. Bush, "Remarks by the President to the Press Pool," Fort Hood, TX, April 20, 2003.
77. President George W. Bush, "President's Radio Address," Washington, D.C., April 19, 2003.
78. President George W. Bush, "President Bush Honors the Brave and Fallen Defenders of Freedom," Arlington, VA, May 26, 2003. A profile of Tippetoe was published by Jon Ward, "Fallen Army Ranger 'A Man of Faith,'" *Washington Times*, April 11, 2003.
79. Bartlett clip played on *Countdown with Keith Olbermann*, MSNBC, May 1, 2003.
80. Ibid.
81. Damon Wheeler, "My Heroes Are Cowboys," *Front Page*, May 5, 2003.
82. Michael Ledeen, "The Lincoln Speech," *National Review Online*, May 2, 2003.
83. Lisa Schiffren, "Hey, Flyboy," *The Wall Street Journal*, May 9, 2003.
84. Frank Rich, "The Jerry Bruckheimer White House," *The New York Times*, May 11, 2003.
85. In his February 12, 2003, speech opposing the war, Byrd called the Bush administration "reckless" and "arrogant," said its record was "dismal," and accused it of "crude insensitivities" and "disastrous," "inexcusable," and "outrageous" policies and pronouncements.
86. "GAO Won't Probe Costs of Bush Flight to Aircraft Carrier," Associated Press, May 14, 2003.
87. Bob Schieffer speaking on CNN's *Larry King Live*, CNN, May 1, 2003.
88. Chris Matthews on *Countdown with Keith Olbermann*, MSNBC, May 1, 2003.
89. President George W. Bush, "President Bush Announces Combat Operations in Iraq Have Ended," USS *Abraham Lincoln*, at Sea, off the Coast of San Diego, CA, May 1, 2003.

90. Carl Cannon reported that Bush skipped services at St. John's that day so as to avoid images of the president going to a Christian house of worship just after Saddam's capture. Cannon, "Bush and God."

91. "Briefing by General Ray Odierno," U.S. Department of Defense, December 14, 2003.

92. Alexandar Vasovic, "Colonel: Forces Were Closing to Killing Saddam," Associated Press, December 15, 2003.

93. Ibid.; and "US Interrogators Grill Saddam," BBC News, December 15, 2003.

94. President George W. Bush, "President's News Conference," December 15, 2003.

95. "Ambassador Bremer Briefing from Baghdad," U.S. Department of Defense, December 14, 2003.

96. Sources: On December 16–17, 2003, the Middle East Media Research Institute (MEMRI) translated and published approximately thirty Iraqi and Arab media stories on Saddam's surrender. Also see: Bassem Mroue, "Iraqi Media Celebrates Saddam's Capture," Associated Press, December 15, 2003.

97. Published in the Baghdad newspaper Al-'Ahd Al-Jadid, December 15, 2003. Translated by MEMRI.

98. President George W. Bush, "President's News Conference," December 15, 2003.

99. Lieberman speaking on Meet the Press with Tim Russert, NBC, December 15, 2003.

100 Peter Johnson, "Big Story Kicked Off Long and Chaotic Day for Media Outlets," USA Today, December 15, 2003.

101. Bush noted this to the press during his December 15, 2003, White House press conference.

102. This was reported in the State Department's annual report on terrorism. See also: Sharon Behn, "Terror Attacks Fewest Since '69," Washington Times, May 1, 2003.

CHAPTER 14

1. Dean told reporters: "I am still learning a lot about faith and the South and how important it is." The Boston Globe reported: "[Dean] said he expects to increasingly include references to Jesus and God in his speeches as he stumps the South." Source: Sarah Schweitzer, "Seeking a new emphasis, Dean touts his Christianity," Boston Globe, December 25, 2003. Also see: Franklin Foer, "Beyond Belief: Howard Dean's Religion Problem," The New Republic, December 29, 2003; William Safire, "Job and Dean," New York Times, January 5, 2004; Ted Olsen, "'Allegory' Job 'Favorite Book in the New Testament,' Says Howard Dean," ChristianityToday.com, January 5, 2004; David Teather, "Democrat hopeful walks with God in 'Bible Belt,'" The Guardian, January 5, 2004; Jim VandeHei, "Dean Now Willing to Discuss His Faith," Washington Post, January 4, 2004; and Jodi Wilgoren, "Dean Narrowing His Separation of Church and Stump," New York Times, January 4, 2004.

2. Ibid.

3. John F. Harris, "In Ga., Dean Embraces Carter," Washington Post, January 19, 2004.

4. Terry Eastland makes an excellent point with this. See: Eastland, "Bush's Gospel," The Weekly Standard, March 1, 2004.

5. The collective media—from left to right—as well as groups like the Anti-Defamation League and the Simon Weisenthal Center, stood aghast at the political ads, which were not adopted by either the Kerry campaign or Moveon.org. Michael Janofsky, "Critics Attack Efforts to Link Bush and Hitler," *New York Times*, January 6, 2004; Howard Kurtz, "Anti-Bush Ad Contest Includes Hitler Images," *Washington Post*, January 6, 2004; Alessandra Stanley, "Showing Candidates, as They Praise Themselves and Bury Others," *New York Times*, July 1, 2004.

6. Senator Edward M. Kennedy, "America, Iraq, and Presidential Leadership," January 14, 2004.

7. On May 17, 2004, it was announced that a 155 mm Iraqi artillery shell filled with Sarin gas had been found, a fact that was subsequently confirmed. It was the first discovery of an actual WMD. See: John J. Lumpkin, "Tests Confirm Sarin Gas in Baghdad Bomb," *Associated Press*, May 25, 2004.

8. The ABC News poll of Iraqis was conducted on March 15, 2004.

9. Cleric's Supporters Threaten All-Out War With US," *Associated Press*, April 19, 2004.

10. Among others, see: Thom Shanker, "Hussein's Agents Are Behind Attacks in Iraq, Pentagon Finds," *The New York Times*, April 29, 2004.

11. Louis Meixler, "French Journalist Describes Captivity in Iraq," *Associated Press*, April 16, 2004.

12. Senator Robert C. Byrd, "A Call for an Exit Door from Iraq," April 7, 2004.

13. Charles Krauthammer, "This Is Hardly Vietnam," *Washington Post*, April 16, 2004.

14. "Kerry Says Bush Manipulates Fear of Terror Attack," *Reuters*, April 15, 2004.

15. Fred Barbash, "U.S. Firms Add 308K New Jobs in March," *Washington Post*, April 2, 2004.

16. President George W. Bush, "President Addresses Nation in Prime Time Press Conference," April 13, 2004.

17. Jason Keyser, "Agreement Reached to End Fallujah Siege," *Associated Press*, April 29, 2004.

18. Arnaud de Borchgrave, "Looking for the exit," *Washington Times*, May 3, 2004.

19. Among the major findings to emerge from the 9-11 Commission's hearings was the commission's conclusion, shared by the Bush administration, that there was no evidence of a direct link between Saddam and 9-11. On the other hand, both the commission and administration acknowledged links between members of Saddam's government and Al-Qaeda. (These facts were badly bungled by the major media, which misreported them; in turn, commission members Democrat Lee Hamilton and Republican John Lehman scolded the media.) Importantly, after September 11, the Bush administration, and especially the president himself, immediately considered the possibility that Saddam was behind 9-11, and continues to do so. Apparently, however, the White House has found no smoking gun, beyond intriguing (potentially) circumstantial evidence. Most important, the Bush administration removed Saddam because it feared that he was capable (and willing) of sponsoring another 9-11, or, worse, orchestrating a WMD attack on the United States at some future point.

20. Others included Kevin Phillips, Al Franken, Michael Moore, and, yet to come, Joseph Wilson.

21. Bob Woodward, *Plan of Attack* (NY: Simon and Schuster, 2004), p. 421.

22. David T. Cook, "Interview with Ralph Nader," *Christian Science Monitor*, April 20, 2004.

23. The Pentagon had hoped for 28,377 reenlistments, but got 28,406. Kimberly Heflin, "U.S. Soldiers Re-Enlist in Strong Numbers," *Associated Press*, April 23, 2004.

24. Shmuley Boteach, "Burning Bush," *The Jerusalem Post*, March 24, 2004.

25. Katharine Q. Seelye, "Kerry Ignores Reproaches of Some Bishops," *The New York Times*, April 11, 2004; and Seelye, "Kerry Attends Easter Services and Receives Holy Communion," *The New York Times*, April 12, 2004.

26. Kerry Can't Dodge Catholic Issue," *Catholic Exchange*, April 26, 2004.

27. This and other discrepancies were pointed out by Joseph Bottum, "John Kerry, in the Catholic Tradition," *The Weekly Standard*, April 26, 2004. Also see:

28. "It's a Sacrament, Senator! Not an Opportunity for a Photo Shoot," *Catholic Exchange*, March 31, 2004.

29. Joseph Bottum of *The Weekly Standard* says that Kerry's claim on this occasion was wrong. Joseph Bottum, "John Kerry, in the Catholic Tradition," *The Weekly Standard*, April 26, 2004.

30. Senator John F. Kerry (D-MA), U.S. Senate, August 2, 1994, published in the *Congressional Record*.

31. Deal Hudson, "Did John Kerry Lie About Abortion?" *Catholic Exchange*, February 23, 2004.

32. As this book goes to press, Kerry is sending mixed messages on this matter. See, among others: Ron Fournier, "I could appoint an anti-abortion jurist, Kerry says," *Associated Press*, May 20, 2004.

33. Material taken from: "Abortion rights protest packs National Mall," Associated Press, April 25, 2004; Kathryn Jean Lopez, "We're . . . Feminists!" *National Review Online*, April 26, 2004; Kathryn Jean Lopez, "Wax Bush" *National Review Online*, April 26, 2004; and George Neumayr, "Among the Pagan Ladies," *The American Spectator*, April 26, 2004.

34. The bill passed on April 1, 2004 by a 245-163 vote in the House and by 61-38 in the Senate. The vast majority of Republicans supported the bill, whereas more Democrats voted against rather than in favor.

35. Laurie Goodstein, "Vatican Cardinal Signals Backing for Sanctions on Kerry," *The New York Times*, April 24, 2004.

36. "Teresa: Abortion ends a life," *New York Daily News*, April 26, 2004.

37. "Vatican: No Communion for Pro-Abortion Politicians," *Associated Press*, April 23, 2004; "The Bishops Speak," *Catholic Exchange*, April 26, 2004; and Goodstein, "Vatican Cardinal Signals . . . ," April 24, 2004.

38. These individuals acted before the statement from Cardinal Arinze, though others have since followed.

39. George Neumayr, "The New Saintliness," *The American Spectator*, April 21, 2004.

40. See: "American Catholic Support for Kerry Falls Below 6 Percent," *Catholic Exchange*, May 28, 2004.

41. Ted Olsen, "Kerry's Religion Is Today's Big Politics Story," *ChristianityToday.com*, March 29, 2004; Nedra Pickler, "Bush Campaign Blasts Kerry's Bible Quote," *Associ-*

ated Press, March 28, 2004; and Karen Tumulty and Perry Bacon Jr., "A Test of Kerry's Faith," *Time*, April 5, 2004.

42. Showing its disgust, the U.S. Senate unanimously (92 to 0) passed a resolution condemning the abuse.

43. Kennedy made this statement on May 10, 2004. Outside of conservative media, it received virtually no press coverage, a point that was made by Hugh Hewitt in his *Weekly Standard* piece "Under New Management," May 13, 2004.

44. "Berg Died for Bush, Rumsfeld 'Sins'—Father," *Reuters*, May 13, 2004.

45. "Hezbollah Slams Beheading of American as Un-Islamic," *Reuters*, May 13, 2004.

46. Laurie Goodstein, "Bishop Would Deny Rite for Defiant Catholic Voters," *The New York Times*, May 14, 2004. Not all of the church hierarchy shared this view. To cite just two examples, Theodore Cardinal McCarrick of Washington, DC and Roger Cardinal Mahony of Los Angeles disagreed with this position.

47. Interestingly, McGreevey said that he would accept communion in private but not in public, even though Myers made no distinction between the two. Jeff McKay, "NJ's Pro-Abortion Catholic Gov Will Avoid Public Communion," CNSNews.com, May 7, 2004.

48. John Zogby, "The Election Is Kerry's To Lose," released by Zogby International, May 9, 2004.

CHAPTER 15

1. President George W. Bush, "Remarks at the National Prayer Breakfast," Washington, D.C., February 6, 2003.

2. Oswald Chambers, *My Utmost for His Highest* (Grand Rapids, MI: Discovery House, 1995), p. 10/1.

3. On Bush's cursing, see: Woodward, *Plan of Attack*, pp. 178 and 186; and Schweizers', *The Bushes*, pp. 303, 331, 333, 342, 438, and 473.

4. Of those responsible for 9/11, Bush said, "We're going to kick their ass." See: Woodward, *Plan of Attack*, p. 296; and Schweizers', *The Bushes*, p. 516.

5. Discussion with Peter Schweizer, March 29, 2004. Bush's friend Doug Wead goes even further, calling Bush's faith "the good angel of his personality. Without that faith, he is so hard . . . he is so brutal, he is so unapologetic, so self-righteous." Wead interviewed for "The Jesus Factor." *Frontline*, PBS-TV, 2004.

6. President George W. Bush, "Remarks at the 20th Anniversary of the National Endowment for Democracy," November 6, 2003.

7. President George W. Bush, "Remarks Following a Meeting with Congressional Leaders and an Exchange with Reporters," September 19, 2001.

8. Woodward, *Bush at War*, p. 194.

9. In addition to the November 6, 2003, speech at the National Endowment for Democracy, Bush invoked Wilson's democratic idealism and, again, the same general themes about freedom, peace, and democracy, in a November 19, 2003, speech at Whitehall Palace in London.

10. See: Gaddis, "A Grand Strategy of Transformation."

11. President George W. Bush, "Remarks at the National Prayer Breakfast," Washington, D.C., February 6, 2003.

12. Quoted by Mike Allen, "Close Look at a Focused President," *Washington Post*, April 27, 2003.

13. Tim Hames, "Have We Seen You Some Place Before, George?" *London Times*, May 26, 2003.

14. Richard Brookhiser, "Close-Up: The Mind of George W. Bush," *The Atlantic*, March 2003.

15. Bush, *A Charge to Keep*, pp. 239–240.

16. Ibid. p. 6.

17. Chambers, *My Utmost for His Highest*, pp. 1/2, 1/4, and 3/19.

18. President George W. Bush, "Remarks at Yale University Commencement," New Haven, CT, May 25, 2001.

19. President George W. Bush, "Remarks in Address to Faculty and Students of Warsaw University," Warsaw, Poland, June 15, 2001.

20. President George W. Bush, "Radio Address by the President to the Nation," April 14, 2001; and Bush, *A Charge to Keep*, p. 6.

21. Nancy Gibbs, "Person of the Year: George W. Bush," *Time*, December 17, 2000.

22. Quoted in Ron Fournier, "Bush's Test: to Unite the Great Divide," Associated Press, January 21, 2001.

23. Michael Duffy, "Marching Along," *Time*, September 1, 2002.

24. Bush interview with Beliefnet.com editor in chief Steven Waldman, October 2000.

25. President George W. Bush, "Remarks at the National Prayer Breakfast," February 6, 2003.

ACKNOWLEDGMENTS

This book was born in late 2002. At the outset of that year, I had a conversation with *National Review*'s Rich Lowry, who had just spoken at Grove City College, about my then-upcoming book on the faith of the 40th president, *God and Ronald Reagan*. Lowry asked if I'd consider writing a feature for *National Review* on the faith of the current president. I said I'd be happy to. I had been filling a box with material on Bush's faith since the Texas governor began running for president in 1999. Once that article was published, Cal Morgan, my editor at ReganBooks, recommended that my next book be on Bush; my wife, Susan, and a number of others had the same thought. I couldn't resist, especially as progress on my next planned book—a major work on Ronald Reagan's personal role in the end of the Cold War—was awaiting declassification of dozens of documents at the Reagan Library.

The manuscript I produced would not have been possible without key support. Melissa Harvey, a former student who now works at an investment firm in Pittsburgh, called out of the blue one day and asked if I needed any research help. I sure did. She would go on to vet all of the *Presidential Documents* on George W. Bush within just weeks, flagging every document with a religious reference, and refusing pay for her time.

Also crucial was my student assistant, Matt Sitman, who hunted down every biography of George W. Bush and searched for faith-related material and other types of information. Matt is on his way to Georgetown University, where he will get his doctorate in American politics and eventually write books like this.

Others provided research help, advice, and encouragement: Paul Allan Kengor, Mitch Kengor, Bethany Nichols, Melinda Haring, Elaine Rodemoyer, Jen Collard, Drew McKelvey, Dan Solomon, Ben Prince, Darrick Johnson, Cory Shreckengost, Tim Graham, Aubree Rankin, Travis Barham, John Coyne, Michael Coulter, Jim Bibza, Sheila Sterrett, Ralph Pontillo, and Abbey Isaacson. Leona Schecter acted as not only my agent but an editor. Leona, who does not share my political affiliation, helped remove suggestions of partisanship—a difficult step. I'm grateful for Marv Folkertsma's encouragement, and to Grove City College for recognizing the importance of this kind of work by implementing the college's first sabbatical program. That program will allot me the time to promote this book and complete others.

There were numerous people who helped with or sat for interviews—too many to list. I would, however, like to pay special appreciation to Don Browning, who one day in April 2004 spent an hour on the telephone recounting to me (a stranger) the horrible details of the Texas church shooting that took the life of his beloved daughter, Sydney. I'm sure my call ruined his morning. Through that tragedy, Don saw a side of George W. Bush that the rest of us have not, and felt that side needed to be known. I want to thank Tom Brown and Suzanne Tyler for their help in securing interviews. I'd also like to acknowledge those individuals in the Bush White House who shared new material, or confirmed key pieces of information. For reasons that baffle me, these people insisted on anonymity at all times, even when citing their names would only help. Lastly, my thanks to Susan for helping me block out the time to write, and to Chuck Dunn, who has left Grove City College to have an impact on the lives of yet more authors-to-be.

Paul Kengor
Grove City, Pennsylvania
July 7, 2004

INDEX OF NAMES